# VOICES OF HOPE
# FOR MENTAL ILLNESS:
# NOT AGAINST, WITH

# VOICES OF HOPE FOR MENTAL ILLNESS: NOT AGAINST, WITH

Jackie Goldstein

Cover design by Katherine King

ISBN: 1517662958
ISBN 13: 9781517662950

Dedicated to those who live with a diagnosis of mental illness and the accompanying stigma; to their devoted family members; and to all who have chosen a vocation or volunteered their time to serve the needs of those who did not choose to live with mental illness but who inspire us with their courage.

# Acknowledgments and Gratitude

I t's been a long journey from the day I first read about Geel in 1982 to my first visit to the city in 1997 (and six subsequent visits), through visits to over a dozen mental health programs in our own country, and, at last, to the book you're holding in your hands. As I met people along the way, their very existence encouraged me to share their stories—the stories of those with mental illness, their family members, volunteers, and staff dedicated to serving the needs of others. Though I may not remember their names, I can still see their faces and hear their voices.

Because of their consistent cooperation and patience, I can easily remember the faces and the names of those in Geel who made this book possible and whom I have come to consider dear friends and kindred spirits: Marc Godemont, Wilfried Bogaerts, Jan Schrijvers, the loving foster family and their "boys" who made me feel like a part of their family.

Since I am not a mental health professional but rather a keen observer of mental health services, I am grateful for the knowledge and generous input of professionals Eric Maisel, Steve Moffic, and Bernadette Grosjean.

Getting a book published can be a difficult, long, and often fruitless effort. And although I didn't anticipate a best seller, I felt that this book *must be* published on behalf of all of those whose lives have been touched by mental illness and the *stigma* of mental illness. So I sought support using a new twenty-first-century approach: community funding. After all, this book is about "community." It made sense that community members should be my collaborators. On behalf of all of those whose lives have been, or will be, touched by the stigma of mental illness, I offer gratitude to the Community Funding Donors who made this book possible.

Jack W. Berry

Laurence Cantor

Marshall Cates

Marla Corts

Eric Crumley

Jonathan Davis

Elizabeth Dobbins

Pennie Eckman

Lisa Engel

Chris Fellows

Lynette Fifer

Ashley Floyd

Cathy Friedman

Nicole and Antonio Fuentes

L. Jonathan Goldstein

Bernadette Grosjean

Paul Jerome

Meg Kissinger

Susan and Ed Klein

Joan Lorden

John and Sarah Lutes

John and Leslie Lutes

David and Edith Lyon

Steve and Rusti Moffic

Joan Mousseau

J. Alan Neal

Stacey Rippner

Dennis Sansom

Allen Shealy

Michael Sloane

Elizabeth O. Smith

Sandy Steingard

Margie Sved

Diane Tucker

Linda Verin

Nancy Whitt

Sandra Willis

Eleven generous donors who chose to
    stay anonymous

# Table of Contents

# Author's Notes

## IMPORTANT NOTE REGARDING PRIVACY

Please note that whenever I refer to personal conversations or interactions with Geel boarders and foster family members, as well as individuals at other sites – those who have been diagnosed as mentally ill or their family members, fictitious names are used. The exception is that real names are used if the individual has been identified by name in referenced sources.

## FURTHER READING AND/OR REFERENCES

This book is written for the general public, a diverse population with varying degrees of desire to "drill down" on the information contained in the book. Even as I wrote it, using my existing knowledge and resources, I was often inclined to "drill down" myself, sometimes spending hours to find information that would only satisfy my curiosity and provide a phrase of context in a sentence conveying information relative to the chapter.

For those who are curious, I have provided endnotes with additional information and/or links that will lead you to information, should you desire to do further research. Some of you may not have that inclination and will miss nothing by ignoring the endnotes. Information in the text itself adequately covers the theme of the book.

## MENTAL ILLNESS AND VIOLENCE

As I encourage a reduction in the stigma of mental illness with the word *hope*, it is impossible to ignore the way public perceptions are affected by acts of violence and subsequent media coverage, including speculation about or evidence for mental illness in the perpetrators. Even as I worked on this book, multiple acts of violence were in the news. For many people, the mere commission of an outrageous act of violence—surpassing our own capacity for extreme behavior, even in the face of anger or rejection, our value systems, our respect for humanity—would seem to be evidence of mental illness. At this very moment, I'm following the tragic story of nine deaths at an Oregon community college. A little over a month ago, as I sat at the computer working on this book, I listened to news of the on-camera murder of a journalist and cameraman in Virginia. In these two cases, and all the others that have become "too routine," the behavior and actions of the murderer are so bizarre, so inconsistent with what most of us can imagine, that it would not be unusual to think, "That person is crazy!" We may assume that one has to be mentally ill to murder someone. Maybe. But *crazy* and *mental illness* do not necessarily have the same meaning. *Crazy* is not a diagnosis. It's a judgment of irrational acts or beliefs.

So is it correct to assume that anyone who commits such acts suffers from mental illness? The simple answer is no. You will hear it said that those with mental illness are more apt to be victims of violent acts than perpetrators of such acts. That is true when we look at "mental illness"—period. Most people with mental health problems do *not* commit acts of violence, and most acts of violence are not committed by those with a diagnosis of mental illness. But there are many variables that must be factored into the equation. All mental illness is not "created" (or manifested) equally. There are a wide variety of behaviors or thought patterns associated with diverse diagnoses, and some behaviors or thought patterns—some diagnoses—are more likely to serve as risk factors than others.

To complicate matters further, not all of those with symptoms of mental illness are diagnosed or treated, and those who may be most at risk may never be seen by a mental health professional. And that's where stigma is likely to play a role in the sad and tragic incidents in which mental illness may have contributed to the commission of violent acts. Public stigma becomes self-stigma, and, in simple terms, individuals or their family members may be in denial as to what irrational behavior may mean—mental illness—when being labeled as mentally ill is to be avoided.

And so, even as I wrote a book that focuses on *hope* for mental illness, this book does not ignore the acts of violence where there were implications of mental illness in the perpetrator. Rather, it is my hope that through education about mental illness and through the stories in this book—a different kind of contact than what one gets in twenty-four-hour news coverage of shocking acts of violence—there will be a reduction of stigma and, thus, a greater likelihood that individuals or their family members will seek help.

# Foreword

"You can't stop the waves, but you can learn to surf."
— Jon Kabat-Zinn

"All the lonely people,
Where do they all come from?
All the lonely people
Where do they all belong ?"
—Lennon-Mc Cartney

I t takes a village. It does—-a village in which to grow, to feel safe, to learn social skills from role models, to be loved, to care for others, and to belong.

This important book describes communities, from far away Belgium to cities across the US, that have been able to encourage healing in an integrated setting of care—-unique communities for those who have been abandoned by society. It is a book that offers hope for these people while inspiring and motivating community members to create their own "healing communities."

We are living in peculiar times, torn between exponential progress in certain fields and appalling regression in others. It is a time when tools—such as the internet— can both connect human beings from all over the planet, but also endanger the fundamental building blocks of society: real people talking to each other face to face, open to the infinite unknown of another soul, ready to discover the unique and irreducible experience of two living beings changing one another by the simple fact of their physical interaction. It is these personal interactions that make us human.

In the United States---looked at with envy by much of the world as a country of buildings "painted with gold"---millions of American adults and children live in cars, tents, sleeping on sheets of cardboard or in cardboard boxes. Among those wandering between trash bins and jail cells, between unsafe shelters and broken cars are hundreds of thousands of people suffering from severe mental illness.

So many times, as I work among these people, I have wished that I had the money to build for them "a village" -- where they could feel safe and useful, work at their own unique pace, finding a place in a society that would recognize them as full and precious members.

How did we get to this seemingly hopeless place? Several decades ago, in the US, we experienced the shame of gigantic impersonal and underfunded psychiatric institutions. We were then suddenly told that people with severe mental illness could live normally, outside the walls of asylums or hospitals, thanks to high expectations born of pharmaceutical cures dubiously advertised as "miraculous," and with money pledged for community psychiatry. Institutions began closing one after another. But the support money never came.

As for the promise of pills, though many were helpful when prescribed appropriately and in combination with other modes of support, limitations and impairing side effects became apparent over time.

To make matters worse, many entertained the myth of "chemical imbalance" as a single cause for mental illness, and a belief developed that medication alone could cure complex psychiatric illnesses. As a result, and in order for managed care to save money, time allotted for clinical care and therapy---now scientifically deemed useless---was gradually reduced to a fifteen-minute medication visit every few months. By investing mostly in expensive pharmaceuticals, and by preferring computer protocols over the uniqueness of interpersonal relation-ships, psychiatric "Healthcare" systems forgot that one of the most efficacious and valuable healing tools is contact with other human beings.

With time, the difficulties of pharmacological treatments, and more important-ly, the inability to build authentic and personal connections between patients/consumers/clients and mental health workers led to an increasing lack of trust and collaboration between these two groups that were meant to work together. Problems such as attrition, poor adherence, and substance dependence rendered treatment more and more difficult while resources were shrinking. In our cur-rent healthcare system quick surveys, and soulless "check lists" have replaced interpersonal interviews once used to gather information. The value of human beings communicating not only verbally but also nonverbally has been forgotten.

Despite the incredible dedication of peer counselors, social workers, psycholo-gists and psychiatrists in the community mental health field, powerlessness and frustration escalated.

Hence, people who were once institutionalized are living in the community but struggling, most often alone, to find not only good care but a place to live and a job that will support a respectable, meaningful life.

In a world where time is money and productivity is king, many people with mental illness are rejected by systems and machines that ask for more and more, faster and faster. While the general public may think that people on Disability take advantage of the system, in 25 years of psychiatric practice, I have rarely met someone who is not eager to have a job, allowing them to feel useful, pos-sessing a sense of dignity

Without the support of a caring and informed community, very few are able to achieve this humble goal, and too many end up moving between unsafe shelters, jails where they don't belong, and anonymous streets where many will die as a John or Jane Doe.

In this book, Dr. Goldstein demonstrates how a society may step in, by going back to what has been used for centuries to help people with Mental Illness – a community where sufferers can do more than just suffer and survive. They can thrive with a renewed sense of their own humanity

In times of growing isolation, a village, (literally a clustered human settlement or community), that has as its goal, the wellbeing of its members – *all* of its members – is a kind of miracle.

With determination and dedication Dr. Goldstein, has sought out, traveled to, explored, compared and put together her years of experience with communities of care in a book that describes and demonstrates, again and again, the power of faith in human beings, the power of acceptance and tolerance within a dedicated community.

In a world where disintegrating care for the mentally ill could feed our pessimism, Dr. Goldstein's book reminds us of the incredible benefit of basic human connection, of the almost, "miraculous" results that a team or community---a family, a church, a village---offers by providing a sense of belonging for *all* of its members.

Thank you Jackie

Bernadette Grosjean.M.D.
Associate Professor of Psychiatry
David Geffen School of Medicine at UCLA

# Introduction

A voice of *hope*? For mental illness? What kind of hope? The Middle Ages offered hope through exorcism of demons. In the late eighteenth century, moral treatment offered asylum and relief for those suffering symptoms that were thought to be caused by the stresses of life.

As abnormal behavior came to be associated with "disease" of the brain, it was thought that the disease might be "cured" by cutting away parts of the brain or inducing seizures. There was little or no solid foundation for such treatment, but we were desperate to relieve institutional overcrowding.

At last, in the mid-twentieth century, the Mental Retardation and Community Mental Health Centers Construction Act of 1963, coupled with the development of new drugs, seemed to offer *real hope*. Those who once were institutionalized, or would be today, were returned to the community...but *where* in the community? For some, home was another institution—in a jail, behind bars. Others sought any available shelter – e.g., under a highway overpass, on a park bench, in the doorway of a business after closing hours.

Medication? It helped. It continues to help and can indeed be a life changer, even a life saver. But psychotherapeutic medications are seldom "magic bullets" that directly affect the source of a disorder without also creating unwanted side effects. And though drugs can offer relief, finding an effective medication is often a trial-and-error effort. In a nutshell, when it comes to mental disorders, doctors do not have a consistently reliable way to make a specific diagnosis that can be treated with a specific drug.

This book neither offers nor describes any tried-and-true, surefire, specific hope for an end to mental illness. The hope described here comes *from us*—the community—and from our willingness to know and accept *what is* as a starting point. The community does not provide a simple answer, but a stigma-free community optimizes the implementation of any treatment, offering those diagnosed with mental disorders the opportunity to experience what we all desire: meaningful lives. The book's focus is what I've come to call *community recovery*.

The current recovery model of *treatment* operates from an understanding that although a cure or a complete end to symptoms might not be possible, those with a diagnosis of mental illness can live successfully with the realities of their illness given the proper treatment and sufficient social support. In order for *community recovery* to occur, community members must abandon old myths and misunderstandings and show a willingness to understand what *is* known, even though scientific knowledge is incomplete. Since community plays a key role in the recovery process of an individual, it is logical to assume that community recovery is a desirable context for the successful recovery of individual community members.

Poet Robert Frost once advised:

Always fall in with what you're asked to accept. Take what is given, and make it over your way. My aim in life has always been to hold my own with whatever's going. Not against: with.[1]

In 1982, during my final semester as an adult undergraduate student, I first became aware of a community in Belgium that I would eventually come to consider a model for community recovery. For centuries, the people of Geel[2] have taken a *not against, with* approach to mental disorders.

I learned of this community when I was captivated by a picture in an abnormal psychology textbook.[3] The beginning of the caption read, "For centuries the colony of Gheel [sic] in Belgium has recognized that the majority of mental patients are not unstable or dangerous." The caption went on to explain that the "young man [in the picture] is one of many mental patients who live in private homes and benefit from love, warmth, and interaction with family members."

Given what I knew about a frequently expressed negative stigma associated with mental disorders,[4] that statement was particularly meaningful, worthy of a full explanation and discussion. But all I found in that textbook, thirty pages past the captioned picture, was a one-and-a-half-column description of the legend, history, and tradition of "The Gheel Shrine."[5] That was not enough for me, and the dearth of information fed my curiosity about how a legend created the remarkable story of a persistent system of foster family care for the mentally ill.

The article cited in that 1980 textbook was published in 1974 but was based on a Cincinnati neurologist's report after a visit to Geel in 1936.[6] That information was forty-six years old when I first read it, and from time to time over the years I made casual but unsuccessful attempts to find more current information. But my efforts became more focused and serious as I came to know those who were living with both the diagnosis of a mental disorder *and* the associated confusion and fear of friends and family members.

The classic struggle of one particular family haunted me. In 1986, that family began a journey through their teenage son's adolescence—a predictably difficult period of development, once described by a wise and witty friend as the "senility of childhood." It began with troublesome behavior when the teenage son was fifteen. Though he was relatively young, he was approaching the age range of onset for two types of severe mental illness (SMI). The onset for schizophrenia in males falls between sixteen and twenty-five,[7] and for bipolar disorder, late teens or early adulthood. He didn't fit neatly into the age range for either diagnosis, and his symptoms didn't fit neatly into one diagnosis or the other. But as his symptoms persisted and worsened, family members and professionals suspected that he was displaying more than exaggerated adolescent behavior. Multiple hospitalizations and various diagnoses followed, the latter often assigned in response to trial-and-error medication attempts.

I knew of this pattern (which comes first—the diagnosis or the appropriate medication?) but now I saw it unfolding firsthand. At one time, I might have thought that it wasn't supposed to happen to *them*, an *Ozzie and Harriet*-type family. But I have learned that it can happen to anyone. And I became most acutely aware of the social side effect of this particular brand of chronic illness, in addition to the frustration and adjustment that accompanies any chronic illness.

Friends of this young man, who was formerly popular, academically gifted, and athletically accomplished, drifted away—most often out of confusion fed by fear. As I learned how life was changing for this family, my thoughts often turned to the textbook picture and description of Geel, a city where those with mental illness are accepted and visible members of the community.

In the late 1980s, I attended a talk sponsored by the local chapter of the National Alliance for the Mentally Ill (NAMI), where I learned of another story that generated the same kind of interest and hope that I'd felt when I read of Geel in 1982. The speaker was E. Fuller Torrey, noted psychiatrist and schizophrenia researcher. In the context of his talk, Dr. Torrey mentioned an organization that coordinated friendship matches between community volunteers and individuals who had been diagnosed with mental disorders. Was it possible, I wondered, that such a community organization could produce, right here in the United States, the same kind of community acceptance and involvement as did the citizens of Geel, a legendary Belgian city with a seven-hundred-year history of community acceptance?

I soon found that Compeer, the organization referred to by Dr. Torrey, was founded in Rochester, New York, in 1973. In the late 1980s, there were more than one hundred branches of Compeer in the United States alone. By 1993, a group of interested parties, myself included, added Birmingham, Alabama, to that list, bringing to our own community an opportunity for the kind of support and acceptance that had existed in Geel for centuries.

My knowledge of Geel fed my desire to start a new Compeer agency, *and* my involvement with Compeer amplified my lingering interest in Geel. One of the stumbling blocks in my early search for information about Geel was my focus on the role of its citizens, the caregivers in the city's foster family care system. But then I learned, quite by accident, that a directory of worldwide hospitals was available in the medical library of the graduate school I attended. Perhaps, I thought, that might be a better source of the information I sought. And, sure enough, that directory included a listing for the city of Geel, the name of a hospital in Geel (Openbaar Psychiatrisch Ziekenhuis, OPZ, Public Psychiatric Hospital), and the name of the hospital administrator. I soon established communication with the OPZ director and was making arrangements for my first visit to the city in January 1997.

I remember sitting on the train, traveling from Brussels to Geel, wondering what I would find. All I could envision was the old picture in my textbook and an image created by the report of a doctor's 1936 visit to the city, containing information that was now sixty-one years old—not much to go on in anticipation of my visit. But by the end of that day, I would feel a more real sense of awe and hopefulness than what I had felt when I first saw that textbook entry in 1982.

I was met at the train station by OPZ psychologist Marc Godemont, and during that one-day visit, I learned that this was a community with more than a history. I did not find a relic from the Middle Ages. I found a busy, prosperous city of more than thirty thousand, with clear signs of modern awareness. Had I simply passed through the city, unfamiliar with its unique history, I would not have noticed anything unique or unusual. In fact, when I saw a display of Homer Simpson products in a Main Street gift-shop window, it brought a smile to my face. It seemed that this was a typical midsized city with evidence of life much like what US citizens would experience in a city of the same size. But, most important, I found a remarkably modern and realistic approach to mental health care.

That 1997 visit was the first of many visits to Geel and the beginning of an ongoing relationship with staff at the OPZ, an integrated psychiatric center that coordinates four mental health service divisions, including the legendary foster family care services. Determined to share the Geel story with interested parties in our own country, I wrote articles and commentaries and made presentations to professionals and community members, all motivated by a belief that those who learned of this community's experience would be relieved of fear and misunderstanding regarding mental illness. As I developed contacts in the field of mental health, I learned of and visited agencies and programs in our own country whose approach and success engendered as much hope and optimism in me as did Geel. I knew the horror stories relative to mental illness—the stigma and the treatment of those exhibiting symptoms indicative of some type of mental illness or disorder. It was now encouraging to know that these stories were *not* the only tales to be told, and I developed a passion that led me to advocate for those who must live with these symptoms and the accompanying diagnosis.

How, I once pondered, do we come to develop a passion about an issue or cause? Geel, Compeer, personal contact with friends diagnosed with a mental disorder—all of these fed my fervor on behalf of this particular group of people. But I was forty years old when my curiosity was sparked by a short passage in an abnormal psychology textbook. Why did that spark of curiosity become a passion? Sometimes our passion and involvement in issues or interests are so great that we don't bother to, or care to, identify the source of our concern. The credibility seems obvious—to us. And for the most part, that's the way it's been regarding my interest in those *persons* who live with the diagnosis of a mental disorder.

For twenty-four years, I was a psychology professor but *not* a clinical psychologist or psychiatrist or social worker; mental illness was not the focus of my profession. Perhaps I developed this particular interest because I'd personally or casually come to know those who face this challenge and the accompanying stigma. They have taught me about both their struggle *and* their courage. I have met persons, from all walks of life, diagnosed with various mental disorders—persons with diverse personalities, talents, and challenges. And over and over again, in spite of this diversity, I experience an aura of unconditional love when I visit mental health programs or agencies. Though I feel compassion for the enormity and complexity of the challenge faced by those with mental health disorders, I *do not* feel fear or pity. Rather, I am often invigorated and inspired, not only by their courage and persistence, but by their ability to love. Those who too often experience intolerance and rejection still know and practice the art of *tolerance* and *acceptance*. This is not always obvious, nor is it ubiquitous, particularly with those who suffer from self-stigma or who have no support system. But it *is* obvious in those who are on the road to recovery, who have been guided and supported in their efforts to live with and accept the fact of mental illness in their lives.

With that first trip to Geel, I had at last more than satisfied my curiosity about the city. I had observed a reality that was a product of a legend, and I came back to the United States eager to share what I had seen and learned so that others could more readily feel the sense of hope I had experienced in the stigma-free community of Geel. In August 1998, at the annual convention of the American Psychologist Association,[8] I first presented what I had learned in Geel. Those at that conference who recalled reading of Geel at some time in the past had a kind of "whatever happened to..." interest about the city. The nature of their interest inspired the title of a roundtable discussion I led at the 2001 American Public Health Association's annual meeting, "A Community Mental Health Care Legend? Whatever happened to Geel?"[9]

*I knew* what had happened to Geel, and now the city did more than intrigue me as a unique community with a legendary history, for I believed that people with a diagnosis of mental illness could be successfully accepted and integrated into any community. But it soon became clear that if I was going to sing the praises of Geel, I had to provide evidence that the city's success could be replicated in our own communities. If community members and leaders believed that Geel was somehow "different," it would not become an icon for community recovery. But I didn't believe that Geel was different, and that belief was confirmed as I became aware of and visited exemplary programs in our own country. Whenever and wherever I traveled, I looked for, and often found, sites worthy of a visit—programs that appeared to fit my criteria of "exemplary" in terms of opportunities for community integration of those with a diagnosis of mental illness. In 2002, five years after my first visit to Geel, I visited the Way Station in Frederick, Maryland, the first of many sites that I would visit in the next twelve years.

At each site, I shared with staff members and clients the history and modern-day status of Geel, as well as a report on other programs I had visited in the United States. It was surprising to me that sometimes those who were doing good work in one city or state knew nothing of similar successes in other cities and states. And so, as my experience broadened, I gathered encouragement and momentum and a determination to share with others the hope that I had found, not just in Geel, but here at home, in our own country. I spoke to devoted mental health professionals, but it became increasingly obvious that I needed to share my own growing sense of hope with a wider audience—a diverse audience of communities with a common concern. Those who are diagnosed with a mental disorder must live with the fact of their diagnosis. In order to facilitate that challenge, it seems that communities themselves must find ways to live with the *fact, not the fear, of mental illness* in their midst.

It was the people of Geel, the community members, who made a difference in that city. Through the centuries, in a stigma-free environment, they offered hope to those in need. Could they, as a community, offer the same kind of hope to our own communities and to those with a diagnosis of mental illness who live in those communities? It seemed to me that the only way the citizens of Geel could have that effect was if their collective voice could somehow silence the fear and misunderstanding responsible for the stigma of mental illness, a stigma that can paralyze community members. I was determined to channel the voices of Geel into a single voice that would speak to the minds and hearts of those in my own country. This book is that voice.

A sense of hope in dealing with mental disorders of any kind is needed, not only for those who are directly affected—personally or professionally—but for every member of every community. And so, the purpose of this book is to enlighten and encourage even those who have a less intimate or obvious experience with mental disorders, for they, too, are indeed affected by the fact of mental illness. As members of large and small communities, we can all have an effect on the quality of life, or even the behavior, of those who live with the fact of mental illness. Friends, community members, and civic leaders need not feel hopeless or helpless; there *are* ways they can help persons with mental disorders and their family members and, hence, the community itself, to deal with the frustrating facts. Whether those "others" realize it or not, their perspectives may have helped create some of the social side effects associated with the diagnosis of a mental disorder. And, if we have the power to create such obstacles, we also have the power to mitigate them. Thus, this book is addressed to every person in every community. We may not all be consumers of mental health services, but we are all, collectively as a community, living with mental health challenges.

# Part One
## Voices

Stigma stands in the way of our ability to live with mental illness. It deprives us of "hope." To believe in the possibility of hope in the face of mental illness, we must recognize the voices of fear and misunderstanding---the sources of stigma---that are described in the opening chapter. When we understand the source and effect of stigma, we are in a position to minimize or eradicate it. That, in turn, allows us to understand the hope that is uncovered and exists in all of the programs and communities described in this book, beginning with the city of Geel, Belgium, a truly stigma free community. Geel's unique history was born of hope and continues to thrive with the same kind of hope.

In order to understand how Geel came to achieve such a spirit of acceptance and how it has evolved over the centuries, the next two chapters provide a comprehensive history of Geel's legendary system of community mental health care, from its early beginnings and into the twenty-first century. History which, to some degree, just "happens," can shape the future of any community. Though our own history with mental illness in the community is not the same as that of Geel, does that mean that we can't hope to find or create stigma-free communities or programs that provide for our citizens what Geel has to offer?

The final chapter of Part One provides an overview of mental health care in our own country---in the context of community---from colonial America to the early twentieth century. You will read how beliefs and views have changed relevant to medical or political or social developments, within communities, and how these developments have the potential for wielding power---in terms of determining treatment options and the availability of resources for treatment and, most important, in terms of creating a mood of tolerance (or intolerance) toward those who have been diagnosed (or labeled) with mental disorders.

The natural and social sciences will continue in their efforts to advance understanding of the biological and/or environmental basis of mental disorders. At the same time, on a more personal level, we in the community, have much to learn in order to live with mental illness. We can do this by supporting friends and neighbors who are striving to live meaningful lives in the face of stigmatizing diagnoses. We cannot simply wait for a "cure." We must collectively recover while we wait. Each of us has a voice in the choir of "voices" that can determine the kind of life those with mental health disorders will be allowed to live. Rather than a voice of fear, condemnation, or rejection, perhaps the first and most important thing we can learn about mental illness is to speak with a voice of hope, for there *is* reason to hope.

Many human conditions cannot be cured or eliminated. But lay community members don't need to wait for a cure or even medical understanding of those conditions in order to appreciate the value of social support and a sense of worth—for anyone...for everyone. We all have the same needs. Those with any disorder or disability may have specific needs, but those needs do not cancel out their human needs. Those with any kind of disability *also* have abilities. They deserve to hope—have *reason* to hope—that with those abilities and the support of their neighbors, they can live meaningful lives. Communities, too, have reason to hope that they can live with the realities of mental health disorders rather than fearing age-old myths and misunderstandings. One hope nurtures the other—*not against, with*.

# 1

# The Voice of Stigma

There are those who hear voices that no one else can hear—not the metaphorical "inner voice" of insight or inspiration with which we contemplate options and make decisions. No, some have heard what seem to be real voices, coming from without, though there is no one near to utter the words they hear. The perceived source of such voices can depend on historical era or cultural place. In modern times, they may be reported as coming from a television or loudspeakers. Whatever their perceived source, such voices may speak of a distorted world, demanding the listener to acknowledge a distorted reality. Auditory hallucinations (phantom voices) and delusions (the voice of false belief), are two symptoms that can be associated with severe mental illness (SMI). And they have been "heard" long before televisions or loudspeakers or any electronic devices existed.

For those with an SMI diagnosis, such as schizophrenia, who do hear voices (and not all do), the voices are not likely to speak rational truths or make useful suggestions. In fact, they may make demands, potentially harmful to the ones who hear the voices or to those around them. Though auditory hallucinations are not the only symptom associated with schizophrenia, most of us are aware of that particular symptom. In recent decades, many became aware of the disease and its symptoms through the best-selling book and subsequent Academy Award-winning movie, *A Beautiful Mind*, which included details of Nobel Prize-winning economist John Nash's "voices." This symptom is mystifying to those who do not hear what another claims to hear so clearly. Knowing that someone is hearing delusional voices can evoke fear and cause us to wonder, "What if 'the voices' tell this person to harm *me?*"

Stigma is one product of fear. We avoid what we don't understand. In 1999, the United States surgeon general's report on mental illness confirmed the existence of a stigma relative to mental illness and described how it can deter treatment and diagnosis.[1] Typical of any stigma, it can have a snowball effect, increasing its power and, at the same time, blocking opportunities to buffer the private and public trauma of mental illness.

It's true. The voices of schizophrenia do hold the potential for encouraging harmful acts. But there are other "voices" that *we all hear and heed*—voices that guide us through the days of our lives. What is the source of these voices? In our early lives, out of necessity, we are protected by voices of authority. It starts with our parents, and soon classroom teachers join the chorus. And, from early childhood until the day we die, we ascribe authority to real voices heard on TV, from the pulpit or the stage, and in books, magazines, and newspapers. The nation or culture in which we live provides voices that emanate from a host of political and social entities. Indeed, for all who live in the same time and place, in spite of the diversity of voices that surround us, there is apt to be a common thread of authority referred to as conventional wisdom.

As we identify voices to believe in and trust, the voice of our own experience can inevitably stand alone or lead to an intuitive voice some call common sense. We like to believe that we think for ourselves, but we also feel an understandable need to continually seek sources of authority, if for no other reason than to confirm what we believe. They give us something to hold on to and to stabilize us when we feel a lack of confidence or control in a complicated world of mixed messages. Yet we forget that our own voice was, and probably always will be, informed and affirmed by chosen authorities or allies. We can easily forget how our "unique" voice is, in reality, an echo of voices heard through traditional channels.

These "normal," accepted voices of authority are clearly different from the phantom voices of SMI. We don't fear them. We rely on them. But is it possible that voices emanating from the community have the potential to do social harm—even harm to those whose mental disorder may include phantom voices that we openly fear?

There are many horror stories related to mental illness. We are made aware of them when someone whose life has been affected by a mental disorder perpetrates harm to others. What we are less likely to acknowledge is how vulnerable these potential perpetrators are to harm perpetrated *by* others, by citizens acting out of fear or misunderstanding.

Historically, atrocities and embarrassments related to society's relationship with mental illness have existed in a variety of contexts, and new versions of old stories can sound like echoes from the past. The catalyst for these stories can originate with the well-publicized aberrant behavior of someone with mental illness. Or, sad but true, other stories may grow out of the behavior of responsible citizens, based on oversimplified beliefs about the complex topic of mental illness. It would be foolish to deny the reality or terrible consequences that can result from an individual's delusional view of the world. Too real and dreadful to ignore are the death of Kendra Webdale, who was pushed under a New York subway train by a man who was not being treated for what would later be identified as schizophrenia, or the attempted assassination of President Reagan, prompted by John Hinckley's delusional desire to impress actress Jodie Foster. The list of incidents that have made the headlines in recent years and the circumstances surrounding them would demand an entire chapter (or even book). These stories linger in our memories because they make the headlines. In addition, the experience of being verbally accosted while innocently walking down the street can also produce a lingering fear, even if the incident results in no physical harm to anyone and is not worthy of headlines.

On the other hand, just as haunting in their own way are instances of greed, insensitivity, or cruelty—the product of fear or lack of knowledge—embedded in well-intentioned public policy or committed by those who take advantage of the cognitive or economic vulnerability of those living with SMI. Can we separate *those* stories from the tragedies mentioned above? Maybe not, for they are capable of playing a role in creating the very headlines and threatening street encounters that we fear. There is the appalling lack of adequate and appropriate housing for those with SMI, resulting in too many of these individuals living on the streets or ending up in jail. There can be minimal or below standard unofficial "boarding homes" for the mentally ill, with rent based on known disability income, leaving the boarder with hardly enough money to purchase the bare necessities of life.[2] Neighborhoods may refuse to allow residential facilities for those who must live with SMI because of their own delusions and fears, based on a belief that mental illness and violent behavior go hand in hand. Perhaps the most damaging story, one that is both cause and consequence of other tragedies, concerns individuals who avoid or deny treatment for symptoms of a mental disorder in an attempt to escape the stigma of such a diagnosis, as if denying treatment denies the diagnosis, thereby avoiding the stigma, the dreaded "mark" of mental illness.

When it comes to mental illness, what *is* a reliable voice of authority? What voice of authority *does* deserve the attention and respect of the community—of voters and policy makers? That source can, and has, changed over time (e.g., men of God versus men of science). And at any one time, authorities from within a designated group are not always in agreement. In the late nineteenth and early twentieth centuries, neurologists and psychiatrists, both physicians, had different professional perspectives regarding the causes and treatment of mental disorders.

So where can ordinary community members look for the "truth"? How much of public understanding is based on fact and how much is stereotype, shaping biased perceptions and misunderstanding? Unfortunately, when community members, intentionally or coincidentally, are isolated from contact with mental illness, they may give too much power to media reports or literary narratives, both of which are more likely to focus on dire or dramatic stories that will catch public attention. It's less common to read about those who, through proper diagnosis and treatment, are coping with symptoms such that they are living meaningful, productive lives. If dire or dramatic reports are community members' most common exposure to mental illness—the loudest voice, or only voice—the result can be a representation of reality that reinforces myths related to mental disorders. A preponderance of such stories can create a sense of community hopelessness regarding our ability to live comfortably and safely and compassionately with those identified as mentally ill.

In 2005, the potential harm of this media effect was addressed by the United States Substance Abuse and Mental Health Services Administration (SAMSHA) with the creation of the Voice Awards. These awards were designed to recognize, among other things, entertainment programming that gives a positive voice to those with mental illness by writing "dignified, respectful, and accurate portrayals…into their scripts, programs, and productions." Exposure to such programming can encourage a more balanced view of challenges and outcomes related to mental illness.

Still, that does not address the original question. What *is* the truth about mental illness? Where are we to find this truth? How does an individual come to be diagnosed, or labeled, to begin with? What does it mean to the person to live with a diagnosis of mental illness, a medical diagnosis that can become a social label? Why do we need something like the Voice Awards? If a voice of authority is the source of truth, who has the authority to determine that someone has a mental disorder, and how does that person make that determination?

Some lay people may simply "understand" mental illness based on their own personal experiences in some social context. Others' views may be based on our current scientific approach to understanding and treating mental illness, leading to the "medical model," which focuses on reported or observable symptoms and a belief that there is a physical basis for those symptoms. However, the biological source cannot be confirmed directly with, for example, blood tests or imaging or any kind of lab work. It is only confirmed indirectly with the escalating availability of psychoactive drugs (any drugs known to act on the brain) that have known effects on brain chemistry and can produce changes in behavior or mood.

The public's general knowledge of these drugs has led to diverse views of mental disorders. Some community members voice distrust in the necessity, or even wisdom, of taking drugs to cure or relieve mental or behavioral problems, based on a belief that we are all capable of changing our behavior and that the word *illness* is more properly associated with diseases of the body that can be identified with lab work, such as blood tests or imaging—an X-ray or MRI. Even though the brain *is* a part of the body, few diseases or disorders associated with brain malfunctioning can be detected in this way, and certainly none that we know of can be treated or cured with antibiotics, chemotherapy, or surgery.

In spite of the benefits of psychotherapeutic drugs, some people believe that the real antidote to mental distress is to simply develop a stronger will, suggesting that we can personally control brain activity leading to any type of behavior. To some degree, we have involuntary control, in that the brain both "gives orders" and receives information that influences the orders given. But…well, to put it simply, controlling our brain activity is not as simple as telling ourselves, "Oh, too much dopamine? I can take care of that as easily as I can control the temperature in my house." Some behaviors change the level of neurotransmitters (the brain's chemical messengers) *almost* as easily as we control the temperature in our house. But the key word here is *almost*. A great many factors influence the two-way communication between our brains and the world in which we live—many more factors, or variables, than those that exist between the thermometer on your thermostat and your furnace or air conditioner.

On the other hand, perhaps a more common belief today is that those with mental illness who *can* be treated with drugs should be *compelled* to comply. But that opinion can vary with the type of disorder—a belief that schizophrenics should be legally required to take their medication can coexist with a belief that those with depression should snap out of it. Different reactions to, or beliefs about, mental illness are most likely based on the behaviors associated with the diagnosis. People may believe, or fear, that those with schizophrenia can hurt *others*, while believing that people with depression just *hurt*—period—and if they really wanted to stop hurting, they could.

These reactions may define how those with mental illness are viewed or treated by community members, but they do *not* define mental illness. What we now refer to as mental illness has not always been viewed as a medical problem—it was not even designated as an illness. In colonial America, administrators (selectmen) who were in charge of all aspects of running their communities determined the "diagnosis" of mental illness and arranged care for those whom they had diagnosed. Today, the determination of who has a mental disorder is made by qualified practitioners. However, a mental disorder is not a single disorder, but a category of disorder, with a host of possible diagnoses. For practitioners and insurance companies in the United States and many foreign countries, the American Psychiatric Association's *Diagnostic and Statistical Manual of Mental Disorders (DSM)* is the authority for determining which diagnosis is appropriate.

The *DSM–5*, published in May 2013—991 pages, weighing in at 3.4 pounds—is the current edition.

The *DSM* defines current knowledge regarding symptoms that seem to occur together, suggesting the existence of a specific disorder. And we do have reason to believe that certain treatments are optimal for reducing a given set of symptoms. So in an effort to choose the best treatment, mental health practitioners need some kind of common language, an objective way to assess a disorder. (And a code to designate the disorder is required if insurance is to cover the treatment.) Since each new edition of the *DSM* is revised based on what research has uncovered since the previous edition, the sequence of editions can provide insight into how our understanding and definition of mental disorders has evolved. Thus, the *DSM-5* is the sixth revision of the 1952 *DSM-I* and is a reflection of constantly changing criteria based on scientific research. Though we have not been able to use approaches that look at brain function for the purpose of diagnosis, research does make use of such tools in an effort to better understand what mental disorders look like inside the nervous system. We can, for example, compare images of "healthy" brains to images of those with symptoms of a mental disorder.

It should be no surprise that solutions to complicated problems are accompanied by complicating and troublesome side effects. As with other drugs, most psychotherapeutic drugs are accompanied by physiological side effects. Furthermore, there is a social side effect of a classification system such as the *DSM* in that it can feed the fertile ground of limiting labels, among both professionals and nonprofessionals. Professionals have a hard enough time using a complex classification system. Nonprofessionals, even though they may have gained some familiarity with certain diagnoses and terms through the media, are well advised to forget labels, period. Even if they can name, or recognize, the diagnosis given by a professional, how much will they understand about the disorder?

There is great variability in both the prognosis and the most effective treatment for any one individual for any chronic disorder—no matter what bodily system is behaving badly. This is true of multiple sclerosis, diabetes, asthma, and hypertension, to name but a few. The variability among those with a diagnosis of something like bipolar disorder is equally great. And so, difficult as it may be, community members must do their best to minimize reliance on labels that can define a person in a stereotyped, limited, and even inaccurate manner. The language we use can guide our behavior toward an individual as well as our judgment of that person.

A child may respond to bullying, or any kind of verbal attack, by saying, "Sticks and stones may break my bones, but words can never hurt me." Eleanor Roosevelt affirmed that idea, encouraging us with the thought that "Nobody can make you feel inferior without your permission." Don't believe those statements for one minute. While we may find comfort in them and may use them as a way to make our way through a less-than-comforting world, labels *can* both hurt us and make us feel inferior. Words *are* powerful. Words do hurt. Words can test the limits of our ability to stave off a sense of inferiority. Words can negate any reasonable sense of hope. Words *can* hurt you and me, and for those who are dealing with a mental disorder, they can reinforce an already damaging stigma, including the individual's sense of self-stigma.

So, what are we to do when we learn that a friend or neighbor has been diagnosed with a mental disorder? There are at least two ways in which we can be helpful—both motivated by compassion, rather than by fear or puzzled avoidance. Neither of those two approaches suggests that we take on the role of pseudoprofessionals, using words and terms that we don't fully understand. The only knowledge required in both cases is what it means to be a friend and how to offer support rather than advice. There are myths to be dispelled, rather than repeated and encouraged. Even professionals—scientists and practitioners—have much to learn in their understanding of mental illness. And so, it makes sense that our own learning should never be motivated by a desire to become amateur diagnosticians.

Our first chance to help occurs if we observe a noticeable change in behavior in a friend or acquaintance or learn of it from a family member. Mentioning or responding to this information with fear or hesitancy can make friends in need assume a sense of denial about what they are experiencing. But what would you do if you noticed symptoms of a *nonstigmatized* condition—for example, a suspicious skin condition? Your friend would be best served if, in a voice of casual concern, you recommended or offered to find a dermatologist who might help—without giving the skin condition a name. Even having had a similar condition yourself does *not* qualify you to assume that what you're noticing is the same condition. Likewise (or more so), if a friend reports, or you notice, unusual behavior or thought patterns in a family member, you're not in a position to even guess at a diagnosis that could be based on some TV show or news item.

If, or when, a diagnosis is determined, the best thing to do is so simple. You are required to do nothing more than offer support. How? If you don't understand what your friend is dealing with, how can you offer support? If your friend has sought professional help, and a diagnosis and treatment plan is determined, there is more to be done. That's where friends can play a significant role. Friends and neighbors—even acquaintances—can offer open, unquestioning acceptance and support to those who are dealing with an acute or chronic mental disorder, in the same way we would for someone experiencing a bout of the flu (an acute disorder) or diabetes (a chronic disorder). In a kind and caring manner, we can ask nonjudgmental questions and, most important, *listen to the answers*. Try to understand not necessarily the illness itself, but the challenges faced by the family.

Scientific research is a source of information and authority, but understanding good and bad research, or even how to interpret good research, can be tricky for members of the general population. Researchers themselves know that at any one time, they have not arrived at the final answer to a question, for research is an ongoing, open-ended process where one answer leads to further questions and further research...and on and on.

Though you are unlikely to do any systematic objective research yourself, you are constantly exposed to the product of such research, and you're likely to quote it as a source of authority—prefaced with the words *they say*—without fully understanding what it is they're saying or who "they" are and how "they" know. The "they" you hear about and/or refer to may seem to be the researchers, but, in fact, they are most likely members of the media reporting published research in a manner meant to be friendlier to the lay reader. That's understandable and even acceptable, but there are good and bad reporters of science and oversimplified reporting that can lead nonprofessionals to jump to unjustified conclusions.

Let me describe how this might work. I have a young friend who has been diagnosed with SMI, is receiving excellent treatment, is compliant with his medication, has the support of his family, is holding down a good job, and has a realistic understanding of what he'll be dealing with for the rest of his life. The good news is that he is highly likely to be able to live a meaningful life. However, as he was describing to me what he needed to accept about his diagnosis, he said, "I know that my life will be shortened because of this." Though I do my best to keep up with research reports and problems associated with mental illness, I was not familiar with this particular piece of information. I didn't say it was false, but I did make a mental note to check out the accuracy of what he reported with such confident acceptance. Where did that information come from?

A bit of Googling led me to a 2007 *USA Today* article with the headline "Mentally Ill Die 25 Years Earlier, On Average."[3] If one only reads article headlines (many do; I've done it myself), that would confirm what my friend had been told. But in the very first paragraph of the article, I read, "Adults with serious mental illness treated in public systems die about twenty-five years earlier than Americans overall." If you'd already read the headline, you might not even notice an important phrase in that sentence: *in public systems*. Insignificant? Absolutely not. For example, my friend does not receive his medical care in a public system. But if you took the time to read the entire article, you would understand the significance of this two-word phrase. It is not a given that mental illness itself "causes" a shorter life span. It might. But mental illness can also lead to situations and circumstances that can, in turn, lead to a shorter life span; for example, the source of one's health care or lifestyle choices that can affect physical health.

We often hear the words *they say,* but we must be cautious in giving authority to this *they,* not necessarily because *they* are lying, but because you might not have a good understanding of which *they* you're listening to (or reading) and what *they* may have changed or eliminated in an effort to simplify the report of a more reliable *they*—those who *do* the systematic, objective research that is published in peer-reviewed journals or presented at professional conferences where proposed presentations are screened, before they are accepted, to make sure that stringent rules of the scientific method are followed. Gaining that understanding may seem like too much trouble. But since much of what we believe and many decisions we make for ourselves and our family are influenced by the authority of *they*, it is worth your time to at the very least consider who they are, how they know, and what they know. In the case of mental health, misinformation can lead to fear, which too often leads to a stigma characterized by prejudice and discrimination that can complicate our reason to hope. In the face of mental illness, is hope then delusional? Can community members really make a difference?

In a general sense, to have hope means to anticipate a satisfactory outcome. In the case of mental illness, what will we accept as a satisfactory outcome? Is cure the only satisfactory outcome? If cure is not possible, where do we look for hope? Improvement in quality of life for those with mental illness? Improved quality of life for communities such that they can live with mental illness without an accompanying fear? More important, are these two hopes mutually exclusive?

The questions become even more complex and specific. Does our hope reside in the development of medications that will allow management of symptoms? In a more futuristic sense, does genetic testing offer hope for a roadblock to the development of the disease(s)? But let's not get ahead of ourselves. As a starting point, hope must start as acceptance of the current immutable fact of mental illness, rather than a belief that we must eradicate or treat it out of existence. Is it necessary to protect a fearful society and a vulnerable population from one another through structured separation? Or, because individuals with mental illness *are* members of society, can we link hope to an insistence on encouraging socialization and optimizing independence for consumers within the community?

While this book explores such questions, it does not attempt to answer them directly. The intention is to give us something positive to think about and to hope for. It provides evidence, in the form of explicit examples, of how communities can and are coexisting with the complexities of mental illness, offering people with mental illness opportunities to optimize their chances for meaningful lives—providing communities a peek at possibility that might lead to sincere and compassionate efforts. Not against, with.

Though the tragic stories linked to mental illness are purposely not the focus of this book, they are the *reason* for this book. Factual, well-researched media stories and nonfiction narratives are necessities, in that they insist on desperately needed, necessary reform; they are a useful form of protest.[4, 5, 6] However, for reform to occur, people and communities need models and the accompanying sense of hope that such models provide. Reading success stories can give mental health workers, as well as entire neighborhoods and communities, a vicarious sense of efficacy as they seek to implement the twentieth-century movement toward community mental health treatment.

Neither hope nor optimism alone can produce positive outcomes. They can only stimulate the courage to pursue such outcomes. In his book *Keeping Hope Alive*, theologian/ethicist Lewis Smedes[7] described the sequential components of hope: (1) wishing, (2) imagining your wish as fulfilled, and (3) believing that it *can* be fulfilled. Psychological research also emphasizes the power of belief in one's ability to carry out actions that will lead to positive or desired outcomes. *Self-efficacy* is defined by this kind of belief. Albert Bandura, renowned Stanford University psychology researcher and professor, has thoroughly investigated how social situations impact what we come to believe about ourselves, as well as what motivates us. He defines *self-efficacy* as a "belief in one's capabilities to organize and execute the courses of action required to produce given attainments."[8]

Dr. Smedes might say that we dare not wish or imagine if we are not ready to believe. Research says the same thing when it shows that we are not motivated to face challenges if we don't have any reason to believe that we have the ability to meet those challenges. Bandura saw this in groups as well as with individuals, describing *collective efficacy* as a "shared belief in [the group's] conjoint capabilities to organize and execute the courses of action required to produce given levels of attainment."[9] How does this individual or group belief evolve? Where does the inspiration for success begin? Bandura states, "There is nothing more persuasive than seeing effective practices in use." Seeing what *can* happen, or has happened, allows us to imagine it happening again.

The stories in this book offer a new view of mental illness to those who have been exposed to nothing but fear and failure relative to it. These stories can inspire the courage of those who are doing their best to be productive, participating members of their communities. They can inspire hope and courage in fearful community members and beleaguered professionals, both of whom are vital to supporting the courage of consumers. None of us need be afraid to wish, imagine, and believe.

As Robert Frost reminds us, there are many "givens" in life that we would prefer to give back. Most often, that is not an option. It is clear that *all of us*, collectively, have been "given" the fact of mental illness. Once we accept it as a part of our human existence, we may be bold enough to develop a new belief. Perhaps we can "make it over" in a way that allows both those with mental illness and the communities in which they live to "hold their own"—to recover. This is a wish whose reality can be imagined because that wish has become a reality—in Geel, Belgium, and in many communities and programs in our own country. We can believe because of the sense of collective efficacy that we garner from learning of these communities and programs. *Not against, with*—reason to hope.

# 2

# The Voice of a Legend

This is a story, a legend, of lives affected by mental illness. Its origins are sad, even gruesome. It is a story of madness and murder. But it is a story with a happy ending that is still being written. It is a story with a voice of hope.[1,2,3,4]

As legends often do, this one should begin with "Once upon a time." Those words help us differentiate between legend and history. And so...

Once upon a time, in seventh-century Ireland, there lived a proud and powerful pagan king named Damon. Damon was married to the extraordinarily beautiful Odilla. Ironically, in light of his paganism, they lived near Armagh, a city that would become "the ecclesiastical capital of Ireland." You've probably never heard of Damon, but no doubt you know of another man from the same area of Ireland named Patrick. He would become the first archbishop of Armagh in 444 and was ultimately canonized as St. Patrick. In 445, Patrick built a stone church on a site that eventually became the site of Armagh's St. Patrick's Cathedral, which still stands today.

In Damon's day, almost two hundred years after Patrick built his church, Patrick's Christian influence was strongly felt in the area, and, in spite of Damon's pagan beliefs, his beautiful and beloved wife, Odilla, became a Christian. When the couple's daughter, Dymphna,[5] was born, the mother arranged for her to be raised by a priest, Gereberne. Sadly, when Dymphna was in her teens, her mother became gravely ill. To ensure her daughter's Christian upbringing, Odilla asked Gereberne to continue Dymphna's education following her own impending death.

Odilla did die, leaving Dymphna motherless and King Damon overcome with grief. As his advisors helplessly witnessed his daily decline, they suggested that a new wife would offer solace in the face of his inconsolable grief. The king accepted their suggestion, but even after searching the entire country, his advisors were unable to find anyone as beautiful as Odilla; no one, that is, except Odilla's daughter, who was, of course, Damon's daughter as well. Such a match was not unheard of in pagan times, but in the face of her Christian upbringing, her father's proposal of marriage was unacceptable to either Dymphna or her spiritual caretaker, Gereberne the priest. Damon, however, unaccustomed to being denied and eager for an end to his grief, persisted with his proposal. But Dymphna also persisted in her refusal, resulting in an escalation of Damon's stubborn anger.

In response to her father's irrational request and anger, Dymphna requested a forty-day period in which to reflect on his proposal. Though his proposal was meant to put an end to *his* grief, Dymphna hoped that her request would buy her time to find a solution to her own grief in the face of her father's mad insistence. Thus, as her father awaited submission to his demand, Dymphna and Gereberne, along with a lady-in-waiting and a court jester, fled the country across the North Sea to what we now call Belgium[6], entering Antwerp via the River Schelde and moving about twenty-five miles inland to hide in the forests of Zammel, a hamlet of the settlement of Geel. There the party of refugees built a small abode, near Geel's chapel of St. Martin, and settled into a peaceful life, with Dymphna visiting the sick and poor in the area and all of the party believing themselves to be safe from Damon's power and wrath.

If the king had been angry at Dymphna's persistent refusal of his proposal, one can only imagine the tenor of his fury when he discovered that his "chosen bride" had now denied him by vanishing. Damon was not one to be denied, and when he realized that Dymphna was gone, his unrequited desire to make the young woman his wife further infuriated him. He commanded his soldiers to determine her whereabouts. Now his search for a bride became a search meant to affirm the authority of a thwarted king, and his grief appears to have turned to madness. His soldiers soon gathered information indicating that Dymphna's party had made it to the continent, and Damon, along with a party of soldiers and servants, personally went looking for her. As had Dymphna's party, Damon's party also landed in Antwerp. Waiting there, Damon dispatched his men to look for Dymphna—his daughter and chosen bride—in the countryside.

As they searched the area, some of the party, looking for a place to spend the night, happened onto In the Kettle, an inn located in Westerlo, near Zammel. When the soldiers paid for their room and board, the keeper of the inn, intrigued by the unique coins from their homeland, innocently noted that a foreign girl who was living in the vicinity had paid for food with similar coins. The alert soldiers inquired as to where she was staying, and later legend reported that when the landlady stretched out her arm to point in the direction of the young woman's dwelling, her arm remained permanently stiff in that position.

One can well imagine the soldiers' sense of excitement as they returned to Antwerp to report their discovery. On hearing the news, Damon quickly traveled to Geel, found his daughter and the priest, and once again presented his proposal—now a demand—to Dymphna. But even in the forests of a strange land, she refused her father's incestuous proposal. His rage now reached new levels, and the story turned from madness to murder as Damon ordered his soldiers to behead the priest, most likely in an effort to convince Dymphna of his determination. The order was obeyed, but even with her beloved mentor's blood soaking the ground on which she stood, Dymphna still refused to submit to her father's mad demands. Overcome and consumed with rage, the king now ordered his soldiers to behead Dymphna herself. Though they were surely loath to follow Damon's orders to behead the priest, they now expressed defiant outrage. None of the soldiers would obey this shocking demand, and the enraged king beheaded his own daughter, whereupon he and his party left the area, leaving the bodies of Dymphna and the priest unburied.

The fate of the maddened, and mad, king is not included in the remainder of the story, but the fate of the young girl who had martyred herself by choosing death rather than yielding to the incestuous demands of her father was the seed that grew into a larger legend. As with all oral tradition, the legend acquired a life of its own, growing as it fed on the fruits of its telling. Some say that individuals living in the area, knowing of the tragedy, found the bodies and buried them on the exact spots where the murders had occurred; other reports indicate that the bodies were placed in a cave. Still other reports suggest that the bodies were moved at least two times. One version of the legend indicates that when the bodies were first exhumed, they were found contained in white-stone coffins, a material foreign to that area. This led to a belief that they had been buried by angels, feeding an already growing belief in Dymphna's divine powers and, ultimately, her ability to intercede on behalf of the sick. As word of her martyrdom spread, the sick came to pray on the graves of the young princess and her priest. Because the legend came to focus most specifically on her martyrdom in the face of madness, prayers for cures were most specifically for a cure from mental illness—relief for the demented.

Over the centuries, reports of miraculous cures occurring near St. Martin's chapel, the site of Dymphna's martyrdom, continued to be told, luring a continuous and growing influx of pilgrims and the evolution of an increasingly elaborate legend. Finally, in 1247, Bishop Guy I of Cambrai, a large bishopric in the north of France that included Brussels and Antwerp, asked Canon Peter van Kamerijk (or, in some narratives, Pierre) of the church of St. Aubert in Cambrai to commit to writing a story that had been told and elaborated on for more than six hundred years. With that written narrative, the story was documented for the first time, but the canon acknowledges in his "Life of Dymphna" that it was totally a product of oral tradition in Geel. And so, in the thirteenth century, legend led to fact, for based on Canon Kamerijk's narrative, Dymphna, and Gereberne with her, entered Roman martyrdom with a feast day of May 15. Official recognition of Dymphna's martyrdom assured an ever-growing influx of pilgrims seeking religious treatment.

It is fascinating, this story of a young girl with the faith and fortitude to stand up to the incestuous madness of her own father. The story is even more appealing in light of the *consequences* of Dymphna's sacrifice and the miracles attributed to her faith and sacrifice. From the legend grew what is sometimes referred to as the cult of St. Dymphna, and today Dymphna's patronage as a saint also includes her ability to cure or bless sleepwalking, epilepsy, family happiness, incest victims, insanity, loss of parents, martyrs, mental asylums, mental disorders, mental health caregivers, mental health professionals, mental hospitals, mental illness, mentally ill people, nervous disorders, neurological disorders, possessed people, princesses, psychiatrists, rape victims, runaways, sleepwalkers, and therapists.

In the Middle Ages, when the church was looked to for the cure of mental illness, it was only natural that Geel's church became the destination of thousands of pilgrims seeking such a "cure." Additional buildings and additions were erected in an effort to accommodate the pilgrims, but when the church still overflowed, church canons bade the townspeople to take pilgrims into their homes. Thus began, without a committee or council meeting or planning commission, a system of foster family care for the mentally ill that has evolved and exists even today, a system that is considered to be the oldest surviving community mental health care system in the Western world. In terms of the administration of, and motivation for, this system, there have been changes over the centuries, but the general mood of the community itself continues to be one of acceptance for those who, in many places and times, would be shunned or feared by society.

Today, in the twenty-first century, Geel is still the site of not only a foster family care system but a comprehensive system of mental health services that includes the original option of foster family care as well as community-treatment centers, community social clubs, and regional mental health services provided in three different hospitals for the mentally ill. What makes Geel unique, however, is not so much the services provided, but the environment provided by the community itself (as of 2012, a busy, prosperous city of 38,094 inhabitants, representing 117 nationalities), where social interactions between boarders and community members are casual and common. Since the mentally ill have been a part of town life for so many centuries, they're welcomed and even nurtured by the entire community. If a stigma or bias regarding mental illness exists at all in Geel, it is a bias favoring those with a mental disorder. All because of a young girl's courage. Maybe.

The story of Dymphna is lovely, and, while the legend itself inspires and supports those who know the torment of mental illness, few doubt that it is anything but that—a story, or perhaps more accurately, a legend. Ever since the story began to take form, through its existence as oral tradition and even after it was committed to writing, many versions have been told, providing evidence for its designation as a legend. The version you've just read is currently, for the most part, the commonly accepted version. (References to St. Patrick are generally not included in the story, but have been included here to give historical context to "what might have been.") Surely there were many oral versions before 1247, and we have evidence of other versions appearing in print, even in the past one hundred years. One such version identifies Dymphna as having been "driven insane by the behavior of an incestuous father."[7] In the mid-nineteenth century, another legend, though acknowledged as inaccurate at the time, appeared in print, stating that "the legend of Gheel [sic] informs us [that] a certain English lady of high rank and surpassing beauty, when driven to madness by the treachery of a lover, and the cruelty of friends, wandered from her home and from her country, and found refuge in this deserted spot; where she recovered her reason, built a church, and devoted a long life to curing the insane, having received from heaven the power of performing such cures."[8]

Articles on Geel published in 1969 and 1972 state that the miracle was that Damon's sanity was restored after he murdered his daughter.[9] Almost ten years later, a highly respected British psychiatrist repeats and cites another late nineteenth-century version of the miracle in Geel.

> [Damon] attacked [Dymphna], severing her head from her body, and his soldiers decapitated Gereberne. It is reputed that these cruel deeds so greatly frightened several lunatics who witnessed them that they became cured, as if by enchantment.[10]

During the period when the story was passed on orally, there was a strong emphasis on Dymphna's status as an early Christian. In these early versions, Damon was often depicted as a Turk, presumably because Turks were considered to be the enemies of Christians.[11]

When I was a child, we used to play a game called "gossip" at birthday parties. We sat in a circle, and one child whispered a short story in the ear of the next child. That child repeated it into the ear of the next child, with no intentional embellishment. And so it went around the circle until the final child recited aloud a story that began moments earlier and only inches away. At that point, the original teller of the tale would share the original story, and we usually had a good laugh at how the story had changed in the retelling. That is the nature of legend, and since actual legend is repeated and evolves over long periods of time, there is even greater opportunity for transformation. Of course, in the birthday party game, some creative child may have added a word or two to "spice up" the story, and that type of embellishment also occurs in the evolution of a legend. As with any story whose written version is preceded by a long life of oral history, the final product is inevitably quite different from whatever events sparked the original oral version.

While there was surely some event that evoked the beginning of the story of Dymphna, Gereberne, and Damon, there is no evidence that these people, with these names and origins, actually existed; in fact, there is evidence to the contrary. Irish scholars have been unable to verify the existence of a chief named Damon or his daughter, Dymphna, or a priest named Gereberne. At one time, St. Damhnat, who the Irish *do* claim as their own, and St. Dymphna were believed to be one and the same. However, in 1949, an article in an Irish archaeological society journal provided reason to believe that "it is highly improbable that St. Damhnat of Ireland and St. Dimpna [sic] of Gheel [sic] were one and the same person."[12] Nevertheless, in addition to evidence of her legend in Geel, Dymphna also has a physical presence in Ireland, particularly in and around County Monaghan. St. Dympna's Psychiatric Hospital is in Monaghan, and there are St. Dympna's National Schools in Kildalkey, County Meath, as well as in Tydavnet. In County Monaghan, St. Davnet's church is said to have once stood on what is now the village cemetery. There do appear to be two different saints whose names have been linked together in history, and the name of the village, Tydavnet (house of Davnet), would confirm an association with Davnet, rather than Dymphna. But in spite of what scholars may say regarding Davnet and Dymphna, in 2005 a group of Monaghan County officials, as well as citizens from the Tydavnet area, traveled to Geel to participate in the St. Dymphna Procession, traditionally held every five years, on or around St. Dymphna's feast day on May 15. (St. Davnet's feast day is June 14.) While there may have been much of merit about Davnet's life and legend, it appears that she does not offer the living, international legend that can be found in Dymphna and Geel and Geel's celebration of her legend.

So is any of this important? If it is historically inaccurate, does it really matter? A legend is a legend. Certainly there are circumstances in which it can be important or useful to uncover the truth behind historical events. When we emphasize the value of history by saying that "those who fail to remember are doomed to repeat the past," it might be assumed that we will only learn useful lessons if we remember accurately. Legend is a different sort of history, but is it possible for legend in and of itself, accurate or inaccurate, to have positive value? There can certainly be no doubt that in many contexts, what people believe to be true can have power and impact as large as, or larger than, the truth itself. There can be no doubt that over the centuries, many people have believed in some version of a story of miracle cures of mental illness having occurred in the vicinity of Geel. Whether these miracles occurred or not, from this belief has evolved a community that is comfortable with mental illness and hospitable toward those who have been labeled, or diagnosed, as mentally ill. The story of St. Dymphna is a myth with a positive outcome.

For some, perhaps even some in modern times, believing the story is so important that they are not interested in any evidence that debunks it. Perhaps their perspective is to be admired. What is most important is probably not whether the legend is true. What is most important is the ensuing story, a documented history that would not have evolved had it not been for a belief in the legend. *That* history can be documented and is still being written. It is that story that can provide a valuable lesson to communities who still face the difficult dilemma of how to deal with mental illness. It is a story of the evolution of mental health services across the centuries and the history of a community that has supported that evolution by continuously accepting individuals with mental illness. The story of Geel is, at times, affected by outside influences, but it is always affected by an attitude that was fed by a myth. Whether Dymphna lived or not, something caused a community to "hear" a young girl's voice of courage, and that voice echoed as a community voice of acceptance.

There are other myths, legends, or voices related to mental illness that have had a less kindly effect on communities or the lives of those who bear the burden of the illness; these other myths have kept alive a stigma that adds to the burden and often paralyzes the community. Legend and myth and stereotype have at least two things in common: they are tenacious, and they hold within them threads of truth that lend authority to all other elements. The Dymphna legend includes in it truths that may have nothing to do with the legend itself. We all know that there is a city of Antwerp, and we can trace on a map the reported escape route of Dymphna—across the North Sea and up the River Schelde into Antwerp. But does that familiarity, that fact, support the truth of Dymphna's escape? In order to lend historical context to my own telling of the story, I added a reference to St. Patrick, a familiar name even to most modern Americans (particularly those who look forward to a reason for drinking green beer). Does that familiarity make one more ready to accept the story of a less familiar saint? According to legend, the inn where Damon's soldiers found evidence of Dymphna's presence in the area is given a specific name. Does such a precise reference to the inn make the story more believable? And on and on. We often accept the veracity of a story and the conclusions that arise from that story based on recognizable truths or conventions within the story. Though they may not deserve the power or authority to establish the larger truth implied in the story, we readily turn molehills into mountains, trivial detail into formidable fact.

In our own country, what people hold to be truth about mental illness in many instances is most accurately a stereotype. Based merely on the tenacity and the presence of recognizable truths embedded in the stereotype, we see the stereotype as a truth in and of itself. We give it power equal to the power of myth or legend. As with the legend of St. Dymphna, people's beliefs regarding mental illness become their reality, and evidence contrary to those beliefs is easily ignored and even suspect for those who have put their faith in the stereotype.

Today, we take for granted that if a mental illness has been identified and given a name, that designation is based on some kind of medical research and subsequent knowledge or understanding. Some may be leery of what research has to say about the workings or malfunctions of the mind, but most people give some degree of credence to a medical diagnosis. Whether we understand the research process or only casually note brief news stories that describe, or refer to, some current research finding that holds hope for diagnosis or treatment, we trust the "medical model." It is a part of our modern-day culture and our understanding of what it means to be ill.

Before the cataloged authority of the *DSM* and the medical model were established, popular, or sometimes authoritative, *belief* about mental illness defined it.[13] Based on archeological evidence of trephining, it appears that mental illness was associated with evil spirits during the Stone Age. However, it has also been suggested that these trephined holes in the skull were a means to remove physical objects or damaged tissue, rather than spirits.[14] Nevertheless, until the time of Hippocrates (c. 460 BC–c. 380 BC), the standard explanation for strange behavior in an individual was evil spirits, and the standard treatment was exorcism. But Hippocrates did not consider demons to be a part of mental illness, and he stated, "For my own part, I do not believe that the human body is ever befouled by a god." When he began to classify abnormal behavior according to observed symptoms, Hippocrates was perhaps foreshadowing our current *DSM* classification system.

When demons were no longer considered to be part of the cause, exorcism could no longer be considered an effective treatment. Though prescription drugs would not be available for centuries, treatments were prescribed relative to the symptoms and classification. For example, the cure for *hysteria* (literally "wandering uterus") was marriage. Tranquility, a vegetarian diet, and celibacy were recommended as a cure for *melancholia* (extreme sadness, most likely what we now classify as depression), which was thought to be associated with black bile, one of the four natural causes, or humors, associated with mental illness.

Another approach to understanding mental illness came from Plato (428–347 BC), who proposed that mental illness was a "sickness of the soul," implying, at least in part, a spiritual aspect of the human condition. He evidently did *not* associate the "sick soul" with evil spirits, but rather recommended humane treatment within the family as the best approach to cure it. He even went so far as to suggest that the family be held responsible for crimes committed by their insane relatives and be made to pay any penalties related to these crimes. Lest that seem illogical or unfair, parents, even today, are often implicitly, sometimes explicitly, blamed for the mental illness of their children. (For too many years, autistic children were believed to be the product of cold and distant parents.)

Throughout this period, compared to previous eras, civilized attitudes were reflected in treatment approaches for those with mental illness. Galen (AD130–200) represents a summary of the Greco-Roman tradition in stating that mental illness is a brain problem resulting from either disturbed "animal spirits" in the brain or an effect, by consensus, from other organs. His death in AD200 coincided with the beginning of the medical dark ages, and once again understanding of mental disorders was lost in superstition and demonology—an attitude that persisted for more than one thousand years.

In the beginning of these dark days, patients might have been treated with kindness, but it was a kindness motivated by superstition. Patients often exhibited religious behavior interpreted as possession, and since the source of the possession was unknown, the faithful apparently didn't take any chances. Later, when clergy became convinced that possession was a manifestation of Satan's pride, patients were dealt with accordingly, and kindness was replaced first with insults and then curses, which became harsher and harsher. But religious practitioners most likely did not feel any loss of humanity in their harshness, for they did not believe they were attacking fellow humans, but rather *rescuing* them from Satan's possession of their bodies and souls.

Toward the end of this one-thousand-year period, a particularly bitter chapter was written. By this time, the mentally ill were viewed as either heretics or witches and were considered to be dangerous enemies, a perspective that led to a 1484 papal brief from Pope Innocent VIII urging the clergy of Europe to expend all efforts to get rid of witches. Two Dominican monks, Johann Sprenger and Heinrich Kraemer, as a means of implementing the order, offered a handy set of instructions in a manual entitled *Malleus Maleficarum (The Hammer of Witches)*. It was quite successful; over the next three hundred years, nineteen editions of this "divinely inspired" manual were published.

The manual, in three parts, dealt with the issue of witchcraft with authority and thoroughness. First of all, it confirmed the existence of witches and suggested that those who did not believe in them were perhaps guilty of heresy as well. It also described the "clinical symptoms" by which one could recognize witches—for example, red spots on the skin resembling claws of the devil. Finally, it outlined the legal forms of examining and sentencing a witch, with torturing a confession out of the suspect described as the best and most effective way to prove witchery.

Not all were sold on the idea of witches, however, and in 1563, a German physician named Johann Weyer wrote *Deception of Demons*, in which he flatly denied claims made in *Malleus Maleficarum* and argued that many who had been called witches were, in fact, sick in mind or body. While Meyer received some peer support, it was sparse, and he was accused of "progressing the affairs of the devil" in his defense of the dreaded witches.

It seemed that, despite the best efforts of the inquisition, the problem of mental illness would not go away, and toward the end of the Middle Ages, institutions for the mentally ill began to appear in Europe. However, though scientific interest in the mentally ill was increasing, that interest was not reflected in the environment of these asylums.

One of the first of these institutions was St. Mary of Bethlehem, a former monastery converted to a hospital by Henry VIII in 1547. St. Mary's soon became known as Bedlam, and for a penny a look, the public could view the most violent inmates. But Bedlam was not the first mental hospital. During this shameful one-thousand-year period in Europe, the Greek medical tradition was kept alive in Arabia. In the late sixth and early seventh centuries, followers of Mohammadism came proselytizing into Europe. Though they were advancing their own religious cause, they also offered an oasis for philosophy and persecuted heretics. Consequently, the early medical traditions found a haven in the Arab world, and in AD792, the first mental hospital was established in Baghdad. Others followed in the Arab world, offering treatment far more humane than anything known in Christian lands for quite some time.

Despite the shamefulness of the inquisition and the early European mental institutions, in the thirteenth century, the legend of Dymphna was escalating in the village of Geel. Reported miracles over the centuries had surely led to Dymphna's canonization, and, in turn, her sainthood brought a continued and growing influx of pilgrims seeking religious treatment. In an effort to accommodate these pilgrims, a guesthouse hospital was built near the site of the St. Martin's chapel in 1286. Though this was a hospital, it was also the Middle Ages, when mental illness was attributed to devil possession, and even here, priests were the primary practitioners. As pilgrims continued to come to Geel, a new church building was begun in 1349. (Though the church suffered fire and storm over the years, the present Church of St. Dymphna was completed in 1749 and still stands today.[15])

It was in this church that pilgrims received religious "treatment." Upon arrival, they participated in a Catholic confession before beginning a nine-day novena in which they processed in and around the church three times a day for nine consecutive days. The procession required them to pass barefoot and on their knees under the reliquary shrine, said to contain the bones of Dymphna and Gereberne, which had been moved to the church from the site of Dymphna's martyrdom. In addition, they were required to say thirty Our Fathers (The Lord's Prayer) and thirty Hail Marys, a three-part prayer honoring the blessed Virgin Mary. If patients were unable to complete the exercise, substitutes were allowed to recite the prayers on their behalf. The novena included a daily mass with administration of bread and wine sacraments and cleansing of the chalice with ablution water. This water was offered to the patients for drinking, and an exorcism formula was said over the pilgrims to drive out the devil. During this nine-day period, patients stayed in the church sickroom and were advised to sleep in their clothes. Patients were also weighed during this time, and they, or their families, begged grain from house to house in order to offer their weight in grain to St. Dymphna.

Since many pilgrims were unable to care for themselves and because staying in the church became a part of the "treatment," a sickroom was added to the church in 1480.[16] But even with a hospital and a sickroom, there were still more pilgrims than could be accommodated. And so, in about the fifteenth century, a practical solution was found, and the church canons instructed local villagers to house overflow pilgrims awaiting their turns for a cure. Also, if the initial nine-day treatment was unsuccessful, many pilgrims stayed on, and homes were opened to them as well. It was from these spontaneous, pragmatic acts of kindness that Geel's tradition of integrated, community residential care evolved.[17]

What is now called Geel's system of foster family care didn't begin as a system at all. It was merely an opportunistic arrangement agreed upon by the families of Geel and the families of the pilgrims. Each had something to gain. The pilgrims had a place to stay, and the families received some kind of remuneration—monetary or in the form of goods or services. Though there was clearly a *quid pro quo* aspect to this arrangement, given the outcome of this early system, it appears that eventually the families of Geel acted out of a generosity of spirit. Today there is, in fact, evidence that foster families gain a sense of emotional bonding and caring that surpasses any monetary compensation.

In the beginning, the families of pilgrims simply made informal arrangements with villagers for their relatives' room and board. However, in 1532, a college of vicars was established at the St. Dymphna church, and in 1562, when the college became a chapter of canons, they took on various responsibilities associated with the family care system. These responsibilities included "taking charge of the devotion to St. Dymphna, caring for patients, publishing the miraculous recoveries, and disseminating medals and brief biographies of the saint." The presence and type of administration changed over the years, and as the system persisted, authority and supervision were transferred. There was even a time when supervision ceased to exist, but the tradition would not die, even under orders of authority.

In the early years, just as in other cities or countries, patients in Geel were not always treated in a humane manner. From the late fifteenth century to the mid-eighteenth century, various regulatory efforts were enacted to address that issue, but in 1795, during the French Revolution the territory of Belgium that had been under Dutch control came under French control, and in 1797, religious family care was officially ended. The churches were closed, and the priests were dismissed. But the tradition was too ingrained in the culture of Geel. The system belonged to the townspeople, who did not simply respond to the edict of authority. It is also possible that an opportunistic element helped to keep it alive, for the kind of informal financial and work arrangements that marked the beginning of the system resurfaced. The mentally ill from across the region were still brought to Geel by their family members, and as in the early days, private arrangements were made between Geel families and patient families. Perhaps government officials thought that ending religious supervision of family care would end the system itself. Such was not the case, and the government was still left to deal with the fact that a system was in place with conditions that they did not consider acceptable.

Ignoring the apparent fact that it was a care option that was needed by the families of the mentally ill and that the families of Geel were willing to respond to this need, the French Minister of Justice decided to put an end to the family care system itself—not just church supervision—in 1811. Decisions rarely eradicate traditions, however, and the local government used delay tactics to roadblock the decision until, ultimately, in 1838, the family care system came under the jurisdiction of the Geel Municipal Council.

In 1850, Belgium's national mental illness law was passed to address poor treatment of the mentally ill nationwide. Treatment at Geel came under the direction of the state in 1852, and a medical director was named. At this time, Geel was designated as a special region, and the national government assumed responsibilities. The program became known as the Rijkskolonie, or State Colony, and though it still functioned as a normal community, on paper the whole of Geel was considered a psychiatric institute, a sort of hospital without walls,[18] and the system took on an administrative and physical structure. Geel's twenty-seven thousand acres were divided into four sections, each with a doctor, an apothecary, and a guard. In addition, a medical superintendent and a surgeon were in charge of the entire area. Patients were assigned to cordons/sectors according to the extent of their illness. Tranquil and higher-paying patients lived in the center of the village, while the most violent and furious were in the outermost sector. In any section, up to three patients of the same gender could be assigned to homes. Subsequently, in 1862, a central hospital to serve various boarder needs was built in the community.

In 1948, a Ministry of Public Health was formed in Belgium, and mental health care, including the Geel State Colony, was transferred from the Ministry of Justice. A significant change in administration took place on January 1, 1991. Geel's Public Psychiatric Hospital (Openbaar Psychiatric Zeikenhuis, the OPZ) supervises the family care system and in 1991, it gained autonomous status as a Flemish Public Institution subject to Belgian hospital laws.[19] Today the term *Rijkskolonie* is no longer used, and the entire mental health system in Geel is referred to as the OPZ. Having an independent board of directors at the OPZ was considered to be an important change that would allow decisions about the future of the hospital to be made in Geel, rather than in Brussels, hopefully insuring the future of Geel's existence as a mental health facility—a future that has, at times, seemed tenuous.

# 3

# A Dying Voice?

At its peak in the 1930s, Geel's system of foster family care provided homes for close to four thousand boarders. After World War II, the boarder count gradually began to fall, even as the number of patients hospitalized for mental disorders in Belgium remained stable. The boarder population had declined to 2,459 by 1950, and to 1,386 in 1970. This did not go unnoticed by two Chicago psychiatrists, Dumont and Aldrich, who spent two months in Geel in 1960.[1]

In its seven-hundred-year history of integrated community residential care, Geel has often attracted the attention of international visitors interested in the care of those with mental illnesses. In 1821, the system became known to the scientific community when Esquirol, a student of Phillipe Pinel,[2] visited the city and wrote of close to five hundred "lunatics" who wandered freely. While Esquirol was impressed with the system itself, he expressed concern that conditions were not equitable for all boarders, prompting his recommendation to the Minister of the Interior of the Netherlands[3] that "an asylum should be built into which those patients[,] who from their excitement or dirty habits were the most liable to be badly treated by their hosts, might be admitted."[4] To visit Geel today—her foster families and boarders—it is hard to imagine the unacceptable conditions that Esquirol described. However, comparing those early observations to Geel's current environment offers evidence for the way in which approaches to dealing with mental illness evolve over time in response to scientific developments and insights into the behavior and needs of those with a mental disorder diagnosis.

In two 1974 *Journal of the American Medical Association (JAMA)* articles, neurologist Charles Aring shared details of his 1936 visit to Geel and described Geel's success in contrast to problems occurring in the United States relative to dein-stitutionalization.[5,6] To this day, when US psychology textbooks mention Geel, this is the reference most commonly cited. But these articles were based on a visit that occurred thirty-eight years prior to publication, when Geel's boarder population was at its peak. Chicago psychiatrists Dumont and Aldrich had vis-ited only fourteen years before, in 1960, and found a very different Geel than Aring had seen. And thus, in 1962, twelve years before Aring's articles were published, Dumont and Aldrich published a warning cry concerning the future of Geel. They were alarmed at the drop in boarders and surprised to find that this drop was not due to a lack of available foster families.

Historically, families in Geel never seem to give up their desire to house boarders. In early days, when attempts to close down the system failed, Geel farmers continued to make arrangements, on their own, with the families of pil-grims. There is evidence that, in those days, efforts by the town's people to keep the system alive had a practical foundation based on the need for farm labor. It is also true that, as Esquirol noted, treatment of boarders was not always as it is today. While boarders were, at times, poorly treated, some of the things that con-cern us today, ironically, did not concern Geel families in the nineteenth century. For example, today many people in our own country fear what they consider to be a potential for violent behavior from those with a diagnosis of mental illness, even though records indicate that those with mental illness are more likely to be *victims* than perpetrators of violence. Furthermore, the relationship between mental ill-ness and violence is complicated.[7] There is not a clear-cut cause (mental illness) and effect (violent behavior) relationship, in large part because a number of other variables influence this potential relationship. For example, not everyone with a given diagnosis, such as schizophrenia, will exhibit the same type of behavior or delusional-belief symptoms. Unfortunately, while researchers try to untangle the nature of the relationship, the public's understanding can be more decisive, based on what they believe they *know*—most commonly from news stories that make headlines and dominate the twenty-four-hour news networks. The stereotype precedes the news story; what makes the news reinforces the stereotype.

Today in Geel, aggressive behavior, such as that associated with paranoid schizophrenia, would normally eliminate someone as a candidate for boarder status. However, exceptions have been allowed on a case-by-case basis, particularly when there's reason to believe that acceptance and family structure would have a calming effect on the prospective boarder. The decision to accept such a boarder is made carefully, but it has paid off, and there are documented incidents in which those who had exhibited violent behavior in other settings demonstrated successful socialization in Geel. That's today. Violent behavior is not feared, and the family environment can be an antidote, deterring eruptions of violent behavior. In earlier times, consistent with Geel's current attitude, violent behavior was not feared either. But neither was it seen as something that could be changed or cured; rather it was viewed as having potential value. When foster families and the families of boarders made their own matches, the violent behavior of a pilgrim seeking a home was sometimes seen as an asset. It has been recorded that, in nineteenth-century Geel, "raving madmen" who arrived in the town were often considered to be good risks based on a belief that they would have more vitality, and that vitality would be channeled into energy for work once they were freed from bondage or institutionalization. The pilgrims needed a home, and foster families in an agrarian culture needed strong workers. This mutual need kept the system alive.

Even in twentieth-century postwar years, and into the twenty-first century, the boarder population decline has not been linked to a lack of available foster families. In July 2006, only 417 patients were housed in the homes of 350 caretaking families, but, as always, there was a waiting list of families wanting to include boarders into their family lives. In fact, in 2014, with only 285 boarders (10 minors, 120 adults, and 155 elderly patients), there are foster families available who are ready and willing to take in boarders. The drop in boarders in recent decades can be attributed, in some part, to changes in the need for housing of those with a diagnosis of mental illness. In Europe, as in North America, other group or independent-housing options are available, and in many cases, pharmaceutical treatments have allowed greater independence and occupational opportunities to individuals with a diagnosis of mental illness.

There are still those who can benefit from the social environment available in a foster family and are well-suited to the life of a boarder. And it seems that as long as that population exists, there will be foster families in Geel ready to welcome them into their homes. Any decrease in the number of boarders in Geel cannot be attributed to the lack of available foster families nor the lack of desire on the part of Geel residents to share their home and family life with boarders, for in Geel, the centuries-old tradition of foster family care offers as much support to foster families as they offer to boarders. Many Geel citizens have had boarders in their homes since they, the citizens, were children. The boarders, whom they have known all their lives, come to be viewed as family members and are often welcomed as family members in the next generation of those families. A large number of boarders/patients have been in foster care for decades, many still living with their first and only foster families.[8] Thanks to Geel psychologist Marc Godemont, I have had the joy of visiting with foster family members who cannot imagine life without one or more boarders in their homes.

In each of my visits to Geel, Dr. Godemont has arranged for me to experience the hospitality and warmth of a foster family and their boarder or boarders. In every case, he identified a family in which either one of the foster family members or one of the boarders spoke English so that I could converse, at least in part, without translation by Dr. Godemont. During my first visit, in January 1997, I sat around the dining-room table and shared tea in the home of a widow who had two male boarders in her home, each with his own private room, reflecting the diverse personalities of the two boarders.[9] One of the boarders had spent time in Canada and, with a little bit of translation help from Dr. Godemont, we were able to engage in conversation. He had been a boarder in the widow's childhood home, and when she married, he joined her and her husband in their home. The husband had started and built a successful milling business, supplying feed to local farmers, and the boarder had helped him achieve that success. But the husband had died several years before my visit. Their sons helped keep the business going, but the two boarders also played active and important roles, giving them a sense of belonging and purpose.

During another visit, we met with a boarder at Geel's day center. Highly educated and from a European family, he spoke excellent English. I visited with him first at the center and then on the ride to the apartment he shared with his foster mother, an elderly widow with grown children who had been married to an alcoholic who took his own life. Her life had not been easy, but her demeanor was clearly that of a gentle caregiver. Dr. Godemont had indicated earlier that this gentleman was prone to anxiety, and I sensed this during our drive to his home. However, when we got to the apartment, above a small antique shop run by the widow, her presence and the few words that she spoke to him seemed to have an instant calming effect on him. (Indeed, her demeanor had a calming effect on *me*, and I wasn't nervous!)

In the months before this particular trip, I had been contacted by a successful American businessman, Mr. W, whose son had just been diagnosed with a mental disorder. Mr. W found me through my Geel website. He wanted to visit the city and arranged to make the trip with his adult daughter while I was in the city. And so, we all gathered around the table, sipping tea and chatting, with Dr. Godemont translating questions or comments directed to the Flemish-speaking foster mother. In the midst of our conversation, Mr. W asked her why she chose to have a boarder in her home, and Dr. Godemont translated. She paused. And with a gentle shrug of her shoulders, she quietly told us that she couldn't imagine life without a boarder. They had been in her childhood home, and apparently this was not the first boarder she'd had in her own home. The history of Geel was also her history.

During my 2005 visit, I met a foster family who was fluent in English. Jill had been born in the Netherlands, had moved to the United States when she was a child, and had returned to Europe as a teenager. Jill eventually married Thor, a Belgian citizen who was also fluent in English. We established an easy rapport on that first brief visit. I had been in London with a group of my students prior to coming to Belgium, and almost as soon as Jill opened the door, knowing of my background, she asked if I had heard of the bombing on the London tube that day. I had not and wondered if my students who had stayed in London for an extended visit were all safe. Jill was empathetic and comforting, and we soon began exchanging information about foster family care and their current boarder. He was a teenager who had been the boarder of a neighbor but who had become friends with Thor. When the neighbors moved away, the young man asked to live with Jill and Thor. They were honored and more than pleased to welcome him into their home.

Jill invited me to spend more time in their home if I ever returned to Geel, and I was pleased to accept that invitation during my 2007 visit. By then, the boarder who had been with them in 2005 was living independently, and they now had two men living with them in a different, new-to-them home. With Jill's husband, Thor, and their two boarders, Tibo and Axel, occupied for the day— Tibo at a retirement day center, Axel doing grounds work at the OPZ (Public Hospital), and Thor at work—Jill showed me around the partially wooded grounds of their home, describing how she and Axel had worked together to create arbor-covered gardens where they could rest on a park bench and enjoy the beauty of the yard (or observe egg-laying chickens wandering in a pen built by Axel). In the course of the afternoon, during my tour of the grounds and sitting in their living room, we had plenty of time to talk—about OPZ changes; about their new home and current boarders; and about how Jill, with no practitioner training, had been able to help Axel, the youngest of the boarders, to adjust to his first experience of living with a foster family. As Jill affectionately described "the boys" and their diverse but charmingly compatible personalities, I felt the warmth of their family life before they were even gathered together.

By four o'clock—following an afternoon of Jill's affectionate and insightful observations—when "the boys" were dropped off,[10] I was ready and eager to meet them face-to-face. I completely understood Jill's affection for them. It was also clearly reciprocal. Eighty-three-year-old Tibo had a Santa Claus–style smile and demeanor, complete with twinkling eyes. He had been with another family for a long time, but when the foster mother died, the father didn't feel up to having a boarder. Tibo had been with Jill and Thor since 2005, having arrived shortly after my previous visit to Geel. Forty-six-year-old Axel had joined the family in February 2006. He had been institutionalized at one time, and Jill and Thor were his first foster family.

When Axel and Tibo arrived, lively and playful conversation commenced, and, though I couldn't understand Flemish, no language barrier could keep me, or anyone, from understanding their good-humored joking. And then, when Thor arrived home from work at six, there were *three* "boys" thoroughly enjoying mutual "boyish" teasing.

As soon as Tibo arrived home at four, he immediately turned on the TV and occupied his comfortable "throne," a La-Z-Boy recliner purchased just for him, where he could rest his aging body. While I visited with Jill in the kitchen as she prepared dinner, Axel was eager to assume his responsibility of setting the table. But once that task was completed, he joined in the repartee with Thor and Tibo. Though I was neither an official boarder nor a foster family member, I savored the joy of feeling like a part of this warm and hospitable family. In the past, any foster family had to have at least one member who was at home during the day—in other words, did not hold a job outside the home. Today that kind of restriction has been loosened, as all boarders have a place to go during the day. But for a while, Jill did hold a job in spite of the restriction. However, in a January 2008 newsy e-mail, she reported what was going on in the lives of "the boys" (all three of them—Thor, Tibo, and Axel) and in her own life. In updating me about her life, she touchingly revealed what was most important.

> Next week I've got an appointment with my employer, and I hope very much that they'll fire me. Otherwise Tibo and Axel will have to go back to the OPZ next July. I HOPE NOT!!!!! I couldn't live without them anymore. It might be selfish, but true. Keep your fingers crossed. It might help.

We continued (and still continue) to stay in touch, and in January 2013, when I made my next trip to Geel, I was welcomed into their home as a guest for five full days and four nights. What I had observed and experienced during my 2007 "day in the life" of their family was now an exponentially more satisfying experience, offering me even greater insight and respect for all of the Geel families that I've had the privilege of meeting, and for the city itself.

In the twentieth and twenty-first centuries, foster families are simply community members with no special training who want to open their homes to those in need. And so, when Dumont and Aldrich visited in the 1960s, the apparent irony was that, in an era when interest in community-based mental health care was growing in Europe and North America, one of the oldest, best-known, and apparently successful community-care systems seemed to be in danger of demise. Dr. Aldrich was alarmed and unwilling to let the system fade into nonexistence. He shared his concern with Columbia University sociologists who, in turn, contacted and met with authorities from the Belgian Ministry of Health, the University of Leuven, and the Geel Colony (the Rijkskolonie). As an outcome of Aldrich's concern, the interest of Columbia sociologists, and subsequent meetings with Belgian officials, the ambitious multidisciplinary Geel Research Project was born in 1966.

Columbia's Dr. Leo Srole, who had gained fame for his participation in the Midtown Manhattan Study,[11] agreed to act as project director for the study, though he would remain at Columbia with full-time faculty responsibilities. Dr. Jan Schrijvers, a psychiatric resident from Leuven and a native Geelian, would serve on-site as administrative associate director, having taken a joint appointment at Geel and the Leuven School of Public Health in 1965 after graduating from Columbia's School of Public Health.

The primary intent of the study was to rescue the system from extinction through recommendations to the Belgian Health Ministry. However, if that intent failed, it was deemed important to conduct a full-scale study of Geel before it faded into antiquity—for the successes and possible shortcomings of Geel's system of foster family care had never been thoroughly or systematically examined. The project was well motivated and led by experts who were highly qualified for such an investigation. The design was thorough, and data for one portion of the study was made possible when the Belgian government allowed inclusion of a specially constructed survey in their 1971 National Census—special questions asked of all Geel households that provided data for the Foster Family Typology portion of the study. However, in spite of the thorough design and the credentials of the researchers, the study struggled over the course of its entire ten-year life, and much of the project data was never published or even analyzed—*not* due to a lack of effort or perseverance on the part of those involved, but rather due to inadequate staffing and insufficient funding.

Some funding came from a prominent US businessman, John D. J. Moore. A lifelong New Yorker, Mr. Moore had a distinguished career as a lawyer, an executive with W. R. Grace and Company cruise line, and, under President Richard M. Nixon, as the United States ambassador to Ireland.[12] Impressive credentials to be sure, but it was a more personal part of his life story that motivated

Moore's service as vice president of the American Schizophrenic Foundation and his 1960 establishment of the Family Care Foundation for the Mentally Ill.[13]As an ambassador and businessman, he was well traveled, but it was neither of those positions that led him to Geel, a visit that he described in a 1961 *Look* magazine article.[14] What called Mr. Moore to Geel was similar to what had called me when I read of it in that 1980 textbook—knowing people who were living with a diagnosis of schizophrenia and the subsequent social stigma. In his case, that person was his daughter. After touring the city and experiencing firsthand what he'd heard of, Mr. Moore could not help but share his interest in and awe of Geel in an ensuing conversation with his host, Hadelin Rademaekers, medical director of Geel at that time. Moore wrote:

> The wise, calm manner of the Belgian doctor was working on me. I blurted out my own interest in schizophrenia, telling him that one of my children, a 20-year-old daughter, had been hospitalized due to this illness.

The wise and kind doctor could sense Mr. Moore's obvious distress and, most likely, his hesitancy to share information about his daughter, for he responded to Mr. Moore by saying,

> Let's take a drive. I think we'll visit Rosa. She's about your daughter's age. Her parents brought her here two years ago from Rome, where she'd been in a closed hospital for three years. She was starving herself to death and had to be fed forcibly. She had periods of violence and couldn't live with her own family—very few of these people can, particularly if there are other children in the house.

Mr. Moore had already been touched by his visit to the fostering community, but he was now in an actual foster (fostering) home and was able to see the effect that nurturing had on this young woman. In his mind, he compared it to "the forbidding closed wards of other institutions…where young girls were locked in; the screaming, cursing, and violence…the overworked nurses and aides struggling to care for them."

After their visit with Rosa, Dr. Rademaekers took Mr. Moore to another home that provided additional evidence for the devotion of foster families in Geel. Here, the foster mother was about twenty years younger than Helen, her foster daughter, a woman from a distinguished English family. Helen's foster mother had "inherited" Helen from her own mother, and thus had known her since she was a child. In addition, Helen's foster mother reported that "before we had Helen, my mother had an English woman with the same disease, and she inherited her from my grandmother."

As Moore's visit was coming to an end, the medical director reported how World War II and the postwar years had created problems for the city, including the diminishing boarder population that Dumont and Aldrich had observed. Moore wondered what would happen to the community. The doctor thoughtfully responded with his hope, rather than any particular predication:

> I am a Roman Catholic, like most Belgians, but I am a scientist also... We don't know how much of the Dymphna legend is factual...But one thing we do know: Thanks to St. Dymphna, something happened in Gheel, and that something started what we see today...I can't believe that such work for good can halt. The Gheel Idea must survive.

Those were the same thoughts that inspired the Geel Research Project (GRP). The ambitious goals of the researchers were not fully realized, but even after the project terminated, Dr. Srole continued to present information regarding Geel and the GRP at scientific meetings, including the 1976 International Symposium of the Kittay Scientific Foundation.[15]

In November 1997, during my second trip to Geel, I visited with some of the researchers at the University of Leuven. They were amazed that there should be interest in the GRP twenty years after its end. They seemed to feel something akin to embarrassment that such an ambitious project did not produce the intended outcome. For example, data collected from Geel households during the 1971 National Census had never been analyzed, and the "code book" had been lost or become useless. And unfortunately, in spite of a publishing contract and continued efforts at completing the "omnibus volume," Dr. Srole died in 1993 without completing the comprehensive publication he had envisioned. While Srole and his GRP colleagues may have felt disappointment or even embarrassment at not achieving their intended goals, their effort and time were not in vain.

In 1975, as the study neared its end, an international symposium was held in Geel in conjunction with a traditional St. Dymphna Folk Festival, which had formerly been held every five years. At this symposium, papers presented preliminary analysis from eight of the forty study units. A book, *Mental Patients in Town Life*, written by Eugene Roosens, head of the anthropological team, was published in 1979, and at least seven European doctoral dissertations were written using GRP data.

Even with frustration from overextension and underfunding, during the second half of the ten-year study, Srole continued to address lengthy reports, with recommendations, to each new Belgian Minister of Public Health. For example, in a 1974 letter, he reported that GRP data indicated "a progressively larger number of chronic mental patients, once accommodated in Geel's foster families [had], over the years, been placed instead in the country's exclusively in-patient institutions."[16] In this same letter, Srole expressed concern that the Geel system couldn't survive much beyond 1980.

In that report, Srole identified three converging trends that he believed were responsible for the diminished Geel patient population that had caught the attention of Dumont and Aldrich. He observed that, first, established families were leaving the program. Second, fewer new families were applying. This decline, he noted, was accompanied by, and might even be the result of a third, longer-term trend: a decrease in the number of new patient referrals by Belgian mental health professionals. While many, myself included, consider Geel to be an enviable story of compassion and open-mindedness, others—particularly in Belgium—have considered it to be a last stop on the dark road of mental illness. Perhaps this attitude, held by mental health professionals outside of Geel, was the driving factor behind the decreased referrals, or it could have been a lack of receptivity to new admissions on the part of the Colony administration.

Over the centuries, though Geel's foster care system served as a model for the development of systems in other parts of Europe, it was never adopted by surrounding communities. In the region, Geel was often referred to as "the city of fools," where "half of Geel is crazy, and all of Geel is half crazy." It was unclear in the 1970s whether a decrease in referrals or nonreceptivity to new admissions by the Colony administration was responsible for the decrease in referrals. In his GRP study unit on the ambivalent images of Geel among non-Geel residents and mental health professionals, Dr. Leo Lagrou, social psychologist from the University of Leuven, found evidence for both attitudes. A pessimistic view of Geel's system still existed in many quarters, and Colony administrators appeared to be discouraging new admissions. But why would the Rijkskolonie itself adopt policies that appeared to be self-destructive? It could have been due to a problem that often exists in the field of mental health care: conflict between those who are experts based on their education and those who are experts based on their experience.

Foster families, after generations of sharing their homes with boarders, have embraced practical solutions to problems associated with the illness of their adopted family members. But trained, schooled professionals are not always pleased with the authority granted to families who "only" have generations of practical experience. In his presentation at the 1975 Geel Symposium, Dr. Srole summarized what the Geel Research Project had revealed to him. He observed that foster families take in mentally disabled strangers and, in most cases, assimilate them into becoming functioning members of the family structure. He particularly noted that the medical model of the physician treating a somatic illness was not a part of the success. Rather it was the role of the family—as caretaker; teacher; natural, supportive parent; and behavioral model—that allowed the boarders to function in a "normal" social world in spite of their illness. For hundreds of years, Geel's foster families have served as mental health practitioners with no formal training or education and no awareness of, or concern with, the diagnosis of their boarders.

Dr. Jan Schrijvers, the on-site GRP director, left his duties in the Colony in the midseventies, and he was not known to me when I first visited Geel in January 1997. During that visit, I asked Marc Godemont if anyone had ever done research on factors related to the tenacity and success of Geel's foster family system, and that was when I first learned of the GRP. Dr. Godemont had been assigned to Geel after the project had been put to rest, but he knew of its existence. Though Dr. Schrijvers's name was known to him, he was not aware of Schrijvers's involvement in the project. Ironically, though Schrijvers commuted to Antwerp to work as a psychiatrist in the Belgian mental health care system, he resided in Geel, living in a home that Godemont must have passed on his way to the OPZ many times in a week, or even a day. Why Godemont was not aware of Dr. Schrijvers's role in the GRP or his presence in the city of Geel has always puzzled me. Perhaps no one with whom Godemont worked knew of the GRP or Dr. Schrijvers's involvement. But in response to my query, Godemont did tell me, a curious visitor from Alabama, of his desire to locate and examine Dr. Srole's papers.

I love a challenge, and when I returned to the United States, I put myself to the task of locating the Srole papers. As my search began, I quickly made contact with the Srole family (an uncommon, and thus easy, name to Google), who encouraged me to contact a Belgium psychiatrist named Jan Schrijvers who had been involved in the project. This was the first time I had heard of Schrijvers, who seemed to hold the secret to the lost GRP documents and who resided in the city of Geel, unbeknownst to Godemont. In May 1997, I sent Schrijvers a letter, introducing myself and telling him that the Srole family had led me to him. Ironically, the very month that Dr. Schrijvers received that letter, he was being transferred back to Geel as the new director of the Rijkskolonie. And so, with his new position, inspiration from the shelved GRP was brought back to the OPZ, twenty years after the project's disappointing end. Furthermore, the Geel system had not become extinct in 1980, as Dr. Srole had feared, and though the Belgian Ministry of Health did not show an explicit acceptance of his recommendations, it is quite probable that the GRP indirectly influenced the Colony's acquisition of autonomous status in 1991.

In November 1997, eleven months after my first visit, I returned to the city, and Marc Godemont introduced me to the OPZ's newest medical director. The three of us visited the University of Leuvan to meet others who had been involved in the GRP. As that visit to Geel ended, Godemont and Schrijvers hosted a lovely dinner where the three of us toasted the spirit of St. Dymphna and Dr. Schrijvers described his hope for the future of the Colony. Being a native Geelian, he hoped the Colony would not come to an end—not a new hope.

As it deals with the problem of mental illness, Geel is a mingling of old and new buildings, services, attitudes, and approaches. In order to implement this search "for new and creative ways for Geel to adapt," Dr. Schrijvers organized the May 2000 Scientific Congress on Foster Family Care, where speakers from around the world gathered in Geel to continue a dialogue sparked by the spirit of Dymphna and echoed in the Geel Research Project. The Congress was held in a modern Geel conference center and attended by 279 participants. The eighteen speakers included researchers, practitioners, consumers, and family members, and four speakers were from the United States. In this forum, Geel was both student *and* teacher. In his introductory opening talk, Schrijvers noted, "We are aware that we can no longer be teachers, but that we have to become students again, who are looking for new and creative ways to adapt our traditional program to the methods of foster care in urban settings."

During his short tenure as director, Schrijvers moved to bring the old and the new into harmony. Improved communication was the theme of his initiatives. The Congress encouraged communication between Geel and the world. Within the community itself, he implemented techniques to encourage better communication between foster families and the hospital.

Part of Dr. Srole's motivation for becoming involved in the Geel Project was a belief that mental illness is a product of environmental factors. However, ten years of investigation and more than fifteen visits to the city did not support his belief. While mental illness may not be a *product* of environmental factors, Srole did find evidence that the shape of adjustment to mental illness is strongly affected by simple, yet critical, social experiences. This attitude affirmed my own intuition and became a driving force in my continued interest in Geel specifically and, in a more general sense, in the role of community in the lives of those living with a diagnosis of mental illness. In Geel, a diagnosis didn't need to be a label, producing a stereotype. Those with such a diagnosis had the same need for, and from, social experiences that we all do. I was convinced that the effectiveness of community-based mental health care is dependent on understanding those needs and providing healthy social experiences.

Though changes continue to shape the provision of mental health services in Geel, the foster family care system is still offered as one aspect of care. Geel's foster family care system did not die and, in spite of insufficient funding and staffing, the GRP appeared to have had a larger impact on the future of Geel than the frustrated participants anticipated. It offered explanations for the apparent decline, observed in the 1960s, of the centuries-old system and uncovered new insights into the system itself. It probably contributed to the 1991 legislation that many hoped would secure the Colony's future in some form. The history and motivation has been kept alive through those involved in foster family care, sometimes across generations. And at Hobart/William Smith College in Geneva, New York, the site of Leo Srole's first faculty appointment, GRP documents and other material evidencing Dr. Srole's life of dedication to understanding mental illness have been carefully stored and are available for the benefit of US professionals interested in the history of community care for the mentally ill.

I was fortunate enough to be a part of the 2000 Millennium Symposium and traditional St. Dymphna celebration. It was a perfect blending of a centuries-old legend and tradition that led to a modern stigma-free community. The presentations of professionals and laypeople from North America and Europe were reflections of Geel's interest in the today and the tomorrows of community mental health care. Visitors were reminded of the tradition that inspired the Geel of today as we viewed a parade in which community members (including foster families and boarders) and floats commemorated the story of St. Dymphna and Gereberne and the vile but necessary role of the incestuous Damon. An amateur play production that night told the story on stage. Though St. Dymphna is no longer seen as the instrument of miraculous cures, the role her story plays will most likely never be forgotten.

Today, visitors to the city can walk into the church and see the story of St. Dymphna's martyrdom in the beautiful altarpieces. They may walk past a school named in her honor. They may even find themselves shopping in an all-purpose hardware store, the Dimpna Center. And evidence of the way in which modern, industrialized sectors of the city have recognized the agrarian culture that led to fostering families sits in the town square where Amoco Chemical has placed a statue with the name Tribute to Geel's Historical Family Care System.

The story of Geel always seems "to be continued." Today in Belgium, the tradition of Geel's psychiatric foster care system serves as a role model and inspiration for a general European move toward all types of foster family care. At the same time, as Belgium is effecting changes in mental health care, Geel is adapting to those changes. And thus, while Geel's unique history provides an inspirational model, Geel is being inspired by newer models. In response to these changes and to encourage open dialogue, in May 2014—the month of St. Dymphna's feast day—another symposium, Community Care: Foster Family Care as an Inspirational Model, was held in Geel. The six featured presentations covered (1) the role of foster family care in Belgium mental health reform; (2) the current organization of foster family care in Geel today, with special attention to Geel's innovative children in foster families project; (3) foster family care from the perspective of health-care economics; (4) current foster family care practices in Germany, Austria, and Switzerland; (5) a panel discussion on foster family care in the context of community care and current mental health care reform; and (6) a presentation, "Supportive Housing Integrating the Mentally Ill: Geel to New York City," by Ellen Baxter, founder and executive director of New York City's Broadway Community Housing, featured later in this book as one of the exemplary mental health programs in our own country.

I was not able to attend the 2014 symposium. But what of my still dear friends who made me feel a part of their family? In a January 2015 e-mail update, Jill reported that Axel is still his "cheerful 'old' self— 'old' because he is now 50 years old." He has been with his first and only foster family for nine years and says he "never, ever wants to leave." Jill echoed his wishes. Tibo, now ninety-one years old, has been moved back to the OPZ due to declining health and the need for readily available medical staff. Jill also reported that he would be moved to a new nursing home in the center of Geel that was—with a touching symmetry—located right behind the Gasthuismuseum (hospital museum), in a building that was, at one time, a part of the old hospital in Geel.[17] One of Dr. Aring's 1974 *Journal of the American Medical Association* articles was indeed aptly titled "The Geel Experience, Eternal Spirit of the Chainless Mind."[18]

# 4

# Mental Illness and the Community: The Voice of History

How does it feel to be identified as a member of a stigmatized group, marked and feared due to a single aspect of one's being? We all take pride in certain sorts of group membership—religious affiliation and citizenship, to name but two. Yet each of us wants to be viewed and valued as a unique individual, a *whole* that is "me." Those who are identified as members of a stigmatized group are not apt to be judged so objectively or kindly. The potential result? The single factor of group membership—skin color, country of origin, religion, gender, sexual orientation—can determine how the whole person is perceived and treated. The ultimate outcome? They *feel* marked because they *are* marked. They may be avoided, ostracized, feared, or misunderstood, unable to advocate for themselves or win the advocacy of others, left to bear the burden of stigma, sometimes compounded by a sense of self-stigma. Those who face mental health challenges can come to be identified primarily by their "membership" in a stigmatized group—"the mentally ill"—with other aspects of their identities minimized or ignored. Self-stigma can even cause them to minimize or ignore their own value as people, leading to a sense of hopelessness and helplessness.

In Geel, if those with a diagnosis of mental illness are marked in any way, it is a mark that has come to evoke support and respect. Over the centuries, the presence of boarders became so common in town life that those with a mental disorder were welcomed, even nurtured, by the entire community.[1] At one and the same time, the citizens of Geel accept boarders *and* view them with pride, as valued members of the community. Friendly social interactions between board-ers and other community members are everyday occurrences—in stores, local pubs, and at community events.

Seven hundred years ago, the community of Geel did not purposely set out to create a stigma-free haven for pilgrims "possessed by demons." Signs were not posted on lampposts around Belgium and Europe reading, "Come to Geel, the site of St. Dymphna's martyrdom! Experience the miraculous intercession of this Irish princess and the hospitality of Geel's citizens, who will stand by you as you are freed of your demons!" Grant applications were not submitted to fund foster family services. Neither the citizens nor the church canons nor the politi-cal officials of Geel openly encouraged pilgrims to come to their city. But there they were—hundreds of pilgrims streaming into the community, seeking a cure through intercession from a martyred Celtic princess. The citizens of Geel could accept or reject these uninvited visitors, who may have been shunned by the rest of the world. Since residents of the city were aware of the legend that brought pilgrims to their village, rejection was *not* their choice. Instead, they likely felt a sense of responsibility, even honor, to respond in a manner consistent with the city's legend. Whatever their motivation, they used available resources—families in their agrarian community—to find a practical solution, a way to ac-cept and accommodate the never-ending parade of possessed pilgrims who came to the city because of a legendary history of "miracles" attributed to a princess who, we now know, may not have even existed.

We don't really know to what extent compassion played a role in the initial response of citizens and church canons. We are safe in assuming that once the tra-dition of taking in "lunatic" strangers began and took root, the citizens of Geel felt that they "owned" the system, leading them to leave open the doors of their homes to pilgrims, even in the face of closing of the church in 1797 and the French Minister of Justice's subsequent 1811 decision to abolish family care in Geel.

We know that in spite of—or because of—this tenacity, many in Belgium considered Geel to be a "city of fools." We have documented evidence that Esquirol's 1821 visit to Geel lured other members of the scientific community to visit the city. But we also know that not all visitors looked kindly on the sys-tem of foster family care that defined the community.

Although the legend of St. Dymphna did not result in a single form of mental health treatment, the story of her short but inspirational life *is* a common thread that runs through the history of Geel. It is present even today when the sum total of Geel's diverse, modern, up-to-date mental health services goes beyond foster family care and is not based on miracles of intercession. Geel's approach to dealing with mental illness evolved from a legend. The seed of the legend took root, growing into what would become the unique documented history of a community virtually devoid of a negative stigma relative to mental illness. The legend of St. Dymphna grew within the context of miracles and sainthood and the church. Religion and miracles of intercession are no longer an aspect of mental health programs in Geel, yet the long-standing acceptance and integration of those with mental health challenges might be due to what some call the spirit of St. Dymphna, present in a secular context. It is not unreasonable to believe that the acceptance of, and care for, those with mental illness by untrained community members *is* a kind of "miracle" that does not require intercession by a martyred Celtic princess. But what *does* it require? Is Geel so very different from the United States that we can't hope to replicate the atmosphere of acceptance that many centuries ago became associated with miracles? If the intercession of a saint is not available, is it possible that the intercession of a tolerant and caring community, such as Geel, can result in miracles as great, or greater, than the miracles associated with St. Dymphna?

If a collective social history has the power to lead to acceptance of a stigmatized group, as it did in Geel, what can be said of our own history and experience in the United States? In modern times, when we see evidence of fear of mental illness and avoidance of those who have been diagnosed with a mental disorder, is it possible that our own history had a power of its own, albeit with a different outcome—the development and persistence of a negative stigma?

Compared to Geel's story, our story can't be told as simply. We don't have an inspiring personality or legend as a starting point or a common thread running through our experience with mental illness. In hindsight, we can look to some periods of our past with pride, while other periods may evoke a sense of embarrassment—albeit unwarranted embarrassment in many cases. We commonly did the best we could based on what we knew at the time, and often motivated by a hope that *we*, as a community, had escaped the perceived "demon of mental illness" in our midst.

In order to understand where we are, how we got here, and how we, as community members, can help to shape a hopeful future, it is useful to look at the progressive development of our perspectives and efforts, from colonial days to the twenty-first century, when we are still living with community members once referred to as *distracted*,[2] and now more commonly known by a *DSM* diagnosis. In looking at why treatment or care for those with mental illness took various forms, we can sense one consistent theme: hope. If we are to realize our own hope for the future, it is useful to understand the source and outcome of hope in the past. Retrospective insight might encourage us to move forward enlightened, rather than encumbered, by where we've been. In hindsight, we can better understand how events and policies of each era affected the next. In the process we might—just *might*—dare to believe that it is not unreasonable to hold onto "hope" for living with, not against, mental illness. Rather than simply abandoning past efforts or feeling helpless and fearful when mental illness makes the news, we might be in a position to see how fragments of past hopes might encourage us in the direction of new hope.

In order to understand mental illness in the context of community in our own country, it seems reasonable to define the nature of community that developed as this country was born. As settlers began to arrive on the east coast of North America in the late sixteenth and early seventeenth centuries, communities evolved. Though Spanish settlers were responsible for the first permanent North American colony—St. Augustine, founded in 1565—most settlers came from England, bringing with them social and cultural perspectives that guided them in creating social order in a new, raw environment. Compared to the densely populated communities from which settlers emigrated, the overall population of colonial America was much smaller, as was the population of individual communities, confined to a relatively small eastern strip of the continent but widely scattered within that strip. This population density and distribution would affect the way in which community members dealt with mental illness.

In their countries of origin, settlers had most likely been exposed to individuals who behaved in an erratic or disruptive manner, but the *incidence* of such behavior in colonial communities influenced how citizens coped with so-called distracted persons. Historical records regarding incidence and prevalence of mental illness in colonial times are scarce, but in 1996, a report based on eighty-two seventeenth-century cases—taken from both official and personal records, such as diaries, journals, and letters—supports a presumed paucity of mental illness in the early days of our country. This is not surprising. Leaving one's native land to make a home in unsettled territory would not be easy for someone with a disability. Distracted persons would not be apt to emigrate to a new land on their own, and emigrating families were unlikely to bring along a severely distracted family member. And so, while those who came from Europe may have been familiar with mental disorders, in North America there were fewer distracted persons in less dense and more scattered population centers. Still, they were present. So how did North American community members respond to those whose behavior strayed from the norm?

During colonial times, there were no diagnostic criteria for mental illness; indeed, citizens had no strong sense of mental illness as a disease. While individuals could be assessed based on their behavior, treatment and care for those who strayed from the norm was typically left to the family, consistent with what was seen in England and Europe. But in the colonies, this task was facilitated by smaller, more scattered communities that allowed both distracted persons and their family members a certain sanctuary and the possibility of community support.

In essence, colonial American families were on their own. Yet an individual's violent or erratic behavior *could* affect the community as well as family members. Neither England nor Europe had programs to deal with mental illness, so there was no model or tradition to guide colonists. There was, however, both here and abroad, general concern for the needs of "the poor"—including distracted persons, widows, orphans, the aged, the sick, and the disabled. Thus, the *need* created by poverty was of greater concern than any special circumstances that created that need.[3]

There have always been, and always will be, responsible families who know the pain and frustration of trying to care for loved ones who crave or demand independence yet cannot deal with it in a safe or socially acceptable manner. In colonial times—with no treatment or care options—structured alternatives to family care were not available. Then, as today, a family might face financial and emotional burdens, a destroyed marriage, or even physical danger if a family member became violent, leaving the family with a sense of helplessness and isolation. Yet, as in Geel, social circumstances in the colonies offered something of value not consistently available today—informal support from community and neighbors. Historical records tell us that though there were no program-like services (maybe even *because* there were no program-like services), informal community support was available.

Colonial records and archives for Massachusetts provide evidence of tolerance for public displays of behavior that went far beyond mere eccentricity—what we might view as "madness." Records of community response to prominent public figures are most readily available, but there are strong hints that tolerance was not reserved for prominent figures alone. It may have existed in response to any display of madness, by any community member.[4]

How does our own twenty-first-century level of tolerance and acceptance compare to what was documented in colonial records? Ask yourself. Imagine if your church pastor, unable to face a crowd or even his own congregation, wore a handkerchief over his face while delivering his sermon. It is likely that action of some kind would be taken. Yet York minister Joseph "Handkerchief" Moody used that coping method, and his congregation showed tolerant acceptance for three years before they relieved him of his duties. Or what if your minister, after suffering personal losses, could not stem his tears when he spoke, a problem that escalated to the point where his sermons could only be described as gibberish? Such was the case with Samuel Checkley. And rather than relieve him of his duties, his congregation hired someone to *help him* with his problem.

This kind of generosity was shown in contexts other than religious settings, as evidenced by public response to the mad behavior of lawyer James Otis, a political leader in pre-Revolution days who held high positions in colonial governance. His speeches expressed fervent opposition to violation of our rights by the British parliament. In 1769, when Otis was forty-four, a passionately expressed stand led to a violent encounter with the commissioner of customs, resulting in a head injury for Otis. Some blamed that injury for an escalation of his outrage—he went from eloquent speeches to increasingly violent behavior. However, some historians observed that even before his head injury, his behavior was erratic enough to be consistent with symptoms of insanity. But there was no mental health professional with *DSM* in hand to diagnose, and thus label, his behavior as mental illness. His behavior was tolerated by community members, and the source of his passion was apparently valued by many. In a 1770 tirade, during which he damaged Boston's Town Hall and fired guns from the windows of his own home, his friends came to his rescue—perhaps out of concern and kindness, or perhaps due to his valued voice of opposition during difficult times. For whatever reason, friends settled him into a country home to recover from what they believed to be the effect of his head injury and the stress of his passionate political stands.

After a few months, Otis reentered the world of Massachusetts politics, but his insane behavior reappeared within a year, including, from time to time, clear fits of madness. Still, community leaders who valued Otis's political stands were apparently not eager to lose his voice, for he continued to play a role in Massachusetts political life through the pre-Revolutionary years.[5] Early in his political career, his passion was valued by those who supported his views, and even as he became more and more erratic, he was not rejected by the community as a whole. (At age fifty-eight, however, Otis fell victim to "nature's passion" when a lightning bolt struck and killed him.)

Otis's story might suggest that community members were only willing to ignore the madness of one who served some community cause. Not true, as evidenced in the case of Samuel Coolidge, a 1727 Harvard graduate. Coolidge's story provides evidence of community generosity in the face of madness that demanded a constantly renewed effort to offer meaning to one whose life was marked by incessant wandering—mentally, in words and deeds, and on the road from one Massachusetts town to another. Given the severity of Coolidge's behavior and the patient and benevolent community response, Clifford K. Shipton justifiably included Coolidge's biography in his collection of *Representative Biographies from Sibley's Harvard Graduates,* stating, "This dreary story has been given in detail here in order to show how a New England community cared for one of its unfortunate members."[6]

In 1703, Samuel Coolidge was born in Watertown, Massachusetts. After graduating from Harvard, he preached in various frontier pulpits but returned to Cambridge in 1733. One year later—aware of his restlessness—his alma mater appointed him as a Harvard librarian in an apparent effort to help him settle into a useful life. He held that position for a year before his persistent inability to relate properly or kindly to students resulted in dismissal from his job. He was allowed to remain in the city until 1737, when Harvard found a position for him as chaplain in the garrison of Castle William, South Boston's Castle Island. At the same time, they published one of Coolidge's sermons in an effort to find him a position as a preacher. But the published sermon appeared to be "too queer for parishes looking for ministers."[7]

After a year at Castle William, and then six months at the Leicester school, forty-six miles west of Boston, he returned to Harvard, but in 1742, the university exiled him from the city. Once again Coolidge returned to Watertown, a pitiful wanderer through the town in which he was born. Yet his needs were not ignored, and as the cold winter approached, townspeople collected money to clothe him and found him a position as schoolmaster in Westborough, twenty-five miles west of Watertown. Here, he was kindly invited to dine with the minister, Parson Ebenezer, but given Coolidge's reputation, the Parson did not dare invite him to say grace, nor did he feel it prudent to admit Coolidge to communion.

Efforts at lending stability and sanity to Coolidge's life seemed to be in vain. Less than a year after taking the position at Westborough, he was unable to continue his teaching duties, leaving him with a total sense of hopelessness. Community members did not yield to his sense of hopelessness, and Westborough cared for him until he once again began his wandering. However, on returning to Westborough for commencement in 1745, he was removed from the meeting house due to his "destractions [sic] and delirium."[8]

Eighteen years had now passed since Coolidge graduated from Harvard and began his wandering ways. He had been tended to and rescued over and over, yet every effort to offer him a meaningful life was for naught. Once again, in the winter of 1745, he was homeless, and the selectmen of Watertown were told that Coolidge was "under Such Circumstances that he is in Danger of Suffering if Something be not Emediately [sic] done for him."[9]

Through the generosity of the community, he was clothed several more times, but his wandering continued, and behavior that put him in "danger of suffering" could not be ignored or stopped. As one reads of the efforts made on his behalf, one cannot help but feel extraordinary respect and awe for the generous and patient spirit of Coolidge's family and members of the surrounding communities—Watertown, Cambridge, and Westborough. No one ever seemed to give up hope of settling him into a better life, somehow, somewhere. At one time, for his own safety, he was kept in the Watertown jail. When he escaped, efforts were made to rescue him and house him in the Boston workhouse. But he eluded his rescuers and was found disturbing the peace in a community near Watertown. At that point, Watertown selectmen brought him back home but *still* did not give up on him, and when, in February 1751, he seemed to be improved, the selectmen gave him an opportunity to serve as a schoolteacher in his hometown. Sadly, living without supervision was more than he could handle, and he was relieved of his teaching duties but still not abandoned. He was placed in the care of a community member with orders to chain him, if necessary, until he was in his right mind and able to teach again. As long as he was cared for, he *was* able to teach.

When the school year ended, the selectmen continued to find supervised living for him until he was taken back to Westborough to teach but, *yet again*, he was unable to fulfill his teaching duties while living independently. Back in Watertown, his birthplace, he taught off and on for two years, but always with supervision. Community members had learned that Coolidge simply could not take care of himself for any extended period of time. A final effort on his behalf was made in 1763, when a Cambridge gentleman kept him for two weeks but quickly determined that Coolidge required a physician's care. After decades of effort to rescue him, Watertown now bought a lock for Mr. Coolidge, and though his mind was not relieved of the wandering of insanity, his days of wandering from town to town and job to job were over. On January 12, 1767, the selectmen of Watertown were notified that sixty-four-year-old Samuel Coolidge was dead. His funeral was held the next day.

Because of his position as Harvard librarian and the subsequent inclusion of his biography in the seventh volume of *Sibley's Harvard Graduates,* we know the sad story of Samuel Coolidge's life. We know of remarkably persistent community efforts that were, most likely, motivated out of a sense of humane responsibility. We know of the tenacity and futility of those efforts. Coolidge's story is documented primarily because of his position at Harvard. One can only wonder if it is unique or if it is, in some way, representative of the way in which our colonial communities cared for those in need when no other options were available.

Are aspects of what we know about colonial tolerance of mental illness and care for the insane consistent with what we know about tolerance and care in Geel? Perhaps Geel is not as unique as it seems. Perhaps humane treatment of those with mental illness is the product of humankind's practicality and humanity—*not against, with*—a kind of tolerance and compassion that can emerge as needed, at any time and in any place.

Records also indicate that even the mad behavior of those who lacked community prominence was tolerated. There was the churchgoer who consistently taunted other parishioners, using a hook and line to lift their wigs from their heads during services. Another citizen, this one from Taunton, who was clearly deranged in both appearance and behavior, was often seen and heard laughing insanely as he wandered the streets of the town.

Research reveals that eighteenth-century Massachusetts families viewed "mad behavior" as episodic rather than the mark of a permanent state of being, a perspective that may have motivated their tolerance. In Coolidge's case, though episodes were frequent and persistent, a general belief in the possibility of remission may explain tenacious efforts on his behalf. Perhaps colonial Americans persisted in caring for the mentally ill even during difficult times because they had hope that those in their care were not in a permanent state of need and that community efforts served a purpose. That hope may have encouraged them to tolerate unusual or troublesome behavior rather than making assumptions about the life of one who has been *diagnosed* or identified with mental illness.

It would be wrong to minimize or trivialize the challenge early Americans faced in caring for distracted family members. However, if their perspective of the transience of what we now recognize as the disease of mental illness *did* offer hope, that may have been a coping mechanism that served them well. Rather than the fear and hopelessness that accompany a negative stereotype, hope may have encouraged the treatment of distracted family member in ways that would optimize quality of life for the family.

> [E]arly colonists recognized mental illness in their midst, and worked to deal with it as best they could. In the process, they blended reasonable compassion for the afflicted with appropriate concern for families and the community responding at all points in practical ways to the difficulties posed by their "distracted" brethren.[10]

Perhaps compassion and practicality—in colonial times and in the way that citizens of Geel responded to mental illness in the Middle Ages—exemplifies Robert Frost's *not against, with* approach. This approach flies in the face of fear generated by a negative stereotype. It encourages acceptance of *what is*, rather than fear of what seems to be.

Religion played a significant role in the life of colonists, but in what manner? Did it motivate their compassion? Some have believed otherwise. Historians, and even the general public, are familiar with the 1692 Salem witch trials, a piece of history not identified with a spirit of compassion. How can we resolve evidence for compassionate concern with what we know about the Salem witch trials, in which a belief in "the supernatural" seemed to guide perception and treatment of mental illness in the colonial era? While colonial Americans did associate witchcraft with possession, records indicate that they made no *automatic* or consistent association between witchcraft and mental illness. Satan certainly made an appearance when it came to *ideas* of possession and distraction, but there is evidence that colonists viewed bewitched behavior as being far more dramatic than the behavior of those identified as distracted. Noted medical and social historian and researcher Gerald Grob[11] suggests that a loose link between belief and reality was strengthened by historians who—based on their own beliefs about the presence of cruelty, ignorance, and irrationality in colonial times—*assumed* a belief in witchcraft to be a part of colonists' understanding of mental illness. Historical research provides evidence that colonial officials and citizens acted in a responsible and often compassionate manner toward all those who, for reasons beyond their control, were dependent on others, a perspective surely linked to the fact that English law made local communities responsible for those who could not take care of themselves. Eldridge surmised that the colonial American's sense of responsibility was, to a large degree, based on "Christian sensibilities and personal pity."[12] Religious beliefs may have had some impact on how colonists treated the mentally ill, but that impact varied among colonies and, at least in early times, had a more positive influence than some have believed.

As the population of the country increased, problems associated with those in need were complicated by an increase in the number of urban areas, altering the nature of community. In addition, nineteenth-century changes in the labor force and characteristics of family life contributed to a change in the nature of community. Instead of families taking care of their needs within the structure of their own homes, coping with mental illness in the community became fraught with problems more similar to what we know today. In rural areas, those in need likely lived with family or received haven and support as members of the community, whereas in larger urban areas then, as today, a transient poor population with no access to this kind of support was more present and problematic—where and how should, or could, those in need be cared for? In colonial America, almshouses (poorhouses), a European model, began to appear in the mid-eighteenth century as the first form of institutionalized housing. Subsequently, as the number and size of urban areas increased, so too did the number of almshouses, which may have been the product of a community sense of responsibility but also indicated a community sense of little or no hope for those in need.

Larger and more complex population centers required more formal social policy, and laws were enacted to protect those in need, including distracted persons and their families. An interest in the biology of insane behavior began to evolve, but knowledge garnered from that interest did not suggest any specific treatment; treatment was based on need and was primarily the responsibility of the selectmen. And social policy did not develop in a void; rather, it was motivated by "[t]he English principle that society [has] a corporate responsibility for the poor and dependent."[13]

As community environment changed in the colonies, changes took place in Europe that soon affected the approach to mental health care in this country. Earlier, as possessed pilgrims were making their way to Geel, European institutions for the mentally ill were also beginning to appear. Sadly, they would become disgraceful warehouses for those deemed to be insane until Frenchman Philippe Pinel introduced more humane treatment, believing that the environment in which inmates lived was not beneficial and could even exacerbate their condition. Shortly after the French Revolution, Pinel was put in charge of the hospital for the insane in Paris and was grudgingly given permission to act on his belief in the therapeutic effect of humane treatment. In 1793, he took inmates out of dungeons and put them in sunny rooms with freedom to exercise on hospital grounds. Some had been "warehoused" for decades due to abnormal behavior, delusional thoughts, or mental problems associated with advanced stages of syphilis. In addition, political prisoners and poverty cases lived in their midst, in the same deplorable conditions, with many chained for extended periods of time. As Pinel had suspected, freedom and humane treatment—for *all* inmates—produced a behavioral environment of order and peace. This bold approach came to be known as moral treatment, in which mental illness was attributed to severe stress, the *moral* cause.

In the same time frame, English Quaker William Tuke introduced moral treatment to England, establishing, in 1792, the York Retreat, a country house where mental patients lived and worked in a restful religious atmosphere. The York Retreat led to the introduction and spread of moral treatment in the United States after Thomas Scattergood, a Philadelphia Quaker, visited the Retreat during an 1811 visit to England and subsequently encouraged the building of a Retreat-like asylum in Philadelphia. Scattergood died of typhoid fever in 1814, before his dream was realized, but a committee of Philadelphia Friends investigated the possibility of a retreat with Isaac Bonsall, a successful farmer with no experience or expertise in caring for the mentally ill, taking a leadership role. On May 15, 1817, the doors of the Friends Asylum (officially The Asylum for Persons Deprived of the Use of Their Reason), the first of its kind in this country, were opened to members of the Society of Friends who suffered from problems associated with insanity. For the next six years, Isaac Bonsall served as superintendent with his wife, Ann, as matron of the asylum.[14,15]

When pilgrims first began to flock to Geel, it was an agrarian community, and foster homes were primarily farmhouses. Boarders were thus able to do meaningful work in a rural setting. As with the York Retreat, the Friends Asylum was built as a self-sufficient farm, covering fifty-eight acres, thirty of which were cultivated to provide food for six cows, a source of dairy products and meat. Staff and residents worked together, ate together, and lived together in a building with a wing for women that extended from one side of the central house and a wing for men on the other side. Residents strolled and engaged in recreational activities on the land not used for farming. This serene setting was carefully planned so that the Friends Asylum could indeed be called a retreat.

Though Bonsall had no previous experience with mental illness, as a Friend he was accustomed to the Quaker belief in "a compassionate, supportive attitude toward the mentally ill," an attitude and approach consistent with moral treatment. Kindness alone did not resolve all the problems that developed for residents of the Friends Asylum, but Bonsall was an excellent manager, successful in altering unacceptable behavior through intelligent and compassionate use of reward and punishment. The methods were never intentionally punitive but were meant to benefit the patient in achieving recovery or cure—the desired goal. What Bonsall offered in the setting of a serene retreat was the compassion and caring nature of a Quaker coupled with common sense and nonauthoritarian management skills. Compassion without the ability to maintain order might not have been enough. Management skills without compassion might have been too much.

When Isaac and his wife left the Friends Asylum in 1823, he was still dedicated to the principles of moral treatment but despaired about losing his original optimism for the promise offered by such a retreat. But his despair was not well-founded. The Friends Asylum continued to operate and eventually became the Friends Hospital, still in operation today as the oldest private psychiatric hospital in the United States.

Bonsall could also take pride in how the Friends Asylum environment was consistent with the goals of Benjamin Rush, a Founding Father of the United States who was also considered the founding father of American psychiatry. Even before the Friends Asylum came to be, Rush promoted humane treatment of the insane, a goal born of the conditions he had observed during his thirty years on the staff of Pennsylvania Hospital, a tenure that began and ended before the Friends Asylum opened its doors. Rush, one of the first to identify mental illness as a disease, established a medical practice in Philadelphia in 1769, joined the Pennsylvania Hospital staff in 1783, and maintained that position until his death in 1813. Established in 1753, Pennsylvania Hospital was not meant to exclusively serve the insane, but motivation for the hospital included a concern for the "mad," and six of the first patients were psychiatric patients.

Rush's view of mental illness as a disease led to "scientific" treatment approaches that were based on his intuitive medical belief that a malfunctioning circulatory system was at fault. To address this hypothetical malfunctioning, he designed devices that, at first glance, seemed more like amusement-park rides than viable treatments for mental illness. Today the image and purpose of his gyrating chair seems primitive and even cruel, but it is an example of how at any time in history, we use what we know and our best common-sense guess to treat something as puzzling and difficult to understand as mental illness.

Though Rush's devices do not seem to be consistent with moral treatment *per se,* he is sometimes considered a pioneer in occupational therapy, particularly as it pertains to the institutionalized. In *Diseases of the Mind*, published one year before his death, Rush wrote,

> It has been remarked, that the maniacs of the male sex in all hospitals, who assist in cutting wood, making fires, and digging in a garden, and the females who are employed in washing, ironing, and scrubbing floors, often recover, while persons, whose rank exempts them from performing such services, languish away their lives within the walls of the hospital.[16]

The environment of the asylum had been envisioned and developed as a place where the insane could be "cured" by relieving them of the stresses of life. However, some believed that mental illness was curable for some, while others could not be cured. Indeed, not all *were* "cured" by a stay in asylum, yet many sought the new hope of moral treatment—so many that they could not be accommodated by small, private asylums that soon became overcrowded. Eventually Massachusetts state leaders were alarmed and concerned about overcrowding and the shameful care of the insane, who were held in jails with sparse and/or filthy conditions. Several solutions were considered but rejected in favor of the 1833 opening of Worcester State Lunatic Hospital, with 120 beds. Unlike the first asylums, Worcester offered both moral and medical treatment. Again, new hope emerged from what had become the dark valley of shameful care for the mentally ill.

Based on a high recovery rate in the first twelve years of the hospital's existence, Samuel Woodward, the first Worcester State superintendent, and the hospital itself gained recognition and respect in the United States and abroad, leading to the building of thirty-one public hospitals (federal, state, and municipal) between 1840 and 1859. But overcrowding persisted. Public hospitals were ready to accommodate a greater number of patients, but there was a sharp and unexpected increase in the daily census of patients at Worcester—from 107 in its first year to 359 thirteen years later. Once again, there was a need for change. But where might we find a new sense of hope? Care for the mentally ill by family members in the community was no longer the norm. We had moved so far away from it that it wasn't even considered an option. What next?

Enter Dorothea L. Dix, referred to as "the most famous and influential psychiatric reformer of the nineteenth century."[17] Born in Maine in 1802, Dix grew up in Massachusetts and moved into the Boston home of her wealthy grandmother at the age of twelve. As a young woman, she was a teacher, first opening a school in Boston for children from privileged families and then teaching disadvantaged children in her own home. Beginning at the age of twenty-two, she also wrote children's books, but at twenty-eight, poor health interrupted her teaching duties. Improved health allowed her to start teaching again in 1830, but five years later, illness once again interrupted her teaching career, whereupon she traveled to England, hoping to recuperate in the home of a family of Quakers who were strong believers in the active role that governments should play in advancing social reform. During this trip, she was also introduced to the York Retreat, which likely informed her future concern for the insane.

Shortly after her visit to England, while teaching a religious class to women convicts in an East Cambridge jail, she became aware of insane individuals who were living with "hardened criminals" in the jail. Her life experiences began to coalesce, giving her a sense of purpose that prompted her to spend over a year traveling through Massachusetts to observe firsthand where and how the insane were housed. At the same time, Massachusetts physician Samuel Gridley Howe was trying to convince the state legislature to expand the Worcester Hospital. Dix's yearlong visits to jails, houses of correction, and almshouses throughout the state prompted her 1843 letter to the state legislature describing in detail the horrible conditions she had observed and an impassioned plea for support of Howe's proposal to expand the number of beds at Worcester.

Dix's concern for her home state prompted her to carry out the same kind of inspections and pleas in other states, always advocating for more public asylums. In the course of her career, she was responsible for founding or enlarging more than thirty hospitals in the United States and Europe and also for a resultant change in the way the public viewed appropriate care for the insane, as described by historian Gerald Grob:

The presence of a mental institution had the inadvertent effect of altering both the expectations and behavior of the surrounding population.

When offered an alternative to home or community care, many families and local officials opted to use institutional facilities with far greater frequency than was originally anticipated.[18]

With an increase in the number of available hospitals and an increase in those who looked to hospitals as the appropriate place for those with mental illness, overcrowding continued. By 1955 the inpatient population had topped off at 559,000.

Several times in our history, there have been attempts to replicate Geel's traditional foster family care system. Concern regarding overcrowded hospitals probably led to one of the most intense campaigns. During the last half of the nineteenth century, several prominent Massachusetts doctors visited Geel, with many advocating for the establishment of a family care system in their state. From 1886 to 1887, Franklin Benjamin Sanborn, Massachusetts Deputy Commissioner in Lunacy, acting on orders of the governor, moved approximately 180 quiet and chronically ill patients from hospitals and asylums into private family homes.[19] While there was not unanimous support for this decision and the policy was short-lived, by 1914, 2.4 percent of Massachusetts's mentally ill were living outside of hospitals. Proponents of the system found "one of the chief virtues of the…system [to be] that the insane are surrounded by normal, or sane influences, while under our [asylum] system, they are surrounded by abnormal or insane influences." Today the advantage of a "normal" home environment has been acknowledged by mental health professionals in Geel as a key factor in the success of foster family care. However, nineteenth-century opponents of foster family care in Massachusetts prevailed due in part to a belief that "[i]n a country where all prize individual freedom…[t]here is a marked difference…between American lunatics, as a class, and those of more phlegmatic races, [such] as the Flemish."[20]

Even if "American lunatics" were somehow different, did either state asylums or hospitals offer a better solution than family living, which, in fact, had been the norm in early colonial days? History tells us that care in asylums and hospitals, the method that ensued when care within the family was no longer convenient and which had, at one time, offered hope, had instead become a hopeless life sentence for too many.

From colonial days to the beginning of the twentieth century, how did the "story" of mental illness and the community evolve in the United States? What worked, and what didn't? Can we replicate any successful aspects of our history? Have we learned what to avoid?

As settlers arrived and lived in sparsely populated rural communities, they continued the tradition of family care brought from England. Such an approach was not without problems, but the nature of early communities offered distracted persons and their families havens and support from neighbors. As communities grew, with no established social services or mental health treatment available, appointed community leaders, the selectmen, identified those in need and sought solutions to their problems. But with the country's continued growth and increased population, small rural communities were no longer the rule. With the growth of urban communities and an accompanying change in family life, along with an increase in transient poor, those in need were less likely to stay within the havens of their home communities. Concerns and challenges born of the evolution of urban centers are with us even today.

The idea of asylum, meant to provide a restorative environment for the insane, offered a relaxing pastoral setting and, in some cases, the opportunity to engage in meaningful labor. Since many did not experience successful treatment or cure, more remained in these asylums than had been anticipated. Still seeking to establish treatment centers, hospitalization for the insane offered hope, but overcrowding continued as the public came to rely more and more on institutional care for the insane, and, thus, communities had less personal contact with mental illness. It is possible that with a lack of personal contact, fear and avoidance supplanted compassion and care. In addition, though many of those with mental illness *were* among the indigent—those in greatest need—as insanity came to be considered an illness, treatment and care approaches addressed the presence of illness itself, and the medical profession came to play a role in determining the cause and treatment of mental illness. The source of authority had evolved from the family and/or immediate community to the medical profession and institutions. And in the early twentieth century, a new source of authority was heard when one who knew mental illness firsthand shared his personal experience and his name in an effort to inspire and influence the shape of treatment for those who shared his suffering—suffering due to mental illness as well as aspects of treatment that he believed to be cruel.

Clifford Beers, a Connecticut native, Yale graduate, and subsequently a mental patient, is considered to be the moving force behind what came to be known as the mental hygiene movement. The focus of mental hygiene was prevention, negating the need for treatment. In the nineteenth century, prevention focused on religion as its source—meaning through living a "God-fearing" life. However, at the beginning of the twentieth century, as science sought to understand and treat mental illness, a belief developed that mental illness was the product of nature *and* nurture—genes and environment—with prevention coming from science rather than God.

In his book *A Mind That Found Itself*,[21] Beers never denies the fact of his illness or the associated symptoms, but he writes vivid descriptions of those symptoms leading to his attempted suicide, followed by his extended hospitalization and the paranoid delusions that ruled his life in the ensuing years. He also came to be critical of those who were responsible for his treatment. He found psychiatrists to be "ignorant, incompetent, and punitive," but his strongest complaints were directed at poorly paid attendants who earned eighteen dollars a month (the equivalent of less than five hundred dollars a month in the present day) and who had no credentials to serve the mentally ill. Most of them, he observed, showed little or no respect for patients as human beings, believing that their primary function as attendants was to maintain order. Though other books describing inhumane treatment of the mentally ill in institutional settings had been written, none had the impact of Beers's book—both when it was published in 1908 and today, as it continues to inform those who must live with mental illness as well as those who work in the field of mental health.[22]

Beers was determined to do more than write about poor conditions. He sought to start a movement to end them. To facilitate reforms, prior to publishing his book, he contacted lay people and mental health professionals whom he thought would have reason to support his cause and the influence to advance that cause. He received strong support from American psychologist and philosopher William James, and Adolph Meyer, considered to be one of the most influential psychiatrists of his time, wrote a positive review of Beers's book. However, though Meyer and Beers did have some common perspectives and Meyer was willing to collaborate with Beers, the tension that existed between two strong-willed and dedicated men—one experienced, with authority born of his schooling and profession, and one who knew what it felt like to *experience* mental illness—resulted in a less-than-friendly relationship. Both saw the need for organizational support, and Meyer was the one who proposed establishing the Society for Mental Hygiene, with a focus on prevention, but he also suggested that Beers move slowly to gain support for reform. Reluctantly, Beers agreed to begin with the formation of the Connecticut Society for Mental Hygiene in 1908, but with neither man willing to share the reins of reform, tension about focus and financing continued to strain the possibility of a collaborative effort. Beers prevailed once more with the formation of the National Committee for Mental Hygiene (NCMH) in 1909, but by 1910, Meyer doubted Beers's judgment and resigned from the NCMH. Their inability to work together was likely a product of what William James described as "the ox and the 'Wild ass' not working well in double harness."[23]

Though the NCMH may not have been successful in fulfilling its stated goal of "prevention," the organization did stay alive—first as the National Mental Health Association and, since 2006, as Mental Health America (MHA), describing its mission as "promoting mental health, preventing mental and substance use conditions, and achieving victory over mental illnesses and addictions through advocacy, education, research, and service."[24] Clifford Beers would likely applaud those goals. And he would certainly be proud to know that every year since 1976, MHA has presented the Clifford W. Beers Award in his honor at their annual conference "to a consumer of mental health and/or substance abuse services who best reflects the example set by Beers in his efforts to improve conditions for, and attitudes toward, people with mental illnesses."[25]

Though Meyer advocated a perspective of mental illness that included biology of the brain, personality of the individual, and social context, the strongest emphasis early in the twentieth century was on mental disorders as "illnesses" of the brain—a perspective that offered hope that the brain might be "healed" in the way other somatic illnesses could be treated and cured. But this perspective did not offer immediate answers. We did not know the manner in which the brain was "sick," but the search was not deterred by lack of understanding. European researchers and clinicians in the field of neurology, followed by pioneers in the United States, formulated rationales for somatic therapies that "seemed like" they would work. There was now hope for a "cure" through efficient, defined treatment approaches, rather than the extended use of psychotherapy, which had sought to enter and heal the brain through words and responses and insights.

The search for somatic treatment began with pyrotherapy (fever therapy), but as with most of these early somatic treatments, the rationale for success was flimsy. Pyrotherapy was motivated by an Austrian physician's casual observation that coexistence of a mental disorder and typhoid fever could lead to the disappearance of mental symptoms. During World War I, the physician tested his hypothesis by injecting eight mentally impaired soldiers with the blood of a soldier infected with malaria. Four of the eight experienced complete remission of mental impairment, and two more showed improvement. It was a small sample of patients/subjects without the proper experimental control demanded today, but it was an easy treatment, and we were eager to find a cure. The physician, Julius Wagner-Jauregg, continued to use variations of fever therapy, winning the Nobel Prize in Medicine in 1927. In spite of its popularity, there were risks associated with blood sharing in a hospital setting, and there was concern regarding the lack of experimental controls necessary to warrant confidence in its therapeutic value. In the mid-1940s malarial fever therapy was abandoned as a treatment. But it wasn't the last treatment to be used despite shaky scientific support.

In 1928, physician Manfred Sakel made another casual observation: diabetic drug addicts who were treated with insulin to facilitate use and storage of glucose and thus reduce elevated blood sugar level *could* experience *hypo*glycemia (excessively low blood sugar) and an accompanying state of "shock," a deep coma that could only be relieved by administration of sugar. Sakel noticed changes in the mental state of diabetic drug addicts who went into insulin shock, leading him to believe that he had found a treatment for mental illness. There was no biological rationale to support his conclusions, but "it worked," and the need for therapies that would reduce the hospital population of those with chronic mental illness eclipsed the need for scientifically controlled experiments that could *explain* and *justify* such therapy.

Perhaps motivated by Sakel's unexplained success with insulin shock therapy, a Hungarian physician noticed that those with epilepsy seldom developed schizophrenia. Testing his hypothesis that convulsions protected one against schizophrenia, Ladislas von Meduna found that a camphor solution worked with animals *and* patients who exhibited symptoms of schizophrenia, but there were problematic side effects associated with the procedure, leading him to subsequently use a more efficient seizure induction method—electroconvulsive shock therapy (ECT) developed by two Italian psychiatrists.

Neuropsychiatrist Urgo Cerletti had been experimenting with a nonchemical shock therapy approach, using electric shock to produce seizures in animals. At the same time his colleague, Lucio Bini, was developing the idea of using electricity for human patients and, in 1938, Cerletti and Bini were the first to use ECT on humans, finding that agitation due to schizophrenia was reduced, catatonic patients became animated, and there were dramatic effects for those suffering from depression and mania.[26] With the development of ECT, Meduna stated that "chemically induced convulsive therapy is past history for me, and I believe for almost every psychiatrist. I do not believe the original publications have much value anymore."[27] Psychiatry had not abandoned seizure induction as a treatment, but it did find ECT to be a simpler approach.

In light of its success in Europe, the newest form of seizure induction soon made its way to the United States as clinical success with shock therapy continued to override any undesirable side effects. By 1940, shock therapy of one form or another was commonly used in virtually every mental hospital in this country in spite of its almost brutal side effects: severe thrashing movements, sometimes resulting in broken bones, and a common, often long-lasting, loss of memory. But ways have been found to address such side effects, and shock therapy is still in use today—for example, to treat depressed individuals who are not responsive to antidepressant medication and whose depression is so severe that they are considered suicide risks.

While changes in the use of ECT made it more acceptable, the same cannot be said of another popular and irreversible "therapy" of the same era—psychosurgery. There had been prior attempts to treat mental illness by altering brain function through surgical procedures, but in 1935, a surgical treatment was not only investigated but came to be used extensively for close to twenty years. Leucotomy (or lobotomy) was developed by Portuguese neurologist Edgar Moniz, who shared the Nobel Prize for Physiology and Medicine in 1949 for a simple procedure he developed shortly after attending the 1935 International Congress of Neurology. Stories vary as to the source of his inspiration. At that congress, Yale neuroscientist John Fulton reported on basic research into brain function using two chimpanzees, in which remarkably docile behavior followed removal of the front of their brains. At that same conference, Moniz heard neurologist Richard Brickner report that a patient whose frontal lobe had been removed to relieve the pressure of a meningioma suffered no loss of intellectual ability but *did* show a flattened affect (mood).[28]

Whether Moniz was inspired by Fulton's or Brickner's report (or perhaps both), three months after the conference, he made the quick leap from a single human case study—and/or a basic science experiment with two chimps—to human research, hoping to develop a clinical therapy for mental illness. He used a simple, irreversible procedure to cut or scrape away connections to and from the prefrontal cortex, leaving an important part of the brain isolated from communication with other areas of the brain. A year after Moniz began using the procedure, American psychiatrists Walter Freeman and James W. Watts of George Washington University Hospital began performing lobotomies in the United States. Shortly after its first use, the procedure was modified and varied by others. Though the use of psychosurgery waned during World War II, at its peak as a treatment, five thousand lobotomies a year were performed between 1948 and 1952.[29] Was this to be our last and best hope?

# Part Two

## Community Recovery in the United States

After my first three visits to Geel, I began to seek out what I considered to be exemplary programs in this country, defining *exemplary,"* for the purposes of my search, as sites and programs that met Marc Godemont's definition of Geel's success: (1) acknowledging and accepting the human needs of those with mental illness, (2) responding to those needs by providing opportunities for social interaction within the community, (3) providing opportunities to engage in meaningful work consistent with their individual interests and abilities, and (4) living within not just a foster family but an accepting and fostering community. It is the fostering community that enables the other three experiences, leading me to coin the term *community recovery,* where communities have found ways to live successfully with the realities of mental illness. Geel would certainly be considered a model of community recovery. But were there any examples of community recovery in our own country?

Having defined what I was looking for, I found that it *did* exist in the United States, and from 2001 to 2015, I visited almost twenty community programs that fit the criteria in some way. But they were not all the same, and they were not replications of Geel. Geel is a single city that used its unique resources to serve the needs of incoming pilgrims at a particular time in history. We don't know exactly what symptoms led pilgrims to Geel, nor do we know how many were relieved of their symptoms. But we do know that their presence created a community forever immunized against the stigma of mental illness. We are a large, diverse country. Different communities have different resources and clients with different needs. It was this observation that led me to include flexibility as a fifth criterion for exemplary programs in this country. And I found that flexibility is necessary for the programs I visited, as each had their own challenges, resources, and strengths.

By 2007, I had visited six programs, and in the interest of spreading the word about the possibility for community recovery, I created and launched an informational website describing Geel's history and current status as well as successful community mental health programs in this country.[1] I often get inquiries from those who, having heard of Geel and wanting to know more, find my website. Some of the queries come from students or researchers who are preparing a paper or presentation about Geel. Many are from family members of someone with a diagnosis of mental illness, particularly from parents of adult children. When their children are first diagnosed, parents invariably cope by holding onto hope that these are acute episodes and that successful pharmaceutical treatment will be identified and all will be well. But as their children become adults, they learn that most mental health disorders are chronic—treatable, but not often curable. With that realization, they naturally begin to wonder what will happen to their children when they, the parents, can no longer care for them, help them manage their treatment, or aid them in dealing with the normal aspects of life—finding a place to live, holding a job. In fact, the Health Insurance Portability and Accountability Act (HIPAA) of 1996 allows adult patients, if they choose, to block family members from following the course of their treatment.[2] This is not always a wise decision but one that—for better or worse—offers the grown child a greater sense of independence and control of his or her life.

Queries from parents who visit the website may begin with a desire to move their children to Geel, an option that is not possible. Then they may wonder if a similar place exists in this country. I can't answer that question with a simple yes or no. The good news is that there are exemplary programs in the United States that meet the criteria for success that Geel has achieved, but they are seldom carbon copies. They are developed to meet the needs of *their* communities, using the resources of those communities. Furthermore, Geel's services are provided through Belgium's Ministry of Health, and we do not have the same kind of national mental health care system in this country.

"A voice of hope for mental illness" has been defined, so far, as the opportunity for those with diagnoses of mental illness to live the most meaningful, productive lives possible in a stigma-free environment. Consumers and family members want to find that environment in the context of community programs. There *are* public mental health care programs in this country, and the quality of those programs are determined, to some degree, by policy and funding in a given state or county within a state. Some states are better (or worse) than others. However, in the following chapters, you will read of diverse programs developed with diverse sources of funding by individuals or groups of individuals. You will read of rural residential therapeutic communities, apartment complexes, group homes, and independent living accommodations. You will even read of the many who are able to live totally independent lives.

There is *hope* in the very existence of such programs. And hope is also born of the motivation and imagination of those who are responsible for their development, encouraging individuals or communities who want to *do something* and not just wait for something to happen. It's not always easy, but you will be amazed, encouraged, and even inspired, by what motivation, dedication, and perseverance can accomplish. Once again, you'll read of hope that is most accurately defined in any setting or situation as *not against, with*.

# 5

# The Twentieth Century—
# New Voices of Hope

Somatic therapies focused on a belief that mental illness was a disease of the brain, suggesting new approaches to treatment or cure. But these approaches were not based on solid scientific foundations and were fraught with unpleasant and sometimes permanent side effects. Overcrowding of patients and overworked staff in hospitals was still the rule. Then, in the 1940s, the discovery of medications that actually reduced psychotic symptoms offered a new burst of hope for treatment of serious and persistent mental illness as we entered the modern age of psychopharmacology. It is a hope that lingers, dominating the treatment of mental disorders and providing evidence that mental disorders are likely associated with imbalances in biochemistry.

The discovery of antipsychotic drugs occurred quite by accident, with the development of antihistamines. Since histamine can lower blood pressure, which is a problem during surgery, doctors wondered if *anti*histamines might prevent presurgical shock. They did. This was good news for surgeons and surgical patients. But what observant physicians didn't expect was that this new class of drugs appeared to reduce anxiety. Interesting. At least a large French pharmaceutical company thought it was *very* interesting, a hope-inspiring observation. Riding this new wave of hope, they went to work to synthesize antipsychotic drugs.

The amazing thing about these new drugs was that they were not simply sedating the patients. They reduced or eliminated specific symptoms associated with schizophrenia—delusions and hallucinations. These drugs were known to reduce the activity of the neurotransmitter dopamine, and the dopamine hypothesis of schizophrenia was born, leading to the ongoing development of drugs that could reduce dopamine's effect on brain activity. However, the very nature of scientific research produces situations in which answers simply open doors to more questions. Thus the original dopamine hypothesis was just that— a hypothesis that didn't offer a complete explanation. Drugs that addressed the hypothesized role of dopamine "worked," but we didn't know (and still don't know) exactly *how* they worked. Attributing mental illness to a "chemical imbalance" is commonly an oversimplification, hinting at the truth of what is happening in the brain but not fully explaining what is happening.[1]

A psychoactive drug is any drug that alters the activity of neurons, the messenger cells in the nervous system that communicate with each other when chemicals, known collectively as neurotransmitters, are released from one neuron and bind to a receptor on an adjoining neuron, changing the activity of that neuron. This was not well understood until 1921, when Austrian pharmacologist Otto Loewi, after seventeen years of trying to resolve the issue of whether neurons communicate via electrical signals or chemical signals, literally "dreamed up" a simple experiment that provided evidence for his belief in electrochemical communication.[2] On Easter Saturday, 1921, Loewi dreamed of how he might test his long-held hypothesis. In the middle of the night, he woke up and wrote down the necessary steps that he had envisioned in his dream, but in the morning he could not read his notes and had no memory of the details of the dream. All was not lost, however, for the next night he had the same dream. Not trusting his own note-taking, he immediately went to his laboratory to conduct a simple experiment using two frog hearts. He later acknowledged that he never would have conceived of such a simple experiment while working in his lab, where he was immersed in so much knowledge that the obvious and simple became obscure. Thanks to the filter that dreams provide and to Loewi's persistence, his frog heart experiment supported the role of chemicals in neural transmission. He identified the first known neurotransmitter and named it *vagustuff*, because when the vagus nerve was stimulated, the chemical was released onto the heart. Loewi's discovery earned him the 1936 Nobel Prize in Physiology and Medicine and—given the doors to understanding the brain that were opened by his discovery—unofficial, but deserved, recognition as the Father of Neuroscience.

Since Loewi's discovery of vagustuff, more than one hundred neurotransmitters have been identified, and the discovery process continues. Everything we do, think, or feel is controlled by the action of neurotransmitters—more accurately, a harmonious choir of neurotransmitter-induced activity. With a scientific understanding of the ways in which neurotransmitters are manufactured, used, and broken down in the nervous system, we were offered the opportunity to develop drugs that could alter the "song sung" by any given group of neurons. Pharmacological treatment of mental illness offered a vast new area of hope. Today, with a more sophisticated understanding of the molecular structure and action of neurotransmitters, drugs are often designed specifically to normalize some type of disruption in healthy brain functioning. In addition, when we know the biochemical effect of a given drug, the drug itself can offer an understanding as to what neurotransmitters are related to certain functions (or malfunctions) of the brain. And so, drug effectiveness can lead to new treatment approaches as well as to new knowledge about the function of naturally occurring chemicals that are manufactured and stored in our brains.

Still, we must learn to be humble in spite of what we do understand. Drugs that affect the activity of neurons are seldom "magic bullets," and if we view them in that manner, we may miss out on their more useful roles as "magic shotguns," affecting the harmonious activity of neurons, rather than trying to understand or rely on any solo role of single neurotransmitters.

This new approach to treatment could not have come at a more opportune time. There was hope that these drugs would be to schizophrenia what insulin treatment was to diabetes. It seemed possible that mental hospitals would no longer be necessary, and those institutionalized due to a diagnosis of mental illness could return to the community. Indeed, after a 1955 peak in the number of hospitalized patients, deinstitutionalization began. Patient population numbers dropped from over half a million in 1955 to about sixty thousand at the beginning of the twenty-first century.[3] However, it was not only this new treatment option that led to deinstitutionalization. Another significant development was emerging at the same time.

Mental health professionals, supported by public demand, wanted to know how they were doing in the field of mental health and, in general, what we could do better. In July 1955, motivated by a need to understand clearly where we'd been and where we were, Congress passed, and President Dwight D. Eisenhower signed, the Mental Health Study Act, which included provisions for a Joint Commission on Mental Illness and Health (JCMIH) whose goal was "to find the nature and prevalence of…mental disorders in the country and…forces in the community tending to [either] promote mental health…[or] produce mental illness."[4] In 1961, the JCMIH released their report, with the primary recommendation that mental hospitals be replaced with mental health centers. Subsequently, in 1963, President John F. Kennedy signed the Community Mental Health Centers Act (CMHCA), a blueprint for grants to finance construction and staffing of centers that would provide thorough and comprehensive services: inpatient and outpatient services, partial hospitalization, emergency services, and consultation. The act also provided for diagnostic and vocational education for agencies and professionals along with program evaluation and precare and aftercare training and research.

Two new sources of hope had come together. New drugs offered hope that severe and persistent mental illness (SPMI) could be dealt with as were other illnesses. The CMHC Act offered hope that those with SPMI, such as schizophrenia, would not be isolated behind fences and in brick buildings; as members of the community, they would experience no more stigma or rejection than did those with any treatable chronic illness. Community care was to be the norm, but a decade and a half into the twenty-first century, reality has fallen short of an idealized promise.[5,6,7] Though impressive and successful examples of progress exist, many communities are still discouraged by what they perceive to be an overwhelming, complex problem with no simple solution. Community care is meant to be the norm, but caring communities do not yet appear to be the norm in the face of fear and misunderstanding.

When we take a long view of our country's history with mental illness in a community context, it can seem that we have sometimes moved backward, even as science offered hope for forward movement. Mary Ann Jimenez[8] described that kind of dance-step progress in the context of colonial days, that has, to some degree, persisted even into modern times:

There is likely to be a wide range [of] reaction to madness and the amount of anxiety it causes. Some of this variation may be related to the kind of society in which the insane live. The relationship between madness and society is a dynamic one; the tensions created by the mad reveal much about what is important in a particular period, and the reaction to insane behavior is the most important measure of that conflict.

It is likely that our willingness to interact with the mentally ill at any point in time is influenced by what we *believe* about the causes and consequences of mental illness—the voices we have heard or chosen to heed. Jimenez's observation regarding the dynamic relationship between insanity and society may help to explain why society's view of mental disorders at any point in time isn't necessarily a reflection of scientific understanding. Though it often stumbles or encounters detours, science does strive to move forward by building on existing or new scientific knowledge and learning from past errors. Social acceptance is more erratic and subject to the public's emotional response to economic, political, or social circumstances of the times. Historian Gerald Grob confirms that trend, observing that, historically, "Explanations and perceptions about the nature and etiology in insanity, however important, did not by themselves shape the way in which society dealt with disturbed individuals."[9]

So where are we today? Has our experience and scientific progress produced a significant change in the lives of individuals—those diagnosed with mental illness or their family members? What of community understanding and acceptance? Compared to colonial days, for example, how does the twenty-first century community respond to those with mental illness? There *have* been changes and undeniable progress. We have moved in a positive direction. We have a better understanding of mental illness as a disease that is, at least in part, the product of abnormal brain function. We have a weighty manual to assist professionals in diagnosing mental illness, and with each revision of that manual, there has been an effort to incorporate new knowledge gained from recent research, offering more precise, objective guidelines to diagnosis. But there is still no definitive way to specifically identify the presence or type of mental illness—no blood test or X-ray or MRI. When it comes to diagnosis, professionals must rely on observed or reported behavior along with a survey style of questioning. And an individual's response to various drugs can lead to a diagnosis almost as readily as a diagnosis suggests an appropriate drug treatment.

Addressing the focus of this book, where are we in terms of the *stigma* of mental illness, the way in which we in the community view and treat those identified as mentally ill? If diagnosis is difficult for medical and mental health professionals, it should be summarily avoided by the public, who can turn a diagnosis into a label and then into a stereotype. Education is necessary, but though it may be a cliché, in many cases, a little education *can* be dangerous, especially in the hands of nonprofessionals. The purpose and value of educating the public about mental illness is *not* to create lay experts and certainly not diagnosticians. If we are to believe what historians have uncovered about how the mentally ill were treated during early colonial days, when neither professionals nor citizens were diagnosticians, it seems that colonial community members were more accepting and tolerant than we are today, when too many lay people freely, and often inappropriately, use diagnostic terms.

Treatment of mental disorders and public reaction to these disorders have a patchwork quilt quality—treatment approaches or public perceptions are pieced together but are missing pieces that could provide a complete and reliable picture. And invariably, one thing that is often ignored is the critical aspect of simply *living with* a diagnosis of mental illness or, for that matter, any chronic disease—living with both the illness itself *and* the inconvenience and complications associated with necessary treatment.

Evidence does point to a physiological basis for mental disorders, although it is probably a more complicated picture than we might imagine or than scientists yet understand. For example, recent pioneering research suggests that schizophrenia may be at least eight different disorders, each with a different set of symptoms and a different genetic basis.[10] But initial recognition of a brain-based disorder begins at a psychological level—a persistent or abnormal change in behavior, mood, or cognitive function. Prescribed medication can, and usually does, play an important role in dealing with mental illness, but physiological regulation through the use of drugs does not enter the picture as a part of treatment until symptoms are recognized.

One hope that would seem to grow out of an understanding of the bio-chemical basis of mental illness is that social stigma would be reduced if we do not "blame" the one who is diagnosed. But the use of psychotherapeutic drugs is not as simple as (1) diagnosis, (2) prescription, and (3) fast and total relief of symptoms. When that is what we expect, we can lose the kind of patience that leads to compassionate support. While psychopharmacology is an improvement over demonology, exorcism, and lobotomies, it is not an end in and of itself. There are chemical and social complications. Though we're closer to develop-ing drugs that treat target symptoms, even when an appropriate drug is found, there are often side effects that must be treated with other drugs. For example, schizophrenia is currently linked to too much dopamine activity. Another brain disorder, a movement disorder—Parkinson's disease—occurs when dopamine cells in a particular area of the brain die. Thus, drugs that treat schizophrenia by reducing dopamine can produce abnormal movement as a side effect. Likewise, drugs that increase dopamine as a treatment for Parkinson's disease can produce mild psychotic symptoms as a side effect. We do know, however, that the in-crease in dopamine associated with schizophrenia and the decrease in dopamine associated with Parkinson's disease do *not* occur in the same part of the brain, offering new hope in the form of *targeted* pharmaceutical treatment. Newer an-tipsychotic drugs can more specifically control dopamine release in the area of the brain considered to be responsible for schizophrenia, thus avoiding problems associated with a general reduction in dopamine throughout the brain.

Medication as a way to treat behavioral symptoms is no doubt a lifesaver for some. But as with drug treatment for any condition, there is the additional burden of managing the treatment regimen. An effective medication is not al-ways identified on the first try, and once an effective therapeutic drug is found, many, if not most, psychoactive drugs come with uncomfortable side effects. If that isn't enough, a diagnosis of mental illness demands that one cope with the associated social stigma, influenced by whatever science and public policy have to say about the cause and consequence of the illness—sources that may be reli-able, but only in that moment. Extensive media coverage of isolated but tragic incidents involving someone diagnosed with mental illness may draw as much, or more, attention than science news. And even when the media tries to inform the public, they can inadvertently induce a greater sense of fear, for the social stigma of mental illness is often bubbling beneath the surface of public opinion. The bubbling volcano of fear can erupt in the face of public knowledge of tragic events in which the perpetrator has a history of mental illness or when, after the fact of tragic events, mental illness symptoms are recalled by friends or family members for the first time because the stigma of mental illness discouraged them from seeking help and/or failure on the part of the patient to comply with treatment. There are those who *are* living a life of dignity based on their resilience and courage, in spite of a mental disorder diagnoses, but their stories do not readily make the news and are too easily overlooked or forgotten in the face of extensive news coverage to the contrary.

Even well-intentioned news stories have the power to induce fear. In June 2014, following the shootings at Seattle Pacific University, CNN's Anderson Cooper reported on and televised his participation in a demonstration of what it is like to have auditory hallucinations—to hear voices that no one else can hear.[11] "Exercise in Empathy: Hearing Voices" was designed by Pat Deegan, a clinical psychologist who knows what it is like to experience auditory hallucinations, not simply because they've been described to her by her patients, but because she has lived with schizophrenia since she was a teenager. She has heard those voices.

In his narrative introduction, before showing the video of his participation, Cooper clearly and carefully informed the audience, "It's important to know that only a tiny number of people who hear voices engage in violence of any kind." It was an excellent demonstration that could, or should, elicit empathy in response to education, as was intended. The demonstration was compelling, even frightening—both for Cooper, as the subject, and probably for many in the viewing audience. I couldn't help but wonder if the "tiny number of people" part of Cooper's introduction carried as much weight as what audiences saw and heard during the demonstration, including Cooper's description of and reaction to his experience. In his interview with Pat Deegan, the audience *did* hear from someone with schizophrenia who indeed lives a life of dignity and courage. One can only hope that his warning and her demeanor helped to reassure those who, in response to the demonstration, may have experienced as much fear as empathy.

During my first visit to Geel, when I observed the natural community integration and acceptance of those with mental illness and asked my host, psychologist Marc Godemont, what he believed to be the secret of Geel's persistent success he described community factors that have been present, in some form, throughout Geel's history of foster family care. Geel acknowledges and accepts the *human needs* of the boarders. Today the community responds to those needs by providing social clubs, safe inclusion in the community's "pub life," and opportunities to do meaningful work consistent with individual interests and abilities. And, most important, is the existence of not just foster families but an accepting and fostering *community*.

These factors may be the product of Geel's long history with mental illness, but only a narrow view of human capability for kindness and tolerance would insist that they are *dependent* on such a history. Geel provides evidence that those with severe mental illness can be successfully integrated into community life. Acceptance by the community itself—any community—is likely one of the most important factors in achieving that success. These factors may have grown from and been nurtured by Geel's centuries-old legend and the community's need to accommodate the influx of pilgrims. But these factors need not be uniquely linked to such a history.

In looking at our own history and how we have continually sought new sources of hope, our early colonial days, when family care was the necessary rule, seem to be more akin to the early days of Geel. As our own country grew and care for those with mental illness first left the home, and then the community, becoming the responsibility of hospitals, one can't help but wonder how institutionalization influenced what is now our current view of those with mental illness. Whereas those with severe mental illness have always been visible members of Geel's community (just as they were in our own colonial communities), when asylums and state hospitals became the norm, the mentally ill were removed from the community. The CMHCA offered new hope, but deinstitutionalization came quickly, before we were prepared to accommodate and integrate those with mental illness into our communities. Then, as in the years of our young country's urban expansion, many came to associate mental illness with homelessness.

Both of these historic experiences—institutionalization and deinstitution-alization—have likely influenced the development and perpetuation of stigma in our own country. Institutionalization led to the physical separation from, and lack of direct experience with, those who have been diagnosed with mental disorders. But did deinstitutionalization resolve the stigma born of earlier sepa-ration? Did the promise of hope, in the form of community care, find life in the context of caring communities? Or, for those who are no longer institu-tionalized, does social isolation continue such that individuals with a diagnosis of mental illness may only be visible in the face of a homeless stranger on the street—assumed, sometimes erroneously, to be "mad"[12]—or on TV screens in news of tragic acts of violence or through characters that appear in dramatic books or movies? Are those who live meaningful lives in spite of a diagnosis of mental illness unwilling collaborators in perpetuating the image of "madness" associated with mental illness because they dare not let their secret be known, thus robbing us of the hopeful faces of mental illness?

Steven M. Gillon, University of Oklahoma history professor and the *History Channel's* resident expert, in writing of the effect of deinstitutionalization, has wondered if "bringing the mentally ill in closer proximity to the general public has increased social fears."[13] Professor Otto F. Wahl of the University of Hartford has dedicated his research to fighting discrimination and stigma, and in his book, *Media Madness*,[14] he emphasizes the damaging effect of impersonal awareness of mental illness, in which "contact" is seldom direct but rather occurs primarily through slanted media images presented in an unfavorable context.

Today, in the city of Geel, treatment and services for those with mental illness include all of what we offer in our own communities. So what, if any, lessons might we learn from Geel? More than anything, Geel demonstrates the importance of the community *context* in which treatment and services are of-fered—how community integration is naturally facilitated in the absence of a negative, myth-based stigma. We can observe it and read about it, but can we *do* it? Can we only admire from the distance of time and an ocean what a small Belgian town achieved many centuries ago when forced to resolve a problem by looking to its own resources? One thing is certain: our ability to create that kind of environment is dependent on a *desire* to do so and a belief that we can create such an environment. We must be honest about the way stigma kills desire by keeping fear alive. Today, Geel provides a full array of services for the mentally ill, reminding us that "one size does not fit all"—not in life in general, not between different communities, not within a single community, and not in the lives of those who have been diagnosed with a mental disorder. Rather than one simple solution to challenges that surround care and treatment of those with a diagnosis of mental illness, flexibility is another important secret to success. Flexibility must be exercised in the care of individuals with diverse symptoms (and diagnoses) and in the use of resources to provide services for these individuals. In the following chapters, as I describe sites that I've visited in this country, you will notice a common theme of helping those in need, but you will also detect diversity in clients served and services offered. One size does *not* fit all, and if we try to make that happen, there is a chance that we will be seeking *not with* but *against*.

# 6

# Pioneers and Innovations

As a result of the 1963 Community Mental Health Centers act, by 1977 close to two million individuals a year were being served by 650 community mental health facilities, even though implementation of the act suffered from inadequate funding due to the Vietnam War and an economic crisis. President Carter's 1980 Mental Health Systems Act promised improved services for those with chronic mental illness, but a year later, Carter's act was repealed by passage of Reagan's Omnibus Budget Reconciliation Act and a resulting 30 percent reduction in federal mental health spending.[1] With the hope of an extensive community mental health system dampened and continued deinstitutionalization, mental health professionals and community members were concerned about those who would return to the community without access to adequate mental health care. That concern led to the development of several programs that started in a small way but still exist today and have grown to the degree that they readily meet the criteria for success described by Geel's Dr. Godemont. I have visited some of these programs, and with each visit I felt a stronger sense of hope—for the possibility of a meaningful life for those who personally *live with* mental illness and for a reduction in fear and misunderstanding for communities who live *in the midst of* mental illness.

The exemplary mental health programs I've visited are a small sample, but they offer hope that fostering communities are possible. These pioneers were early responders to the needs of deinstitutionalized consumers. They have continued to grow in terms of services provided and clients served.

## THRESHOLDS—CHICAGO, ILLINOIS

Founded in 1959 by Chicago's National Council of Jewish Women (NCJW), Thresholds was a pioneer and, as client numbers have grown over six decades it has also become a model in terms of services provided. The need for an organization such as Thresholds became apparent to a small group of Chicago NCJW members when they attended an educational conference on mental health and learned of the troubling status of those with mental illness who were released to fend for themselves after long-term hospitalization. In too many cases, they had neither supportive social networks nor the experience and know-how to find homes or jobs. They were physically returned to the community unprepared to function within the community, leaving them at high risk for rehospitalization.

As Chicago's NCJW saw community members being pushed out the door of institutional living, they were motivated to start a support organization that would guide patients across the *threshold* to community living. Today, Thresholds provides that guidance for more than seventy-three hundred adults through delivery of thirty unique programs including individual and group therapy, vocational rehabilitation, outreach to the homeless, residential programs, and research. Services are provided by over one thousand employees in clinical, administrative, leadership, facilities, and internship positions. In 2014, the *Chicago Tribune* named Thresholds one of the 128 top workplaces among Chicago companies and organizations.

It's relatively easy to identify a community need, but where could these concerned, nonprofessional women begin? Mental health experts advised against a support program run by nonprofessional staff. But that advice fell on the deaf ears of those motivated by compassionate hearts. Refusing to be discouraged, the women sponsored a five-year project focusing on social rehabilitation. First step? Funding, of course. It's nice to "think big," but it's often wiser to think practical, show the public or the powers-that-be what can be done, and then hope you've gained their confidence and support, allowing you to "grow big." Thanks to corporate donations, government grants, and individual contributions from NCJW members, Thresholds' first annual budget was $53,365, the equivalent of about half a million dollars in 2015. In terms of supporting their vision, that's not much, but when you're determined, you use what you can get. It was enough to get started.

A program needs a home, and we might assume that the home of such a program would likely be located in a lower income district where rents are low. In fact, the organization was able to find a *low-rate* lease in a high-rent neighborhood, made possible by a prize-winning author who owned a gray stone house in Chicago's Gold Coast, an area developed and inhabited by millionaires a decade after the Great Chicago Fire of 1871. The low rent left enough money in their budget to hire a full-time executive director and a part-time psychiatrist to train forty volunteers.

They were ready to provide services—to learn what services were most needed and how they could best be delivered. Initially, Thresholds was open six days a week, when members could participate in a variety of social activities. But a psychiatric social worker noticed that many members dropped out of the program within a few weeks or months. That could be interpreted in a variety of ways, but she didn't jump to conclusions. She observed and learned and reported. Thresholds needed to provide more than just social activities, which only made up one aspect of any person's life. Though they did not look to Geel as a model, what *we* know about Geel is that their success over the centuries is linked to the fact that boarders/patients are able to live balanced, meaningful lives. Understanding that members wanted more than social activities, Thresholds added to their staff two full-time professional social workers who provided counseling and help with training for seeking jobs and resolving family problems. Thresholds had listened and learned. Members responded by reporting a feeling that staff was now concerned with their *total adjustment*—at the center and in their life outside it. Dropouts fell off, and membership grew to 120.[2]

Highlights of accomplishments and services from the organization's 2013–2014 annual report include the fact that they currently offer thirty innovative programs at more than ninety locations throughout Chicago and adjacent suburbs. Services include assertive outreach, case management, housing, employment, education, psychiatry, primary care, substance abuse treatment, and research. While the target population for their services is persons with severe mental illness, services are also provided for others in need, such as youth and adolescents, young mothers, and veterans.[3]

A primary requirement for all of us is a place to call home. Just like those in the general population, individuals with severe mental illness may have diverse housing preferences, often based on the amount and kind of support they require. In 2014, Thresholds housed 651 members in seventy-five different Chicago-area residential developments—supervised group homes, single-room occupancy (SRO) settings, and independent apartment settings. With any of these options, residents are provided with more than a bed and a roof over their heads. They are taught basic living skills that will facilitate integration.

In May of 2004, I spent three days visiting some of Thresholds' programs and sites (it would take many more days or weeks to fully grasp the scope and significance of what Thresholds provides for those with mental illness). My first day began with a morning visit to the Dincin Center, located in Chicago's upscale Lincoln Park community. The building has served Thresholds members well, but came to require more upkeep due to its age, and it recently became clear that the physical layout of the building itself could no longer accommodate programs for those with disabilities. Thus, sale of the Dincin Center was finalized in June 2015. But back in 2004, when I visited, the Dincin Center housed Thresholds' Recovery Team and two Outreach teams, as well as psychiatry and supported-employment services.

Each day at the Dincin Center started with a short community meeting, attended by both clients and staff. On the day of my visit, I was at the center at nine o'clock in the morning to sit in on the meeting and to observe and participate in the day program, allowing me an opportunity to meet some Thresholds members. One, a former practical nurse, won my heart with her pleasant, gentle demeanor but surprised me when she shared that she could no longer work in the field of nursing because of a felony conviction. She expressed her eagerness to do *any* kind of work, stating that she had done all kinds. However, she was in the Catch-22 situation faced by those who must use medication to manage their mental illness. If she couldn't get a job with benefits (health insurance), she was better off, medically, on disability. A part-time job was not a practical option in terms of health care benefits and some full-time jobs could be stressful for her or might require a waiting period before she had access to affordable health insurance. Her story was not unique. She needed benefits that would provide necessary pharmaceutical treatment. She was eager to work and support herself, but circumstances road blocked her ability to finance the treatment that allowed her to manage her illness. Many may view individuals on disability as a financial drain, unaware of their desire and ability to live independently. Such a perspective can feed the stigma of mental illness.

That evening, I returned to the Dincin Center with my niece—who lived near the center and with whom I was staying—to observe a rehearsal of Thresholds' Theater Art Project. This program started in 1988, as a collaborative effort between Thresholds and some Chicago theaters, with the intention of creating vocational, social, and artistic opportunities for members. In 1989, the project received a three-year grant from the US Department of Education, allowing an artistic and administrative collaboration between Thresholds and Chicago theaters, including the well-known Steppenwolf Theater. And in 1991, they presented their first live performance in front of a community audience. The six-to-seven-month program begins early in the calendar year when participants, primarily Thresholds members, get together to share their stories and then participate in movement-oriented exercises and games. About halfway through the program, the ensemble will have gelled, and actors begin to build a show based on their stories and the work they've been doing. And then… it's show time, with seven to twelve performances and an opportunity for the public to see and hear stories of real people who are living with mental illness. Interaction between those in the theater seats and those on the stage provides true community integration—a therapeutic outlet for the actors and education and insight for the audience. (The program was still in operation in 2011, though struggling with budgetary constraints.)

During our visit, my niece and I watched the rehearsal as the actors (a few professionals but mostly Thresholds members) did an exercise where, two at a time, they struck poses of their own choosing and then described and discussed what they'd done and what it meant to each of them. We watched with rapt interest and attention, but when we were invited to do the exercise ourselves, our interest was replaced with self-conscious hesitation. But we did it, and we felt a sense of pride and accomplishment, creating a stronger appreciation for what participation in such a project must mean to those who have been stigmatized—made self-conscious—by a mental disorder diagnosis.

The next day started with a visit to a nonprofit flower shop located in the lobby of a bank building, in the heart of Chicago's financial district. Urban Meadows—a division of Thresholds Rehabilitation Industries (TRI)—was established in 1998 by expanding the Dincin Center's horticultural therapy program, which had grown into a small business, delivering plants and floral arrangements to clients who, for the most part, knew of Urban Meadows through word of mouth or, eventually, a website. But in 2002, a property-ownership and management firm provided space in the American National Bank building, and Urban Meadows gained status as a lobby flower shop, allowing more visibility to potential customers; providing more jobs for Thresholds members, allowing them to learn and develop new skills; and creating community integration beneficial to both Thresholds member employees and Urban Flowers customers. Thus Urban Meadows was added to the list of TRI small businesses, which, at the time, included laser-cartridge recycling, commercial cleaning, and light manufacturing.

Horticultural therapy offers those with mental health problems opportunities to observe and participate in the forgiveness of nature—its rhythm of death and renewal. A flower shop is an excellent work site for members whose symptoms make it difficult to work in, for example, a restaurant or grocery store where job responsibilities and a lack of understanding from coworkers can create anxiety. Working with plants and flowers relieves social stress yet allows the satisfaction of being a caregiver—for flowers and plants.

For twelve years, the Urban Meadows lobby shop was a source of employment and pleasure for Thresholds members. It is still in business with the same name, but it is no longer affiliated with Thresholds or any other nonprofit agency. In 2014, it was sold to the shop's former manager, who continues to hire individuals with disabilities. Sale of Urban Meadows accommodated a change in Thresholds' employment services, which now operates as a Supported Employment Program, helping members to find jobs through Thresholds' partnership with over 150 area employers, including Banana Republic, FedEx, Jewel-Osco, and Kohl's. With this approach, members can find meaningful and

competitive employment with an even greater degree of economic independence and community integration. In 2014, 40 percent of those in the Supported
Employment Program found jobs.

On the afternoon of my second day, Thresholds staff introduced me to one
of their residential facilities, Rowan Trees Apartments, located in a neighborhood with a very different socioeconomic profile than Lincoln Park and the
Dincin Center. In 1998, a building in Chicago's Englewood community was re-
habilitated to a forty-five-unit building of affordable housing—thirty-nine single
units and six one-bedroom units—for very low-income homeless people with
mental illness and substance abuse issues. These tenants participate in a daily
schedule of drug-rehab activities presented at four levels, with residents spending six months in each of the levels. Englewood is one of the poorest neighborhoods in the city, an area of old buildings, some of them abandoned, and vacant
lots. However, prior to Rowan Trees opening, Englewood community groups
began to revitalize and redevelop the area, adding new housing units for seniors
and families. In 1999, Mayor Richard M. Daley announced a $256 million re-
vitalization plan for the area. But in 2010, the median household income was
just under twenty thousand dollars (compared to Lincoln Park's median of just
over eighty-two thousand), with 42.2 percent of the households living below
the poverty level. In spite of efforts to revitalize the community, Englewood is
still known for its high crime rate; in 2014, it ranked eighth in violent crime out
of Chicago's seventy-seven community areas. However, residential facilities for
those with a mental health disorder are not always located in poverty-stricken
neighborhoods.

In 1999, a year after the opening of Rowen Trees, Thresholds opened the
Grais Apartments to serve the same population—homeless with a dual diagnosis
of mental illness and substance abuse. Chicago's Rogers Park community, where
the forty-four-unit Grais Apartments is located, has an environment quite different from either Englewood or Lincoln Park. Located on the far north side
of Chicago, it has a racially diverse population, with 39 percent white citizens,
26 percent black, 25 percent Hispanic, and 10 percent Asian or "other." Every
Sunday, Rogers Park's historic Baptist Church has services in three languages for
a multicultural congregation.

Rogers Park is home to Loyola University, with Northwestern University only a few miles north. Likely due to its proximity to two universities, the rate of residents with postgraduate degrees is higher than the state average—and the rate of residents who work for nonprofit institutions is almost twice as high as the state average, perhaps affecting the median household income of forty thousand dollars, less than one might expect with so many highly educated residents.

Does the socioeconomic and educational status of community members have an effect on a potential "not in my backyard" (NIMBY) attitude? If so, it's difficult to tell what kind of community would be most likely to adopt that attitude. When a Thresholds board member was asked how Rogers Park neighbors reacted to their facility, he observed that, while there may have been some initial community resistance, it was quickly overcome when they realized that Thresholds rehabilitates both people and derelict buildings by maintaining their properties and supporting their clients. He added, "Within six months, people forget we're even here."

While the scope of Thresholds' services, the number of clients served, and the number of staff employed has grown almost exponentially since 1959, their goals have not changed, even though the "business" of helping people to live meaningful lives continues to be a political, social, and fiscal challenge. Because the mental health of any community member affects the entire community, it is a social challenge that feeds the political, policy-making, and funding challenges. At the root of the social challenge is fear of mental illness due to stereotypes and stigma. That fear, along with the fear of spending by taxpayers, are factors that feed the fiscal challenge. However, just as misinformation gets in the way of understanding and living with mental illness in our communities, so, too, does misunderstanding about the cost of mental health services unnecessarily exacerbate the challenge of providing adequate and appropriate treatment. Compared to hospitals, jails, and nursing homes, community-based treatment is both a bargain and a dividend-paying investment—it is not just a "holding bin" but a source of appropriate and practical services that encourage autonomy and allow individuals to be socially and economically integrated into the community in which they live.

# COMMUNITY ACCESS—NEW YORK CITY

A group of NCJW members in Chicago recognized the challenges created by deinstitutionalization, and Thresholds was born. Fifteen years later, in New York City, family members and friends of patients released from state psychiatric hospitals had similar concerns when it appeared that only two housing options existed for those without support or assistance waiting for them: "flophouses" or municipal shelters. Neither seemed to be a satisfactory or humane alternative. But magazine editor Fred Hartmann, whose own sister had been hospitalized, envisioned a better solution for those moving from overcrowded state hospitals to life on the street, "victims" of both their illness and a lack of community concern. His idea of a better solution was safe, supportive housing, and in 1974, Community Access (appropriately named) was founded by a group of New York City volunteers, led by Hartmann.

As with Chicago's NCJW members, Hartmann didn't wait until he could implement a grand plan. He formed and headed up a board of similarly motivated individuals—primarily family members and mental health professionals—who pooled their own money and used those funds to rent apartments for friends and family members in city-owned, tenant-managed buildings on Manhattan's Lower East Side. Not only was the housing decent, but Community Access was one of the first in the country to provide support for its tenants through community integration and an explicit emphasis on the *abilities*, rather than the *disabilities*, of tenants—*not against, with.*

Three years later, Community Access hired their first staff person and, for five thousand dollars, purchased two small apartment buildings to house forty-four tenants—half with psychiatric disabilities, and half low-income families. Community Access continues to provide housing for those with psychiatric disabilities as well as the working poor, creating a tenant population that includes the homeless, HIV/AIDS patients, veterans, those struggling with substance abuse, formerly incarcerated individuals, and youths aging out of foster care. Other agencies that began to serve the needs of those with mental illness have also evolved to serve those in need for a variety of, and sometimes multiple, reasons. When I encounter this pattern of service, I am reminded of our own early colonial days, when communities naturally served those in need for any reason.

In 1981, an operating license and funding from the New York State Office of Mental Health (OMH) allowed Community Access to lease apartments from private landlords, rent their first office, and hire additional staff. Since then, private donations and contracts have allowed continued growth. While an organization's success story is the product of many people working together and should not be bound to the reputation and personality of a single person, two people who have had a significant impact on the growth and success of Community Access deserve mention.

In 1979, Steve Coe was studying for his master's degree in public policy at New York City's The New School. Having met Fred Hartmann, Steve showed up at Community Access that summer as a summer intern. He didn't care what kind of work they could offer. He was happy to paint hallways and tar paper the roof, just so he could expose himself to the professional environment in which he would soon be seeking work. By the end of the summer, he "was hooked," and he's still there today as chief executive officer.

During my October 2007 visit to mental health sites in New York City, I met Steve, and he showed me around Community Access. But before I met him face-to-face, I "met" him through an e-mail I received after he became aware of a 2003 conference presentation I made, "An International Perspective: The Geel Story." Reading that presentation prompted him to introduce himself in a November 2006 e-mail expressing a belief that we shared the same point of view regarding mental illness and a sentiment that "it's important to let people know that someone else shares your point of view, since it's not the prevalent thinking in our country." I became convinced that we indeed shared a vision regarding mental health and community services when I read: "[as] director of Community access in NYC for 27 years, I've developed a keen appreciation of any approach to community integration and recovery that deemphasizes what is 'wrong' with someone, and instead promotes opportunities for healthy, meaningful relationships and work." He went on to say, "I also don't believe [in] models; there are many interesting and effective programs. I do believe in a system of values and principles that must inform the work."

My visits to exemplary mental health programs in this country and my awareness of people, such as Steve Coe, who are implementing those programs in a *not against, with* manner sustain my belief in a voice of hope for mental illness and my determination to let that voice be heard—by those with psychological disabilities, their families, mental health professionals, and entire communities. Steve noted that we share a point of view that is not the prevalent thinking in this country. Maybe it isn't. But maybe it's more prevalent than Steve and I know. Maybe there are those who share that view but don't express it, because they feel they're a solo voice in the forest of mental illness—a voice that will not be heard or even acknowledged. We'll never know if that's true until our solo voices become a harmonious chorus that won't be silenced by the same stigma that deters the pursuit of meaningful lives by those whose life includes a diagnosis of mental illness.

Fred Hartmann and his friends formed a section of that chorus in 1974. Steve Coe joined it in 1979. I recognized my solo voice when I read of Geel in 1982. It became stronger with my first visit to the Belgian city in 1997—stronger still with each of the site visits to programs described in this book—not just programs as described on the Internet or on paper. It's the people who keep my hope alive—*all* the people who serve and are served by these programs.

Community Access would likely have experienced success even if a twentysomething Steve Coe hadn't shown up to help fix up some of the buildings. But there is no doubt that Steve and his *not against, with* value system helped to facilitate that success. In fact, it was Coe's concern about "cultural drift" in the 1990s that led him to another man who came to play a significant role in the 1995 development of an award-winning Community Access program.

Coe felt that cultural drift was the product of state-licensed programs and the accompanying increase in professional social workers. He feared it had caused Community Access to stray from its original value system—what had drawn him to the agency in the first place. The mere fact that residents were now referred to as "patients" was, to Coe, troubling evidence that Community Access was becoming "too medical." He sensed that the agency would continue to experience significant growth. That was good. But he didn't want growth at the expense of a loss of respect, consumer choice, or human rights that had been a founding hallmark of the organization. Not wanting to stand by and watch those values slip away, Coe arranged a series of meetings where staff and board members developed an explicate philosophy and principles that would maintain and strengthen their original cultural identity.

During this time, Coe met Howard Geld, better known as "Howie the Harp," who was running a consumer-led program in Oakland, California. When Coe met Geld, he recognized traits that he believed would make him an excellent community organizer. Geld was funny and driven—consistent with Community Access's value system—and he believed that, in spite of any disability, people deserved to control their lives through recognition of their *abilities*.

Geld was born in New York City in 1953. At the age of fourteen, he tried to commit suicide, which led to over a year of hospitalization in a school for emotionally disturbed adolescents. During that year, he earned the nickname that stayed with him for the rest of his life when an attendant taught him how to play the harmonica (the "harp") in order to relax. Though Geld returned to his home and family, he was labeled with a host of mental illness diagnoses. He later acknowledged that he did, at times, have what were likely manic episodes, followed by severe depression, but he didn't believe the diagnostic labels defined who he was. At seventeen, he ran off to be on his own and to discover what life was like for others like him, whom he met in the single-room-occupancy buildings in which he lived. During this time, the same thing that had helped him relax while he was institutionalized now helped him earn money for food and a place to sleep; he played his harmonica on the streets of Greenwich Village.

His harmonica and nickname provided part of his identity, but Geld was also a pioneer in advocacy for mental patients, and in 1993, recognizing his talents, Steve Coe created a management position for him as Director of Advocacy. With Geld, who believed in giving people control over their lives, serving as a staff member, Coe envisioned a program that would train consumers to serve as peers in treatment programs. Could anyone better understand the challenges of living with mental illness than someone who lived with the same challenges?

Geld developed a curriculum and secured funding from the State Office of Mental Health to support a Peer Specialist Training Center. However, in 1995, two weeks before classes began, the one who made the center possible—who had devoted his life to the mentally ill and homeless—died in his home of an apparent heart attack at the age of forty-two. The center was appropriately re-named The Howie the Harp Peer Advocacy Center and is still active in fulfilling its purpose through the HTH Peer Training Program. Twenty weeks of intensive classroom training and a twelve-week internship prepares graduates to work as Peer Providers in Human Services. Though those with a diagnosis of mental illness can be certified as New York State Peer Specialists[4] without HTH peer training, HTH training offers unique opportunities and benefits. Applicants must have a mental health diagnosis and at least a high-school diploma (or equivalent), and they must be residents of New York City.[5] In its first fourteen years of existence, more than seven hundred individuals with psychiatric disabilities graduated from the program, trained as Peer Specialists for professional positions in hospitals and clinics throughout New York City. The program is still active, offering four different Peer Specialist programs.

Community Access began because of one man's concern for his sister and others like her who needed an affordable place to live a decent life. Today, that volunteer organization—founded forty-one years ago using funds donated by volunteers to rent apartments for deinstitutionalized family and friends—every day provides independent living in transitional or permanent housing for sixteen hundred consumers, along with job training, counseling, education, and advocacy. As a result, many Community Access clients are able to continue their education and pursue new careers. Community Access started with less concern about the diagnosis or disability of their clients, focusing instead on the *whole person*—not against, with—a perspective that helps create a stigma-free environment, encouraging clients to set goals that allow them to optimize their potential. The goal of, and for, all their clients is to experience the kind of success that allows for meaningful lives within the community. Their success has not gone unnoticed, and their programs have served as models for the development of other programs across the country.

## GEEL COMMUNITY SERVICE, NEW YORK CITY

In the next chapter, you'll read about two more New York City nonprofit organizations that also provide supportive housing. These are sites that I visited, based on the recommendations of those I know who are familiar with mental health care in that city. However, they are only a handful of examples out of hundreds of supportive-housing programs in the city that collectively provide more than twenty-eight thousand units,[6] some of which surely deserve as much attention as

I've given to my small sample of four. I can't visit them all, but I hope my experience and discoveries will encourage you to investigate what's available in your part of the country—not necessarily because you or a family member might need such services, but because, as an *informed* member of your community, you can help reduce the effect of stigma on your friends or neighbors—creating a more meaningful life for your entire community.

I'm including in this chapter one more New York City organization that responded to deinstitutionalization by providing supportive housing, though it does not serve as many clients nor offer services as broad as the other three. I include it to illustrate that an organization doesn't have to be big to make a valuable contribution. During my 2007 visit to New York City mental health programs, I felt compelled to visit Geel Community Services because of its name and the source of its motivation.

Geel Community Services (GCS) was founded in 1976 by mental health professionals and community members in the Bronx. They chose their name because it was their specific intention to replicate what they knew of the centuries-old tradition of compassionate care in Geel. GCS started with the simple but necessary intention of providing counseling services for and a roof over the heads of a handful of people with mental illness living in the Bronx. Today, at any one time, GSC can provide housing to approximately 340 individuals with a diagnosis of mental illness.[7]About 230 are housed in one of three buildings, where they live independently in fully furnished apartments. In addition, the Apartment Treatment Program provides two- and three-bedroom apartments scattered throughout the North Bronx and can house fifty-four adults, who receive personalized rehabilitation services at one of two levels of care. These are named after Belgium's two largest cities: Antwerp level is simply referred to as Supportive, while Brussels level is designated as Intensive Support. (I've often wondered how they determined which level deserved what city designation? I'm a stickler for detail, but some things aren't worth the "drilling down" time. Maybe someday I'll find out by accident.) Residents of this program are referred by New York City area outpatient service providers and inpatient psychiatric facilities, and an average length of stay for Apartment Treatment residents is twelve to eighteen months.

Along with independent living and the Apartment Treatment Program, GCS also offers Supported Scatter Site Housing, with ninety-five beds "scattered" in regular neighborhoods and apartment buildings. Scatter-Site residents can live independently or with roommates in fully furnished studio, one-bedroom, or two-bedroom apartments. Though the housing is scattered, and residents are capable of managing their own apartments, they have access to case management and housing-support services at the GSC office located in the Bronx.

The only GSC facility I visited during my New York visit was Archie's Place—named in honor of Archie Hollander, former executive director of GSC, who passed away a year before the 2003 opening, when fifty-six formerly homeless individuals with mental illness who had been living in shelters for as long as nine years could now enjoy *permanent* housing in a *new* structure built on six city-owned formerly vacant lots. When they moved into that new building, they also moved into a new living experience—their own studio apartments, with private baths, stocked kitchenettes, furniture, linens, cookware, and dishes. They can also enjoy a sense of community with fellow tenants in a furnished community room, an outdoor patio and recreation area, and the convenience of a laundry room. They can avail themselves of onsite services, including prevocational job training, social programs, and twenty-four-hour crisis intervention. With their new social and physical environment, residents feel a sense of self-worth that is often lost in shelter living. One new Archie's Place tenant expressed that transition from shame to hope when she said, "I could not bear my family seeing me while living in the shelter system. Since moving into Geel [Archie's Place], I have reconnected with my family, which is the real road to true recovery."

## WAY STATION—FREDERICK, MARYLAND

When I set out to visit exemplary mental health programs, I didn't have a funded, planned itinerary. I simply took advantage of annual travel funds made available to professors and combined that with my own personal travel funds. So wherever I traveled—for a conference, to visit friends or family—if I was aware of a mental health program of note in that area, I made arrangements to visit. I don't recall how I came to know of Way Station, but it was the first program I visited, in November 2002, and it was a good place to start.

As with the programs described above, Way Station began providing services in 1978, during the deinstitutionalization era, when formerly hospitalized individuals had no place to go. Mental health professionals—members of the Frederick County Mental Health Association (FCMHA)—addressed the need for community services when they met in a small room in a downtown Frederick office building. Though it is the second largest city in Maryland, with a population of sixty-five to seventy thousand, and is fifty miles northwest of our nation's capital, the community of Frederick is decidedly not Chicago or New York City. It is the seat of Frederick County, but the county population is only a quarter of a million. In terms of mental health and the community, compared to large urban areas, Frederick has different resources. In the beginning, FCMHA addressed the same concerns as did urban programs. Today, the organization provides services similar to what is offered in urban programs, but the size and resources of Frederick led to subtle, and sensible, differences in the development and delivery of Way Station services.

As with other programs, Way Station developers were highly motivated to create a sense of community and belonging for the population they would serve. Thus Way Station adopted the psychosocial rehabilitation "membership club" model in order to create a sense of ownership and pride for those who would avail themselves of the club. As with urban programs, they needed space—in this case meeting space—and the Evangelical Lutheran Church was a resource for a city such as Frederick. Though Way Station did not, and does not, have any religious affiliation, the church offered to loan them space in its large downtown facility for a day program. Interested members of the congregation also became involved: a lawyer in the congregation was the first chair of the board of directors, and a retired nurse served as Way Station's first volunteer.

In 1979, one year after Way Station became a reality, they began a small housing program using a "scatter-site approach," with Way Station renting a few three-person houses in existing neighborhoods. This was not meant to force integration, and it acknowledged neighborhood sensitivity while offering a normalizing community environment for Way Station clients. Today Way Station provides or helps members find housing in a variety of residential settings—depending on their needs and desires—including, for some, independent living in their own home or apartment. In some cases, members live in group homes, located in a neighborhood of single-family dwellings. For any type of housing arrangement, sensitivity to neighbors is always considered. They may be invited to a gathering at the Way Station's clubhouse/office where they can learn about their new neighbors and ask questions of Way Station staff and members. In the case of a group home, neighbors may be invited into the home itself. Under any circumstances, a sincere effort is always made to encourage community acceptance in a manner that fosters open relationships among Way Station staff, members, and the entire community, acknowledging "the right of persons with serious mental illness to live in the least restrictive environment, and their right to enter that environment with the *same privacy and dignity afforded any citizen.*"[8] (Emphasis added.)

Community integration for members is also encouraged outside of their neighborhoods, using approaches that are readily facilitated in a city the size of Frederick. The Way Station began to address employment for members using a Transitional Employment Placement model. Arrangements were made for jobs at community businesses, with members working six-month rotations and Way Station staff filling in if members needed to miss work. The program grew to provide job development and placement, job coaching, and (in some cases) self-employment for members through their partnership with over fifty local businesses.[9] The national average employment rate of those with serious mental illness is 10 to 15 percent. Way Station members have a 26 percent employment rate, working in settings such as restaurants, business offices, nursing homes, and machine shops. Some members who may not be able to hold jobs experience community integration by participating in volunteer work. In either case, when members are offered the opportunity to do meaningful work, many report that they feel like givers rather than receivers for the first time in their adult lives.

Initially, Way Station avoided the medical model, believing that clients were overmedicated. However, they came to see the necessity for medication, offered in the context of dignity and normalization, and a traditional outpatient clinic with psychiatrists was eventually added to their services. Today, due to physical-health needs of those with SMI, primary-care nurses are also a part of the mental health team.

In 1990, Way Station services and programs were consolidated to operate in, or from, a new thirty-thousand-square-foot facility, serving approximately thirty-five hundred clients/members in Frederick County and surrounding communities. The large building allowed them to include clients with intellectual disabilities, including employment services for this population and mental health services for children. They also provide employment services for unemployed veterans who may or may not have mental illness or substance abuse disorders. Administrative offices that oversee fourteen different program categories are located within the two-story building.[10] Some clients work within the building; many participate in one of the diverse Day Program activities that include classes in healthy living and the arts along with more practical classes on income tax preparation and voter registration.

## THE VILLAGE—LONG BEACH, CALIFORNIA

Thresholds was started by a group of concerned nonprofessionals. A businessman's concern for his sister led to Community Access. Both Way Station and Geel Community Services grew out of the concerns of a small group of mental health professionals. In each case, the initial purpose was to address the specific needs of those who had been moved out of institutions but, too often, had no place to go in the community. Two overlapping approaches addressed the needs created by deinstitutionalization: supported housing and avenues to community integration. For the most part, these programs began and/or soon evolved to create residency options and explicit or implicit opportunities for community integration.

The Village also serves those who are both homeless and mentally ill—*and* who do not have access to existing services. Their concerns are consistent with the programs I've just described, but their history and structure is noticeably different. The impetus for what would become the Village emerged in 1987, when private citizens and a few mental health professionals expressed concerns about the state's mental health system to California's lieutenant governor. He was receptive, neither turning them away nor justifying what did appear to be a poor system. Instead, he offered to support formation of a task force that would study various systems of mental health care and make viable recommendations for change. Two years later, their study and recommendations led to the passage of a bipartisan bill that provided three years of state general funding to support what seemed to be the most sensible approach to revamping the state's mental health system: integrated services, in which persons with mental illness would be matched to existing community services on an individualized basis, allowing them greater independence to live, work, and learn within the community by using available support services.

A pilot study was launched in which Integrated Service Agency (ISA) projects were established at three levels: county, urban, and rural. The Mental Health Association in Los Angeles County (MHA/LA) was awarded the urban agency contract, and in April 1990, the Village was founded as a pilot project with psychiatrist Mark Ragins as director and 120 members who would, at the end of the three-year project, be compared to 120 members in the rural project as well as a matched set of 120 consumers who would continue to receive existing traditional services.[11] Before proceeding with long-term funding, the pilot study would evaluate the effectiveness of ISAs. Sometimes what sounds good on paper doesn't work as well as predicted. However, outcomes from the pilot study were so successful that the ISA became a model for future California legislation and reform, and MHA Village received recognition and honors from President Clinton in 2000 and President Bush in 2002.

In 1993, Boston University psychiatrist William Anthony published a paper in which he predicted that "recovery" from mental illness would guide treatment in that decade, noting that on the heels of failure associated with deinstitutionalization, those with severe mental illness "want and need more than just symptom relief." Living in the community, they had the same needs and desires as the general population in terms of housing, work, education, and social interactions.[12]

Mark Ragins was not aware of Anthony's prediction when he headed up development of the Village—not as a residential facility and not with a focus on symptoms, but rather as a support service for community integration and member recovery. Ragins had been trained for his profession in the context of the medical model, but when he came to the Village, he wanted to do things differently in terms of how he viewed those with mental illness—most importantly, how he viewed the potential of those designated as mentally ill. But based on his training, the recovery model seemed, to him, to be too extreme to become acceptable. And then in 1991, when Ragins was a year into building the Village, Anthony visited the program. Ragins asked Anthony what *he* thought would be the next big movement in mental health. When Anthony responded with one word, *recovery*, Ragins later reported, "[I] nearly fell off my chair."[13] But he soon learned that other consumer advocates were confirming what Anthony had predicted and what Ragin sensed as an outcome of "integrated services." Subsequently, the Village became a model recovery community, offering members with severe mental health problems, often coupled with substance abuse—many of whom were homeless or had been in and out of jails and hospitals—the opportunity to turn their lives around.

The Village is concerned with the life of the whole person, but while having a place to live is part of a stable, meaningful life, the Village does not provide housing. However, the consequences of homelessness *are* addressed in the context of an ISA. The Village's Homeless Assistance Program (HAP) connects members to whatever services they, the individuals, need. Every day of the week except Saturday, Street Outreach workers go to those in need, wherever they might be—on the streets, in parks or encampments, in homeless drop-in centers, at shelters, or in hospitals. They know where to look, but they also respond to requests from those who are aware of, and concerned about, people who live on the streets: businesses, social-service agencies, churches or faith organizations, law enforcement, or members of the general public. Street Outreach workers do not provide psychiatric intervention or crisis response, but if needed, the Long Beach Police Department's Mental Evaluation Team will respond.

What outreach workers do by going to those in need in the scattered and impoverished corners of their street communities is *build trust*—by something as simple as offering blankets or by encouraging individuals to get off the street for even a day or a night and into emergency housing or a drop-in center. There are many drop-in centers in Los Angeles County, and HAP runs one of them. Many in Long Beach know of its safe and welcoming environment; it is a place where they can find help with something as challenging as benefit-application assistance, as practical as day-labor work opportunities, or as comforting as a warm shower. While the drop-in center only offers transitional services, that assistance can serve HAP's ultimate purpose of connecting those in need to established services. And, for those who do show up at the HAP drop-in center, short-term case management is also available, offering a promising door through which people can connect to consistent mental health and community services, the door to turning their lives around, as many have done.

The Village pilot project started with 120 members in an environment where everyone could know everyone else. In 2003, with 476 members, three neighborhood teams were formed to provide services, each with a director, an assistant director, a psychiatrist, a financial planner, a community integration specialist, and nine personal service coordinators with at least one registered nurse, Licensed Psychiatric Technician (LPT) or Licensed Vocational Nurse (LVN). While the increased membership has diluted the "everyone knows everyone else" environment, each of the three neighborhoods has evolved to have its own unique culture and internal operations.

When I visited the Village in January 2008, I started my day at the drop-in center to sit in on the weekly community meeting where members and staff were invited to talk about whatever was on their minds. Were they happy? Sad? Worried? (The only rule was "don't ask for money"—spoken in earnest but softened by a friendly tone.) It was a small group that day, and no one had a lot to say, but neither did anyone seem hesitant to make a contribution. I listened to them either share what was on their minds or respond to announcements: there would be no service providers that day at the West free clinic; two members were celebrating birthdays—an announcement that evoked the traditional "Happy Birthday to You." I smiled that no one seemed to be at the same place in the song at the same time. But my smile was bigger in response to how every member contributed to the traditional birthday joy that filled the room. A staff member, Kelly, announced that she was leaving and expressed the joy she had experienced at the Village as she observed and shared in the celebration of recovery success stories. Many subsequent comments from individual members or staff included "Good-bye, Kelly"—indicating reciprocal gratitude for their time together. There were sad announcements: after a long illness, a hospitalized member had passed away; another member had suffered either a heart attack or a stroke and was hospitalized in an intensive-care unit.

And, finally, someone made it known that "free oranges" were available for a morning snack.

There weren't any earth-shaking announcements or comments, but I thought about what they had shared and found that if I closed my eyes and imagined settings and situations that were more familiar to me—the break room at work, a shared meal with friends—what mattered to Village members was what matters to all of us. If we don't have a casual social setting in which to share bits and pieces of everyday living news, we can feel isolated and alone. If Village members weren't sitting in the drop-in center, would they have a place to share? Where would it be? In an alley, lying on a collapsed cardboard box? On a park bench? The drop-in center is a place where members are allowed the simple human satisfaction of small talk, of belonging. There are so many little things that make life meaningful. When we naturally have access to them, we forget how important they are. We can also forget that not everyone has access to the satisfaction of that small human need.

One announcement at the meeting that was of particular interest to me was made by then associate director Paul Barry, who assumed the position of executive director in 2009. Barry reported that he met with the president of the homeowners' association for new condos located across the street from the drop-in center. He was pleased to note that the president was supportive and understood that a building such as the drop-in center was a part of the "urban experience." Barry was encouraged and indicated that he would ask the president to be a member of the Village Advisory Board, which meets bimonthly. While the board has no administrative or oversight authority, it includes local community members, allowing them to stay abreast of what's happening at the Village and encouraging communication between Village staff and neighbors.

Noting the general interest in neighborhood acceptance of those with mental illness, I wanted to know more, and I sent a follow-up e-mail query to Barry asking him about the general value to the neighborhood of a program such as the Village, and for more detail about his meeting with the president of the condo owners' association. His reply was not short, but I was interested in all of his remarks as representative of NIMBY-type concerns that could affect or be affected by any stigma of mental illness. His points seemed obvious once I read them, but without good communication between a mental health site and the neighbor-hood, any of the points could go unnoticed. Barry enlightened and encouraged me in his e-mail of January 27, 2008.

- Police see the Village as a functional resource where they can bring homeless individuals with apparent mental illness when they don't know what else to do.
- The Village does not have formal security in the building, but welcoming "ambassadors" work in areas surrounding the building and wear shirts that say Security. (The source for these unofficial security officers is a credible recovery house that makes the job part of their member program.) They keep Village members from loitering on sidewalks and protect Village members by keeping away uninvited street visitors who sometimes vic-timize members away from Village property and even the building itself. Security also walks the neighborhood to discourage loiterers and, if neces-sary, will call the police if a problem requires "more muscle."
- When the opportunity presents itself, the Village reminds neighbors that their presence upgraded "the hood" from its previously "seedy" streets. Some locals may suggest that the Village still makes a contribution to the "seediness," but this is a talking point that can be considered from a "half full vs. half empty" perspective.
- While cleaning around their own building, the Village maintenance crew also cleans adjacent sidewalks and alleys.
- When it becomes necessary to ask members to leave the building due to inappropriate behavior, they are walked out of the building *and* down the street, away from immediate neighbors. This prolonged approach removes the member from the area and also gives the member and the situation a chance to deescalate.

In addition to being a calm and sensible "PR man," as a Village administra-tor, Paul Barry has made employment for Village members a significant factor in the process of mental health recovery. A supported-employment program assists members in choosing, getting, and keeping a job with local employers.

Paid work opportunities in the Village office include receptionists and data-entry operators as well as tellers and money-management coaches at the Village bank. In all cases, the relationship between supervisor and member offers members the valuable experience of being in an employer to employee relationship, not simply one of mental health professional to dependent client.

Two businesses also operate out of the building. Deli 456 is a catering service and walk-in deli, open Monday through Friday from nine to two, that offers fresh food daily.[14] The Village Cookie Shoppe is an online shop that won the *Long Beach Press Telegram* Reader's Choice award for "best dessert in Long Beach" four years in a row.[15]

And there's more. The MHA Long Beach Wellness Center, a program of MHA Village, provides health services to Wellness Center members and the community at large. The Village supports and encourages educational growth of members, fostering a love of learning by recognizing that individuals learn at their own pace. Village staff work with members to integrate their interests and strengths and overcome barriers. Education has obvious benefits in terms of finding work, but it is also, in and of itself, a tool that helps to guide members through the four sequential stages of recovery: hope, empowerment, self-responsibility, and a meaningful role in life.

The Substance Abuse and Mental Health Services Administration (SAMHSA) has identified integrated services and the Village as exemplary practices. Thus, in addition to serving their own members and community, operation of the Village is of interest to mental health professionals, system planners, and people with mental illness and their family members and has become a training center for interested parties from at least a dozen states who would like to better understand and/or replicate the integrated-services model. Immersion training was developed in 1994 and provides information about the structure and key elements of integrated service as well as suggestions for how the approach can most successfully be incorporated into the work of other organizations.[16]

After attending the morning Village community meeting, I stayed to observe an immersion-training session attended by representatives from programs serving two diverse populations: a greater Los Angeles mental health program for elderly adults and a state forensic psychiatric hospital. Diverse though they were, they both had a concern regarding the structure of the program, wondering if members might become slaves to the structure, unable to comply without someone telling them what to do once they returned to the community. The Village trainer discussed it with the two trainees and was able to make useful suggestions that would facilitate implementation of the program at each site.

The Village is different from other programs described in this chapter (and in subsequent chapters) in that it was not founded specifically to provide housing for those with mental illness. Yet the bulk of their services are under the umbrella of their Homeless Assistance Program, acknowledging the fact of homelessness and providing integrated services for individuals where they are and, at the same time, offering members an opportunity to end their homelessness and live more meaningful lives.

You've had a taste of some programs that were innovative in terms of their timing. The first four responded to the need for support as those who had been hospitalized returned to the community. As we look at those programs, we can say that there have been, and are, caring communities. The Village, in its own way, responded to the post-institutionalization era by using a recovery model to go beyond the "disease" of mental illness, offering opportunities to live a meaningful life in spite of a diagnosis of mental illness.

You've met a few individuals who illustrate what it means to *live with* mental illness and to *live beyond* that label. Hopefully you've seen that a diagnosis of mental illness does not negate the need for respect from community members and for oneself.

In some ways, these programs offer the same success factors that have been observed in Geel. Yet just as it's not practical to try to replicate Geel's services, it is not wise for *any* program to ignore its own needs and resources to replicate a program in this country. Hope for successful community programs begins with a realistic evaluation of who the community will serve and what resources are available in order to provide necessary services. In the next chapter, you will read about the successful effort to build a program in New York City that was explicitly inspired by one person's experience with the "spirit" of St. Dymphna, in Geel.

# 7

## The Spirit of Dymphna
## Comes Alive in New York

In a 1970s scientific journal, a young Ellen Baxter first read of Geel's legacy of care for the mentally ill. During her sophomore year as a psychology major at Bowdoin College, wanting to know what it was like to be institutionalized due to a mental disorder, Ellen convinced a psychiatrist to commit her to Maine's Augusta State Hospital, where she feigned symptoms of mental illness. But the length of her stay was cut short, to just one week, after she observed and experienced the cruel treatment of patients and chose to leave the hospital, not because of her inability to tolerate this treatment, barbaric though it was, but because she had become friendly with the patients ("inmates") and did not want to deceive those whom, in such a short period of time, she had come to view as friends.[1]

## BROADWAY COMMUNITY HOUSING— NEW YORK CITY

Today Ellen Baxter is executive director of New York City's Broadway Housing Communities (BHC), which she founded in 1986 to provide supportive housing for individuals with mental disorders. BHC might not exist if, after graduating from Bowdoin in 1975, Ellen's interest in Geel's system of foster family care for the mentally ill had not led her to seek and earn a Thomas J. Watson Fellowship[2] that allowed her to spend a year in Geel. Though born in New York, Ellen had grown up in the Netherlands and was fluent in Dutch, a language similar to Flemish, the language of Geel, which is located in the Flanders region of Belgium. This allowed her to live as an active, participating member of the Geel community, observing firsthand the lives of those with mental illness who, unlike state-hospital residents, were surrounded by a social environment of support and community acceptance.

Ellen's personal interest and inspiration led her *to* Geel. She took *from* the city a belief that supportive housing and community integration could exist anywhere, even in the urban environment of New York, our largest city. But upon returning to New York City and observing the plight of the homeless, including many with mental illness, Ellen became aware of a maddening lack of community care for those in need. Dymphna, the young Irish princess, did not succumb to the madness of her father. Ellen refused to succumb to the madness of a system devoid of compassion. She became even more determined to serve those who were victims of both their own illnesses and this community "madness."

In the days when I was seeking information regarding the Geel Research Project (GRP), I first heard Ellen Baxter's name, as both Jan Schrijvers and the family of Leo Srole encouraged me to contact her (I did) as a source of information (she was). But we first met face-to-face in Geel when we were two of twenty-one presenters from six different countries at Geel's 2000 symposium, "Celebration of Seven Hundred Years of Foster Care." In Ellen's talk, she described how her year in Geel had led her to seek out ways to provide compassionate service to the homeless of New York City.

Seven years after meeting Ellen at the 2000 Geel Symposium, I traveled to New York City to see firsthand what she had accomplished. What I saw during that visit and a subsequent 2014 visit was, in its own way, as amazing as what I had seen in Geel. It seemed that the spirit of Dymphna that had first come to life in a small agrarian Belgian city in the thirteenth century was still alive in twenty-first-century urban neighborhoods, where supportive community residential buildings had been established. Ellen's dedication to the spirit of Geel began in 1989 with BHC's first building, and it continues to grow. By 2014, BHC had established seven supportive-housing communities. Each community of residents is housed within a separate building, located in a different neighborhood of Washington Heights or West Harlem, and integrated into the surrounding neighborhood. The BHC model doesn't simply provide living space, it provides "humane, cost-effective permanent housing for homeless populations" and the opportunity for tenants to live independently while receiving medical and mental health care, vocational training, and job placements.[3]

When Ellen spoke at Geel's 2014 Symposium,[4] she began with an expression of gratitude to families and boarders whom she had come to know forty years earlier. She expressed personal gratitude and, more significant, gratitude for what *their* spirit had helped to create in New York City for, during her year in Geel, Ellen had come to understand the possibility and power of supportive housing and community integration; she had been convinced that this environment could be created in any community willing to utilize its resources to care for those in need. A *"not against, with"* attitude could create environments that welcomed and supported those with mental disorders and, at the same time, provide support for entire neighborhoods: services provided in BHC buildings for those with a diagnosis of mental illness are also available to neighbors who could benefit from such services. Ellen understands that since we all have the same human and practical needs, integration and support are "go-togethers." Neighbors became neighbors based on mutual need and interests, overlooking differences born of a stigmatized label. *Not against, with*—in other words, *not separation born of stigma, but inclusion born of a shared humanity.*

That is the why and the how of BHC. But none of it came to be quickly or easily. When Ellen returned from her year in Geel, she was eager to replicate the stigma-free care she had come to know in Geel. What she found in New York City, however, made her task seem daunting and, at the same time, more necessary. But this admittedly shy, physically small, but gracious and determined woman does not give up easily. In Geel, she had come to know boarders and foster family members by listening to their stories—riding her bike from place to place, conversing with them in their homes and in community meeting places. The New York City stories she heard were told in settings different from those she had visited in Geel. As part of the New York Community Service Society's Quality of Life Project, Ellen and fellow Columbia University graduate student Kim J. Hopper sought out and listened to the stories of homeless mentally disabled adults living in the most desperate of circumstances: sleeping on the streets, in subways, and in parks.[5,6,7] As in Geel, Ellen and Kim learned by asking questions of the homeless, honoring their humanity, and empowering them by *listening* to their stories.

In spite of her quiet and gentle demeanor, Ellen is a woman of action who gathered support from those who shared her concerns and goals. Subsequently, in 1979, she, along with concerned activist friends including Robert M. Hayes, a young corporate attorney, brought a class-action lawsuit to the New York State Supreme Court on behalf of the state and city's homeless and against the state and city of New York.[8] The New York State Constitution states, "the government shall provide food, shelter, and clothing to the destitute." In other words, there are constitutional provisions reminiscent of what was spontaneously done for those in need during colonial days. But what *actually* happened in the twentieth century was not consistent with State Constitution requirements. In fact, during an interview with a Bellevue/New York University faculty member and medical provider, Ellen and Kim learned that the New York City medical examiner, a friend of that faculty member, estimated that during the coldest months of winter, thirty to fifty people were delivered to the morgue with hypothermia as the cause of death (E. Baxter, private communication, March 23, 2015). Whether for humanitarian or legal reasons, the State Supreme Court ruled in favor of the homeless, and a 1981 consent decree affirmed a legal right to shelter for the homeless of New York City.

That's *sort of* the good news. However, in practice, it wasn't as good as it sounds. It is true that due to a court order, every night more than fifty thousand men, women, and children (close to half being children) now had a place to sleep in New York City's emergency shelters. And every new governor of New York and mayor of New York City seems proud to say that their city and state does more for the homeless than any other state. Maybe…depending on how they define *more*. Emergency shelters can be expensive; likely as a result of cutting budgetary corners, the environment of these shelters led them to be referred to as New York City's "refugee camps." A cot in an emergency shelter is not a home—not even close to the supportive housing or community integration that Ellen had seen in Geel and envisioned for New York City.

She knew that to be true, because she lived across the street from the Fort Washington Armory emergency shelter. Every night, throughout the night, she would hear buses bringing the homeless from around the city to lie their weary bodies down on 1,450 rows of cots, positioned on painted lines, with assignment to a cot based on one's health condition—red lines for the actively psychotic, blue for known TB cases, yellow for known AIDS cases. Though Ellen was relieved that these people were not freezing to death on the streets, she was reminded of what else they were *not* doing. They were neither living in supported housing nor integrated into any communities. From Ellen's apartment, she could see and smell the Fort Washington shelter. Though lights were kept on all night for safety, she knew that did not deter unbridled acts of violence and theft. There was more to be done and, based on *who* she is and *what* she had experienced in Geel, Ellen did not stop believing that things could be better. She knew that it wasn't simply the lack of available money that stood in the way. Ironically, as primitive and sparse as were the accommodations in the Fort Washington Armory, the cost to the city for a person sleeping on a cot on the floor of the armory was forty dollars a night. Yet subsequently, in 1985, a private room in the first BCH residence could be provided for less than twenty dollars a night per resident.

Ellen would not abandon her belief in the possibility of a better life for those she had met on the streets, and in 1980, she found evidence confirming that it *was* possible to provide that better life. She became aware of the St. Francis Residence I, established by two Franciscan priests who converted a single room occupancy (SRO) building into affordable housing with onsite social and mental health services. At St. Francis, rent for one hundred formerly homeless citizens was a mere $215 a month (equal to $623 in 2015). Ellen now had evidence that she was not pursuing an impossible dream. She found an abandoned building from which to launch the first phase of BHC's program to provide supportive housing as a long-term solution to homelessness. Still, it would take patience and persistence to sell the idea to those with money and influence. There is no doubt that Ellen has a strong sense of both, and it is no surprise that she got the job done. The building was renovated at a total cost of $1.2 million, financed by multiple funding sources, including Federal tax credits. In 1985, nine years after Ellen brought her dream from Geel to New York City, BHC's first residence, the Heights, was ready to open. Even better, its success resulted in New York City's

1987 Supportive Housing Loan fund. Subsequently, in 1988, New York State established the SRO Support Subsidy Program.[9] The Heights did more than provide fifty-five single units for formerly homeless residents. Funding initiatives motivated by the success of the Heights are considered to be responsible for seventeen thousand supportive-housing units throughout New York City and fifty thousand across the nation.[10]

With the building ready for occupancy, Ellen wanted to make sure that tenants were ready for the responsibility associated with their new lifestyle. Community is about more than finding and renovating a building. A community is a social, as well as a physical, entity. Geel's tradition began because of a need to house pilgrims, but it didn't stop there. In Geel, without any real planning, circumstances led to the evolution of other aspects of community and acceptance. In New York City, it *would* take planning, but Ellen was up to the task. She didn't want to merely house people. She believed in their ability to live independently. She also knew that in a modern, urban environment, they would need guidance in establishing this new way of life. And so, as the Heights was ready to house the formerly homeless, Ellen hosted a gathering at the site for potential tenants whom she had met during interviews on the streets of the city. She showed her guests around the building, allowed them to pick out their space, and discussed the responsibilities of being a community member. Ellen's belief in the possibility of bringing supportive integrated community housing to New York City had been affirmed.

In 1988, three years after the opening of fifty-five single units at the Heights, BHC's second building, the Stella[11] opened with twenty-eight single units. Once again, the New York City Supportive Housing Loan Fund, born of the Heights project, financed renovation of the building. Where did the name Stella originate? In spite of misfortune in their pre-Heights days, early tenants rose above their pasts to live responsible lives in response to the "gift" they had received. Tenant meetings are held in all BHC buildings, and the Heights has the most widely attended meetings of all BHC buildings. Stella Levine, one of the early tenants of the Heights, likely set that tone. Before taking residence in the Heights, Stella, a thin, barely five-foot-tall heroin addict, would have had nowhere to live if not for the kindness of a George Washington Bus Terminal cleaning attendant who gave her a key that allowed her to live in the bathrooms of the terminal. As did other tenants, Stella impressed Ellen. Stella's flashy dress, jewelry, and makeup were hard to ignore, but more importantly, Ellen found her to be "one of the most generous survivors, demanding, yet kind and aware of her rights."[12] The name of BHC's second building honored a woman who was a survivor, a role model for others striving to survive, and an inspiration for Ellen Baxter. Stella called the Heights home until her death from cancer in 1987, only two years after she finally had a home of her own. Yet in spite of her death, Stella's spirit continued to motivate both her fellow residents and Ellen's work.

In 1989, BHC opened its third residence, the Delta, with thirty-two apartments for singles in a building that had previously been operated as a transient hotel with rooms to rent by the hour. It is fitting that the first of many renovations in that building was the removal of an unnecessary bulletproof security booth located in the entryway.

BHC was expanding, and as it grew, the first step was always finding a building. A Harlem building had been designed by a prominent architect in the late nineteenth century for members of a successful publishing family, Agnes and Nicholas Benziger. After its life as a family residence, the building had served as part of a medical institution and even as a brothel for a time. But in 1989, financial support from the Abraham family and the city of New York allowed restoration to provide twenty-one single units of permanent housing for homeless adults. One of Harlem's last remaining freestanding mansions, the building was officially designated an Historic Landmark in 1999. As befits a community building within a neighborhood, an afternoon Family and Friends Day is held annually for tenants and their children, grandchildren, relatives, and friends. In true BHC tradition, tenants and neighbors together enjoy outdoor dining and music in the Jimmy Jervis Garden, named for another tenant of the Heights.

Where we live is an important aspect of our life. Supportive housing is an important element in the life of those in need. Quality of life is dependent on more than a roof over our head and a bed in which to sleep, and those with a disability may have uncommon needs. But BHC does not create an environment where residents are simply "taken care of." The BHC model strives to give residents the opportunity to support themselves and their neighbors and their community—those with whom they share the building, as well as those who live in the neighborhood.

In the presence of diverse needs and abilities, BHC does not take a one-size-fits-all approach to achieving community support and integration, providing residents with a sense of meaning in the context of their communities. All potential and new tenants are assessed to determine their goals and individual needs—sometimes related to age or chronic health issues. But many tenants have no special needs and are merely seeking what Geel offered in the context of permanent housing: lasting reliable relationships that create a sense of trust and tolerance for one another. This is what we all seek, and hopefully find, in the communities we call home. Though individual limitations are considered, close to 20 percent of BHC tenants work as part-time, paid employees managing the front desks of their buildings, thus providing income for tenants and reducing employment costs for BHC. Tenants who do serve as front-desk staff are trained to provide supervision of their fellow tenants and rapid response to urgent or critical needs. Since they are well acquainted with the unique traits of neighbors and tenants, they are able to recognize a need for policy change if it occurs and to provide practical input during meetings with supervisors and other staff members as to how these changes might be implemented. For some, these front-desk jobs are perfectly suited to their limited educational background or compromised physical health.

Residents of BHC communities are *not* all the same, and their needs may be diverse. But diversity is an asset in terms of creating an integrated community. BHC tenants may have mental or physical disabilities. They may be living with HIV/AIDS or some other chronic illness. They may even be in recovery from addiction related to substance abuse. For diverse community members with diverse needs, BHC offers individual support, either within the residential buildings or through collaboration with community agencies, helping tenants to live independent and stable lifestyles.

BHC is not the only supportive-housing program in New York City or across the country. What made BHC a unique model is the inspiration for *integrated residency* that Ellen brought from Geel. The opportunity to create that environment emerged when, in 1991, the abandoned Rio Vista Hotel was renovated and opened as the Rio, BHC's fifth supportive-housing facility, unique in that it included not just seventy-five studio units but five family units, making it New York City's first project to include children in integrated supportive housing. The Rio also introduced practical, but pleasant, amenities. Located on the penthouse level, added to the roof, is office space, a community lounge, an art gallery, and a garden of perennials and evergreens tended, of course, by Rio tenants. And, in 1998, the Rio began to offer weekday after school homework assistance and weekend cultural and art activities for resident *and* neighborhood children.

Ellen's years in Geel convinced her that there was nothing to be gained from any kind of segregation—within or between BHC communities. In Geel, Ellen had witnessed single adults, families with children, the young and the old, the healthy and the disabled all living together as a diverse, but unified, community. It worked in sixteenth-century Geel when pilgrims poured into the city, and Geel used its available resources—the homes of citizens in an agrarian community—to accommodate the overflow of pilgrims. Ellen believed it could work anywhere as long as the resources of the community were used to meet the needs of community members. But, there was not unanimous support for what she had observed and learned in Geel. In this country, we can become trapped in models created by bureaucratic interests associated with professional and public funding biases. For example, some deemed it inappropriate for homeless families with children and single homeless adults to live in the same building. But with five family units and services for both tenants and neighbors, the Rio introduced *integrated* supportive housing to New York City. With BHC's next project, Dorothy Day apartments, this concept was further advanced. Yet once again, Ellen had to call on her indefatigable determination and patience to make that happen. Though the construction of Dorothy Day apartments was delayed for a full year, Ellen would not yield to tenacious illogical bureaucratic interests. Finally, in February 2003, in a turn-of-the-century building donated by an anonymous benefactor, BHC's sixth supportive-housing project opened with seventy apartments ranging in size from studio to one, two, or three bedrooms, housing approximately 190 children and family members. The physical environment of Dorothy Day is different from that of Geel. The social environment is a close cousin.

Why the name Dorothy Day? This project was not named after a former BHC tenant, building owner, or original building name. Though BHC has no religious affiliation, this building was named after a Catholic convert who, in 1933, cofounded the Catholic Worker movement, intent on making "works of mercy" the center of her life.[13] In 2007, when I visited Ellen in New York City for the first time, I walked down West Harlem's Riverside Drive sidewalk, enjoying a lovely view of the Hudson River, across the street from Dorothy Day apartments, which also houses BHC's executive offices. On entering the building, I walked down a glass-walled, sunlit entryway. In front of me, on the wall facing the entry, I met the face of Dorothy Day in a painting of a humble woman with downcast eyes whose work inspired the building where I met the spirit of Dorothy Day—and Geel and Ellen Baxter.

The aforementioned anonymous benefactor who donated the building to BHC did so as a tribute to Day's work for those in need. It was totally renovated with seventeen million dollars in funds derived from private equity, philanthropic foundations, and all levels of government. The tradition of serving families *and* the community, begun at the Rio, continued on a larger scale at Dorothy Day, with programs to serve tenants and neighbors from infancy through adulthood. The building houses a licensed childcare center and a federally funded Head Start Program that emphasizes parental participation and literacy. After school, technology, and cultural arts programs are available for tenant and community school-aged youth, including academic and community service programs for adolescents. Onsite comprehensive employment and social service programs are available for adult tenants.[14] And, as at the Rio, the top floor has an art gallery where neighborhood artists can schedule exhibits and, on the roof, lovely gardens enhance the view of the Hudson River.

Dorothy Day illustrates the good sense and success of not just asking the community to accept those in need but of bringing the community *into* the homes of those in need, where neighborhoods can satisfy some of their own needs. Considering the tenacity of stigma and rejection, it is remarkable that, in just thirteen years, the neighborhood no longer even thinks of Dorothy Day as providing housing for the mentally ill and formerly homeless. It is a part of the neighborhood, a home to tenants, serving tenants and neighbors alike.

In the mid-1970s, Ellen Baxter brought her belief in supportive housing and community integration from Geel to New York, not knowing if it was possible to replicate a rural Belgium success story in urban New York. That did not discourage her. Neither did the many obstacles she encountered on the way to establishing six BHC residences between 1986 and 2003. But the work of BHC was a community investment that paid dividends. In a December 2008 letter to BHC supporters, Ellen reported that among BHC residents, graduating high-school seniors were being accepted by colleges of their choice. High-quality, individualized education offered in BHC buildings services 150 children, allowing them to attend better schools across the city; in 2008, 80 percent of Head Start graduates were attending charter, magnet, private, and small public schools. Close to 25 percent of tenants are part of front-desk management—offering them work experience and assuring twenty-four-hour coverage for all six housing sites.

In that same letter, Ellen announced that she was not ready to stop, for in the coming year, BHC's seventh project would create a model of urban revitalization. The Sugar Hill Project was to be located in West Harlem, a racially mixed community with a high poverty rate, overcrowded housing, rising housing costs, and low educational performance. When Ellen began her campaign for supportive housing of the mentally ill in New York City, she first became aware of, and addressed, the problem of homelessness. Yet it's not surprising that in our nation's largest city, with shifting political promises, an issue as complicated as homelessness is not likely to be resolved once and for all. For over twenty years, the New York City housing program has offered supportive housing in rent-subsidized apartments. However, from 2006 to 2007, Ellen reported, there was a 17 percent increase in the number of homeless families living in emergency shelters. Furthermore, the New York City housing program is set to expire in June 2016 unless a new agreement is reached, even though the number of those living in homeless shelters has risen to 58,000 in the past year. Those citizens are the focus of the Sugar Hill Development.

In BHC's first three buildings, approximately one-third of the units were reserved for adults living with mental illness. That tradition continued at the Rio. A new model emerged at Dorothy Day where parents living with mental illness and custodial responsibility for children were served along with low-income individuals and families. However, Sugar Hill apartments were assigned using a lottery approach, resulting in 124 families (out of 50,000 applicants) who moved into ninety-eight apartments when the building opened in December 2015. There are "set asides" for those with disabilities, but no specific "set asides" for those with mental illness. Given the value of supportive housing in combating poverty, need is the primary criteria for residence at Sugar Hill, and twenty-five apartments are reserved for homeless families, most of whom include children and survivors of domestic violence.

As with other BHC buildings, Sugar Hill will also act on evidence that children benefit from educational and cultural experiences. To this end, a critical aspect of Sugar Hill is the Children's Museum of Art and Storytelling (SHCMAS). In contrast to its current poverty rate and low educational performance, Sugar Hill is, historically, a culturally rich neighborhood, the geographic focal point of the Harlem Renaissance, when a short list of Sugar Hill residents included W. E. B. Du Bois, founder of the NAACP; Supreme Court Justice Thurgood Marshall; civil rights activists Roy Wilkins and Reverend Adam Clayton Powell; actress Lena Horne; and musicians Paul Robeson, Cab Calloway, Count Basie, and Duke Ellington. Gaining knowledge of their heritage through intergenerational dialogue with artists, art, and storytelling is an investment that is expected to pay high dividends in terms of helping young people break out of the cycle of poverty.[15] As with other BHC facilities, SHCMAS will serve the entire neighborhood, not just tenants of Sugar Hill. In addition, public transportation links Sugar Hill to the entire city, making the site easily accessible to those going in and out—out to work, in to visit the museum.

## COMMON GROUND—NEW YORK CITY

While BHC was a pioneer in offering a combination of supportive housing and integrated residency, it is not the only project in New York City that offers this environment. My 2007 visit to the city was motivated by a desire to see, firsthand, how Ellen's inspirational year in Geel came to life in New York. But while I was there, I wanted to visit other city mental health programs, and Ellen was the best source for recommendations. I've already reported on one of her recommendations—Community Access, founded in 1974 (see chapter 6).

Another suggestion included a particularly noteworthy organization—Common Ground. Established in 1990, by 2005 it was the nation's largest not-for-profit developer of supportive housing, collecting awards and national media recognition as it grew.[16]

By 2015, Common Ground offered 2,842 permanent units in fifteen different buildings, allowing more than seven thousand individuals to escape or avoid homelessness. While Common Ground serves those who are homeless for a variety of reasons, priority is for those with severe and persistent mental illness (SPMI), since the incidence of homelessness for this population skyrocketed during deinstitutionalization.

When looking at the relationship between community and those with mental illness, recall that, in colonial America, when we didn't have a good understanding of mental illness, concern was more generally for anyone "in need." In small, scattered and isolated rural settlements typical of the times, it was easier for families or the community to give support to those in need. Then, in the nineteenth century, as the population of our country and the number and size of urban centers grew, the number of those in need increased and included transients with no place to call home and no community to care for their needs. That was the start of a problem that escalated in the next two hundred years and is particularly obvious today in our largest cities.

Common Ground's effort to end homelessness focuses on the chronically homeless who suffer from debilitating medical and mental health conditions and who have established lives on the street, rather than seeking shelter and assistance. They are major consumers of public resources but are typically pushed aside or ignored by conventional outreach, shelter, and housing systems. Common Ground's goal is to alleviate that situation—for the sake of the homeless and, at the same time, for the sake of neighborhoods and communities.

Communities benefit because Common Ground's primary source of housing is renovated old, often vacant, buildings. This approach began in 1991 when the organization acquired the once grand Times Square Hotel, a mere two and a half blocks from Times Square itself. I was not familiar with either the original hotel or the crime-ridden blight to the neighborhood it became as it aged. But in preparation for my visit, I did my homework and learned something of its past and current state. However, when I started my second day in New York by reporting to the Times Square Apartments, where I was to learn about Common Ground in general and this residence in particular, I was not fully prepared for what I saw. I entered the elegant two-story lobby, decorated with large urns of fresh flowers and the artwork of resident artists. It was a lobby that seemed prepared to once again welcome a host of grand visitors. Yet in a residence for those who had been destitute, it was an unexpected sight. Former guests likely expected a grand lobby. For current residents, it seemed to have the potential for increasing their sense of worth and self-respect.

The Times Square was Common Ground's first supportive-housing residence, becoming the largest permanent supportive housing residence in the country, with 652 low-income permanent residents in single rooms. (Since these are hotel rooms renovated into apartments, they are not as spacious as those at Dorothy Day.) Consistent with the goals of Common Ground, not only did the renovation bring new life to a once-elegant building, it also revitalized the neighborhood as a whole, a common dividend associated with this approach. Renovated buildings produce renovated neighborhoods. Together, the two encourage the creation of renovated, renewed *people.*

As a physical structure, the Times Square has earned a rightful place on the National Register of Historic Places. As a social structure, it has received numerous awards for its innovative programs. Common Ground serves individuals with diverse needs and, for the most part, each of its fifteen permanent housing projects is occupied by a specific population. The Times Square offers permanent, affordable housing for persons with serious mental illness, those living with HIV/AIDS, and low-income and formerly homeless adults, with the Center for Urban Community Services providing onsite social services for these particular populations.

It is often said that "children learn what they live." The same thing might be said of almost anyone, and residents of the Times Square, as with residents of other supportive-housing facilities, are offered the opportunity to live lives that, unlike street life, offer them a chance to feel a sense of value and self-respect. Also, not only is the building *in the community* but, as with BHC, the community is welcomed into the building. For example, in a large community room on the top floor, tenants can enjoy something as simple, but beautiful, as sweeping views of the city. This room is also available for commercial rental to the general public.

Common Ground generally renovates old, even vacant, buildings, but in 2010, its first construction project helped revitalize the surrounding Bronx community. Common Ground always shows joint concern for person renewal and building or neighborhood renewal, as it creates housing that is safe, afford-able, and an asset to both the residents and the surrounding communities.

One of its most important programs addresses a concern for the chronic homeless, making a significant contribution to breaking that cycle. Covering all of Brooklyn and Queens and close to half of Manhattan, its Street to Home approach, begun in 2004, had reduced street homelessness by 87 percent in the twenty-block area around Times Square and by 43 percent in the surrounding 230 blocks of west midtown by 2007. It is not surprising that, in 2007, the pro-gram was adopted by the New York City Department of Homeless Services as a citywide strategy. This approach targets those who have been on the streets the longest and are, therefore, at highest risk for premature death. One might think that the homeless would be eager to have apartments, homes of their own, but many individuals, often referred to as "hard to house," are reluctant to accept outreach efforts, in part because of the nature of their illnesses, often exacer-bated by alcohol and substance abuse that has become a way of life for them. The Street to Home approach seeks to gain the trust of these individuals by not insisting that the offer of housing carries with it a demand that the individual must, for example, achieve sobriety.

Street to Home most specifically addresses the needs of those with SPMI. In addition, Common Ground has three other programs that target those who are often homeless or vulnerable to becoming homeless: (1) the Foyer Program, for youth who are aging out of foster care, (2) the Veterans' Initiative, and (3) Elder Care Health Outreach (ECHO).

Approximately twelve hundred young people ages eighteen and older leave the New York City foster care system each year, but only 20 percent are dis-charged to the care of a parent, relative, or other adult. It is not surprising that, with a lack of family guidance during their foster care years and a common failure to successfully complete high school, the remaining 80 percent are often ill-prepared to find and keep jobs or manage housing and health issues on their own. To serve the needs of this population, and hopefully to reverse the current trend, Common Ground has adopted a housing model for youth that was first developed in Great Britain in 1992. Foyer programs seek to forestall homelessness for this group before it happens. In addition, they strive to end homelessness for young adults who did not make successful transitions from foster care to independent living. Through collaboration with other nonprofits, it is the first New York City program to target young adults without families.

The first of two Foyer programs was initiated in 2004 in collaboration with Good Shepherd Services, with more than 150 years of service to homeless and troubled youth. The Christopher—once the site of a YMCA that provided affordable housing for the likes of Andy Warhol and Tennessee Williams and now a renovated one-hundred-year-old building—is home base for this program. The Christopher provides 207 housing units, 40 of which are designated as Foyer units. The remaining units are occupied by low-income working persons and formerly homeless single adults.

In light of the Christopher's success and the scarcity of affordable housing for young adults, in 2010 Common Ground developed a second Manhattan Foyer Program at the Lee, a Lower East Side twelve-story "green" building with features that qualify it for Leadership in Energy and Environmental Design (LEED) silver certification. The building houses 55 young adults, 104 formerly homeless single adults, and 103 low-income working adults from the Lower East Side. Services include self-sufficiency workshops, a computer lab, and a gym. Bike storage is available in the courtyard, giving tenants the freedom to ride to the store, the subway, and nearby Hamilton Fish Park, where tenants can mingle with long-time area residents.

Common Ground's special-need segments include veterans who can fall victim to homelessness for a number reasons—medical and/or mental problems, substance abuse (often as a way to self-medicate mental problems), or joblessness. The very nature of homelessness makes it difficult to collect accurate census data for this group, and nationwide trends are not always representative of regional (state) trends,[17] but in New York City, about 10 to 12 percent of Common

Ground's total residents are homeless veterans. In 2008, to serve veterans as a separate group with unique needs, Common Ground opened a ninety-six-unit transitional home in a wooded rural setting located on the Hudson River, forty-six miles north of New York City. Here veterans receive onsite support to mend family relationships, find jobs, and save the money necessary to establish homes of their own in the community—in other words, to transition back to the life they knew before their lives were redefined by traumatic experiences during service to their country.

In recent years, in light of the aging of existing residents, a trend that is expected to continue, Common Ground recognized a new population in need—those with geriatric problems that did not exist when they first moved into a Common Ground building. In 2011, Common Ground opened the seventy-two-unit Domenech in Brownsville, Brooklyn—their first residence designated specifically for low-income seniors, some of whom have a history of chronic homelessness. Almost half the residents are homeless seniors with special needs; the remaining residents are low-income seniors. The Domenech provides health and medical support as well as self-sufficiency workshops, allowing seniors to maintain as much independence as possible. In order to create a pleasant and friendly environment, there is a community garden space, a library and computer lab, onsite laundry facilities, and accommodations such as wheelchair access for those with limited mobility.

All of the Common Ground buildings and services offer affordable housing, security, and opportunities for the homeless to become productive members of a community while offering savings to the taxpayers. Common Ground's buildings provide housing for thousands of men and women, including low-income tenants who work in the creative fields as actors, dancers, artists, and fashion entrepreneurs and can contribute to the character of a city that proudly calls itself the Big Apple. Foyer programs help former foster children establish an independent life. Elder Care Health Outreach (ECHO) helps aging residents to live independently for as long as possible, thus avoiding the expense of institutional care. We like to say that in this country, everyone has the opportunity to pull themselves up by their bootstraps. The problem is that not everyone has bootstraps. A public investment that provides those bootstraps pays dividends in a *not against, with* manner.

# 8

# A Meaningful Life

Concerned citizens or mental health professionals addressed outcomes associated with deinstitutionalization in the middle of the twentieth century. Several decades *before* deinstitutionalization, those diagnosed with mental illness were believed to face a life of hopelessness. Six patients in the Rockland State Hospital in Orangeburg, New York, were aware of this stigma, and, anticipating a need for assistance and support once they left the hospital, they began to plan ahead. Their foresight led to the development of a program that would not only help them but would come to have significance around the world.

What was life at Rockland like for those patients? Construction of the hospital began in 1927. In 1931, it opened with 5,768 beds and sixty male patients on a six-hundred-acre campus with its own farm and shops where patients made items such as brooms, mattresses, or furniture for the hospital. It was one of many asylum environments in the era of moral treatment, when it was believed that symptoms of a mental disorder could be relieved by removing patients from the stresses of life. In its early days, Rockland was reputed to be the best-planned state hospital in history. But even in its first decade—likely out of desperation when many patients failed to respond to moral treatment, resulting in an exponential growth of the patient population—Rockland began to use questionable treatment methods. By 1959, the peak year for admittance, Rockland had more than nine thousand residents (including a staff of two thousand) and no longer provided a quiet, *therapeutic suburban* environment. Today, at what is now called the Rockland Psychiatric Center, the buildings are mostly abandoned, and less than six hundred patients, mostly outpatients, are served in newer buildings on the campus.[1]

Some patients may have responded to moral treatment, but in general, Rockland's history leaves little to be admired—*except* for the legacy of those six inpatients who, while still hospitalized in the 1940s, formed a self-help group called We Are Not Alone (WANA). After leaving Rockland, the group stayed active with meetings on the steps of the New York Public Library. In 1944, they held an official meeting in Manhattan's Third Street YMCA, with ten former patients and one former volunteer present. Four years later, in 1948, they purchased a four-thousand-square-foot brownstone on West Forty-Seventh Street. Inspired by a fountain on the grounds, which founders saw as a symbol of hope and renewal, they renamed their group and incorporated as the Fountain House Foundation.

## FOUNTAIN HOUSE—NEW YORK CITY

Anticipating the needs of former inpatients, Fountain House was established as a "clubhouse," primarily organized and administered by members, for use by members—not for treatment, but as a place where former patients could go for work, education, and entertainment activities. The purpose was reinforced by the physical environment, meant to resemble a private home. Many early members had been institutionalized for up to thirty years. Unlike the hospitals and asylums where they'd lived, there were no bars on windows or closed doors at Fountain House, and members were not restricted from any area of the building.

That was the seed for the original clubhouse, planted in New York City. In the city itself, Fountain House has expanded its programs and physical presence over the past sixty-seven years. The model has led to hundreds of clubhouses in the United States and around the world. By 1962, the original building was inadequate to house the diverse programs that had been added, and construction of a new building, directly across the street from the original building, began. That building was completed in 1965, and it wasn't the last expansion. Today, Fountain House owns five buildings on West Forty-Seventh Street: the original building, the current Clubhouse Center for Education and Research, and two residences. Four other residences are located around the city. In addition, in 1977 Fountain House inherited 477 acres in northwestern New Jersey from a former board member, with the stipulation that it be conserved as a natural resource that benefited those with mental illness. Thus, High Point Farm offers the clubhouse concept in a rural setting, with a thirty-acre working farm comprised of housing, gardens, animals, and pastures. Fifteen acres of meadows, twenty acres of streams and preserved wetlands, a ten-acre lake, and dense forest cover the remaining acreage.

Each week, a group of staff and members travel to the farm—living for the week, commune style, in an onsite chalet—to carry out the work of a productive farm. A dedicated group tends the garden that provides flowers to create a home-like environment in Fountain House. One of the biggest jobs is maintaining the organic vegetable gardens that provide most of the vegetables used in Fountain House's culinary unit. In the winter, the focus is on wood—chopping firewood for heating the chalet and milling lumber for various woodworking projects. And then there are the animals. Work on trees, flowers, and vegetables is seasonal, but tending to the chickens and alpacas is a year-round job. Chickens provide eggs for Fountain House, and the award-winning alpacas provide income. Members and staff breed the animals, help farmers develop a herd, and, once a year, shear the animals, providing fiber to produce products that can be sold.

During my 2007 visit to New York City mental health programs, I enjoyed a day at Fountain House, touring the multistory building to see the active work going on in various units, sitting in on member/staff meetings, and visiting casually with individual members. It was a warm and welcoming atmosphere. Members were industrious and friendly. (In planning my trip, I became aware of High Point Farm and hoped to include a visit to the farm, but no luck. It's about seventy-five miles northwest of New York City, and needless to say, the subway doesn't go out that far.)

In 1976, as communities around the country established new programs to deal with the fallout of deinstitutionalization, Fountain House had been operating successfully for twenty-eight years. As the clubhouse model was often integrated into these new programs (for example, Way Station, described in Chapter Six), Fountain House was awarded a National Institute of Mental Health (NIMH) multiyear grant to establish a national training program for the community. For those unfamiliar with the Fountain House model, the structure and function of a clubhouse could be interpreted intuitively or subjectively. But the model is more accurately linked to a structure and elements that had evolved, through experience, to define their success. NIMH funding led to the development of a three-week immersion program, describing the foundation of clubhouse culture and including daily discussions with trainees to clarify clubhouse practice.

By 1987, training had produced 220 clubhouses in the United States, providing evidence that a clubhouse culture could be implemented in diverse locations within our own country. In addition, clubhouses had been established in Canada, Denmark, Germany, Holland, Pakistan, Sweden, and South Africa. The clubhouse culture was apparently consistent with universal human values and therefore was compatible with cultures on a global scale. With continued expansion and increasing clarity and standardization of the clubhouse-model definition, in 1989, at the Fifth International Seminar on the Clubhouse Model, six hundred participants reviewed, discussed, and accepted thirty-five International Standards for Clubhouse Programs. Growth of the clubhouse movement resulted in changes in the organizational structure, which came to be contained within the International Center for Clubhouse Development (ICCD) in 1994. In January 2013, "doing business as Clubhouse International" was added to Fountain House's name, and it is still operating out of New York City. Today there are over three hundred clubhouse programs in thirty-four countries modeled after Fountain House.[2]

Before expansion of the model itself, program expansion at Fountain House helped define the model. In 1958, ten years after Fountain House became a reality, guidelines for an Employment Placement Project were created, and placement of workers quickly followed. Then, as Fountain House membership grew, there was need for an employment program to accommodate the diverse abilities and interests of their members (flexibility—a key to success). The project, now known as Transitional Employment, provides part-time temporary employment for six months. Supported Employment provides ongoing part-time or full-time jobs through Fountain House's long-standing partnerships with New York City corporations. As with Way Station, which was established using the clubhouse model, if a member is unable to work on a given day, a Fountain House staff worker will fill in. In addition to these two programs, many members secure employment on their own or with the help of a Fountain House job developer.

Recently, social-enterprise and social-cooperative programs have been developed, offering job opportunities through the creation of new businesses. Social enterprise, with Fountain House's own microbusiness incubator, encourages entrepreneurship in members and has resulted in businesses that provide services to clients (e.g., bicycle food couriers, floral arrangement and plant installation, janitorial work). Though members provide the workforce and may help to create the businesses, social-enterprise businesses belong to the clubhouse. But they still offer learning experiences for members, and skills learned from that experience can lead to future employment. The social cooperative program offers administrative and financial support to help members start and run their own small businesses. One cooperative that has grown out of this program provides front and back support services to for-profit partnerships. Another provides janitorial services for government parks and nonprofit organizations.

Also in 1958, recognizing that some members needed assistance in finding housing, Fountain House began to secure leases for apartments in the community. Then, in 1984, Fountain House opened its first residence building. Today the organization helps more than five hundred members a year find safe, permanent, affordable housing.

Fountain House programs also address a problem associated with the onset and progression of severe mental illness. Onset often occurs in the late teens or early twenties, with 75 percent of psychiatric illness diagnosed by the age of twenty-four, thus stalling or disrupting one's high-school education and/or progress to higher education. Fountain House now operates the nation's largest Supported Education Program, providing academic, financial, and social support to those who want to continue their education or return to school. It addresses the needs of any member—from those who have not learned to read to those who are working toward a graduate degree. Each year, the program also distributes scholarships to hundreds of members for both academic degrees and technical certification. Education opens the doors to employment. Employment is an escape from poverty. Poverty can be a roadblock to advanced education. It's a vicious cycle that Fountain House has helped break for many of its members. The school-completion rate for those with mental illness in the general population is 32 percent; for Fountain House members, it is 65 percent.

And there's more. The Wellness Center provides a variety of services, including simple health education, important to a population that is more vulnerable to chronic physical problems. In a separate program, young-adult members make presentations to groups of young men and women, aged eighteen to thirty, who are vulnerable to the initial onset of mental illness. Self-stigma regarding mental illness can discourage them from seeking treatment; public stigma can create social challenges. Speakers with mental illness provide those in this age group the support and confidence they'll need to overcome the negative outcome of stigma should they be diagnosed with a mental disorder. Fountain House also carries out research, collecting data to investigate the efficacy of existing programs as well as providing insight into the need for new programs.

And it all began with six inpatients in a New York state hospital in the early 1940s, twenty years before Robert Frost advised, "Always fall in with what you're asked to accept. Take what is given, and make it over your way…Not against: with." They didn't need Robert Frost's inspiration to know they would be asked to accept the effects of stigma when they returned to the community. Yet they took what was given and made it over, allowing them the chance for meaningful lives—in spite of a stigma that wasn't apt to vanish in a moment. Over one hundred thousand individuals with mental illness have reaped the fruits of the resourcefulness and courage of those six people.

The vision for Fountain House began in a state hospital. It was kept alive on the steps of a New York Library. The first official meeting took place in a New York YMCA. In 1948, it was incorporated, and Fountain House Foundation blossomed in its own building with a name, inspired by a fountain in the garden of that building. Fountain House and other clubhouses, in this country and around the world, are physical buildings. But more important, these buildings are home for a culture that is kept alive by a partnership between members and staff, with members involved in all of the activities and at every level of the organization.

Inaugurated in 1996, the Conrad N. Hilton Humanitarian Prize is the world's largest humanitarian award, presented each year to a nonprofit organization judged to have made exemplary and extraordinary contributions to alleviate human suffering. It's appropriate, and not surprising, that the 2014 winner of the $1.5 million prize was Fountain House. We can only wait in eager and confident anticipation to see what wonders they will perform with that gift. And it can't be repeated often enough—it all began with the courage of six state mental-hospital patients who persevered and thrived in spite of the stigma of mental illness—*not against, with.*

## PREMIER LODGE—SOUTHFIELD, MICHIGAN

You've now read of programs started by concerned citizens, mental health professionals, and in the last case, individuals who had been institutionalized due to mental illness. In most of these cases, a need was recognized, a plan was put in place—often on a small scale—to address the need, and the program grew from there. As the programs grew, additional services were often provided, or when services weren't being accepted or met in the intended manner, changes were made in the delivery of those services.

In 1963, however, a unique program began as the product of research, funded by a grant from the National Institute of Mental Health (NIMH) and carried out by George W. Fairweather, associate consulting professor of psychology at Stanford University and chief of the Social-Clinical Research and Service Unit of the Veterans Administration Hospital in Palo Alto, California. Dr. George W. (Bill) Fairweather earned his PhD in psychology and sociology at the University of Illinois. His expertise in those two social sciences guided research that led to development of an alternative to hospitalization based on experimental testing.

In the 1960s, those who were hospitalized for mental illness commonly faced either long-term institutionalization or a return to the community after a very short stay. The second alternative would seem to be favored, except, as we've already seen, communities were often not willing or prepared to accept former patients. Neither were those patients prepared to be integrated into the community to take care of themselves as responsible community members. Within a mental hospital, however, Fairweather found that many fared quite well in terms of integration and autonomy, *if* they were members of a small group that functioned within the hospital community.

Since small groups worked well within a hospital community setting, Fairweather wondered if they would have the same success in the larger community once group members were released from the hospital. Thus he carried out research to address the question: Could meaningful roles and social status be created for those with mental illness who had been hospitalized, allowing them to participate in the social processes of ordinary community citizens? The experimental approach required (1) one or more control variables that would be kept constant for all subjects; (2) random assignment to an experimental group or a control group; (3) an independent variable that would create two different experiences—one for the experimental group and one for the control group; and (4) one or more measurable dependent variables to determine if there were different outcomes for the two groups.

Subjects for this experiment were all *patients* on a *selected open ward* (the control variables). They were asked if they would like to volunteer to live in a lodge society, and those who volunteered were randomly assigned to either the *lodge* or the *control group* (the independent variable), with *lodge group* as the experimental group that would be compared to the *control group*. Those who did not volunteer offered a second independent variable by which researchers could see if the act of volunteering, in and of itself, had any effect on the outcomes. Once the experiment was completed, researchers would compare various outcome measurements for three groups: (1) volunteer lodge, (2) volunteer control, and (3) nonvolunteer.

On a specified date (another control variable), groups one and two began thirty days of testing and planning for how their group would function. The lodge group also planned for their move into the larger community—determining who would play leadership roles, how they would go about purchasing food, and the type of work that would be performed by each member. At the end of the thirty days, the lodge group moved into the community, occupying an old hotel that had been rented for the experiment.[3] Initially, there was confusion due to an environment that called for *participation* in group work rather than the *avoidance* behavior that was more typical of hospital life. Adjustments were made, and work-training programs were developed to oversee tasks such as distribution of medication, quality of janitorial and gardening work, and meal preparation. In addition, it was found that things went more smoothly if teams, each with their own leaders, were formed within the group. The expertise of consultants was also added to help lodge members with unfamiliar tasks: a house physician, an accountant, and a janitorial consultant.

There was also a need for supervision by a coordinator, initially an experienced psychologist who was subsequently replaced by a graduate student. With the graduate student as coordinator, a governing body of lodge members achieved increasing autonomy such that lay leaders replaced the graduate students after several months.

Outcomes (dependent variables) emerged in stages. The lodge program was meant to provide a way for people to live and work as a group. As the challenges of living together in a relatively independent setting were ironed out, lay leaders developed and operated businesses that improved lodge-living conditions. Eventually, the original lodge building—the site of the research—was closed, and remaining members chose to continue as a completely autonomous group, living in a new location with the same work and living arrangements but without the help of professionals.

What were the outcomes? First of all, it was shown that a small subgroup of former mental patients *could* exist, be accepted, and thrive within an established and appropriate community. The experimenters were also interested in whether small group membership within a community would *increase the members' time and employment* in the community and, at the same time, *improve their self-esteem.* The answer was yes. Furthermore, since this was a funded experiment, lodge-group expenses were paid, and it was possible to compare the cost of lodge living to the cost of hospitalization. Lodge-group expenses were 50 percent of the cost to hospitalize someone for the same period of time.

The outcome of group processes in the hospital group versus the community-lodge group were also identified and compared indicating a more positive outcome for the community-lodge group. Three processes were identified in the hospital group: leadership, performance, and cohesiveness. However, leadership combined with performance in the community group so that there were only two dimensions. The difference was attributed to the fact that the hospital group could never achieve the kind of autonomy that the lodge group experienced out of necessity. Finally, those who did not volunteer thought they could find better employment and living conditions in the future. That group was compared to the group that *did volunteer* but did not go to the lodge (the control group) in terms of social adjustment in the community. There was no difference between the two.

Fairweather's work produced positive outcomes and was awarded NIMH funding to share those outcomes through the Dissemination Project. Fairweather and his project team toured the country sharing data that provided evidence that through rehabilitation, those who had been hospitalized due to mental illness could live successfully in self-governed residential facilities that were directly linked to self-governed employment opportunities. Consumers could not only live and work together; they were capable of addressing and resolving typical problems that arise in any group-living situation. They did better in a group than they did on their own, *and* they were less likely to be returned to the hospital.

Fairweather's belief that ex-psychiatric patients could govern and support other patients—with mental health professionals merely serving in advisory capacities—evoked skepticism from many in the professional community. However, controlled research supported his belief, and many states developed Community Lodge Programs in the coming years. At the same time, Fairweather became an advocate for patients' rights to participate in decisions regarding their places in community life. Though it has been said that devotion to his belief in the ability of ex-psychiatric patients to care for each other kept him on the fringe of the professional community, in 1985, the Community Psychology Division of the American Psychological Association honored him with the Award for Distinguished Contributions to Community Psychology and Community Mental Health.[4]

In 1978, administrators and staff of Fairweather Lodge programs organized to form the Coalition for Community Living (CCL),[5] which promotes community support systems and educates the public about Fairweather Lodges. Starting a Fairweather Lodge involves, for the most part, the same steps used in the original research when a group of hospital patients volunteered to be Lodge members. Interested parties establish residence in a house where they live together and start their own small business. They divide into small groups according to their skills and capabilities, elect group leaders, and develop group problem-solving abilities. Once a Lodge is established, members are relatively autonomous. There are no live-in staff members, but professionals are on-call twenty-four hours a day to respond to emergencies.

Residents of the Lodge must develop and implement a plan for a business, most commonly a business that provides some service, such as lawn care,

custodial or laundry services, printing, furniture building, shoe repair, or catering. To help them in operating their business, they may hire accountants and
lawyers. However, members have specific responsibilities in the household and
the business. In both cases, responsibilities are matched to the member's interests and abilities. Household responsibilities might entail serving as the cook or
medication supervisor or acting as the crew chief or manager for the business.
Fulfilling these responsibilities provides members with a stable role in the Lodge
itself and, at the same time, increased self-confidence, encouraging them to become more independent.

It is not surprising that individuals who are living and working together can
become as close-knit as a family. Many of us in satisfying jobs have that same
experience. However, our "workplace family" seldom replaces our own families,
and most Lodge members consider their own families to be their main sources
of social support. They keep in touch by mail and/or phone and often spend
weekends and holidays with their families.

The number of states participating in the Lodge program, and the number
of Lodges overall, has varied over time. However, the 2008 National Directory
for CCL listed forty-six Lodges in nine states, with seventeen of those located
in Minnesota and operated by Tasks Unlimited, Inc. (TU),[6] which, in 1970,
opened its first Lodge with residents trained to run a commercial cleaning
business. They continued to open new Lodges throughout the seventies, and by
1980, all the Lodges owned their own business contracts. In the early eighties,
they introduced a JOBS Program for those who were living in stable housing.
The 1990s saw diversification of TU employment opportunities and businesses
as well as the addition of services for TU employees: the opportunity to develop stress control, weight management, and smoking cessation through a
wellness program. TU Mental Health Services became the first official Adult
Rehabilitation Mental Health services provider in Hennepin County and, in an
effort to break through the stigma of mental illness, TU staged an anthology
of mental stories.

Early in the twenty-first century, the organization opened Lodges for target
groups—a residence for women with mental illness and their children in 2003;
in 2007 a lodge-training program for those with felony convictions as a result

of untreated mental illness; and, in 2012, their first Senior Lodge. Clearly, the Fairweather Lodge model has allowed TU to offer a range of diverse programs and services that allow individuals with severe and persistent mental illness to manage their own lives and assist others in doing the same, resulting in successful community integration in a large metropolitan area.

In July 2008, during a summer visit to my home state of Michigan, I visited a Michigan Fairweather Lodge. In 1986, D&M Consultants, Inc., a nonprofit corporation, started two Fairweather Lodge pilot programs for individuals from a "step-down" ward at the Clinton Valley Center in Pontiac, Michigan. A step-down ward allows more freedom for patients who have been moved from restricted-ward settings, making them good candidates for the 1986 pilot program.

In the ensuing years, there were building and location changes, and by the time I visited, in 2008, there had been a decline in Michigan's Fairweather Lodge system, with twelve consumers divided between two lodge programs, both located in Southfield, fifteen miles south of Pontiac. I visited Premier Lodge, located on grounds formerly occupied by an old farmhouse. In 2006, with the financial aid of a private citizen, the land was purchased, and a six-bedroom prefab residence was erected. Eight Premier residents shared typical Lodge duties and ran a business called Ever-Glo Janitorial Service, bidding for contracts with commercial customers throughout the community. In addition to residents of Premier Lodge, three Ever-Glo employees lived in a shared-housing facility, and four lived in the other area Lodge, giving Ever-Glo a total of fifteen employees.

During my visit to the Lodge, I was invited to sit in on a business meeting. The agenda format was familiar: approval of previous minutes, a treasurer's report, old business, and new business. As they reported on their contracts, I learned that they had sixteen customers—sixteen offices to clean every day, with some as large as twenty thousand square feet. They also provided special weekend services, such as carpet cleaning. Under old business, there was a report on the condition of the company's van and cleaning equipment. There were two items of new business: a member would be leaving for a new job in the Ford manufacturing operation, and the October National Fairweather Conference was to be held in Michigan.

Mitch, the president, did an excellent job of running the meeting, though it was his first time to assume that responsibility. He talked about planning related to their janitorial duties from his own personal experience and pointed out that sometimes scheduled workers might not be available, or cleaning equipment could break down. Therefore, it was his habit to always have a spare—a spare crew member or spare vacuum cleaner.

Amy, the treasurer, had lived at Premier for nine years, and though she was very quiet during the meeting, she presented a detailed treasurer's report (balance $7,091.82, payroll $5,329.36, income $10,572, $10,459 worth of expenses; profits for the previous month were around $3,000.) Tim, a gray-haired member, was also quiet and fell asleep at one point during the meeting, perhaps due to the side effect of certain medications. A person taking meds can be aware of that particular side effect, and some will make an effort to fight off the drowsiness. Another member, Steve, was slumped down in a chair. That and did member did make cogent, though mumbled, contributions, perhaps trying to compensate with purposeful but strained alertness. Jones, a bearded, older, gray-haired man, volunteered that he wanted to work as much as possible so that he could earn as much as possible.

Two female staff members and Joe, a staff member in charge of Ever-Glo, were also present, and I was impressed with the way Joe guided and taught at the same time, allowing and encouraging Ever-Glo's autonomy. At one point, members were discussing whether or not they should have two work crews rather than three. The discussion was losing its focus, but Joe easily helped them gain control by going to a whiteboard and showing them the potential problems that could develop with two crews, due to the distance between customers and the time needed to complete their work (twenty to ninety minutes) at the client sites.

Joe also made considerate corrections when a member's social behavior needed improvement. When member Mary's interests, in an almost childlike manner, were more focused on personal matters—what she'd bought at the grocery store and how her hair looked—Joe reminded her to talk about general issues related to the meeting, rather than issues that were directly related to her. Charleen, who apparently hadn't been carrying her share of the load, eagerly volunteered for all kinds of duties, stating that she wanted a chance to help now that her meds were under control. Joe pointed out that she would have to be trained to do any particular job and couldn't just do something like wash windows because she wanted to.

The next day, I sat in on the house meeting, held in the kitchen/breakfast room, with six Lodge members and two staff members in attendance. Items covered were what one would expect to hear around an old-fashioned dinner table (when families were more likely to eat together). A complaint was expressed that people were not cleaning up after themselves in the kitchen, and a great deal of discussion ensued. There were also some hard feelings relative to a misunderstanding regarding bedroom assignments. However, the parties involved were able to discuss and describe their feelings in a mature and clear manner.

Lodge members are encouraged to get involved in state and national mental health organizations and committees. About once a month, Premier holds a Consumer Action Group meeting to discuss their participation. I was not present for one of those meetings, but did get a copy of the June meeting report, which promoted participation in a Walk a Mile in My Shoes rally, in honor of Schizophrenics Awareness Week and Mental Health Awareness Month. It was also suggested that they gather more information on US Representative Robert Kennedy's bill to improve mental health services, and there was a reminder of a Premier Lodge Cultural Awareness event to be held in July.

As I visit various mental health programs, I'm always interested in the history of the program—why and how it came to be. I'm interested in the structure of the program and what it takes to function effectively. And I always hope that I can hear a story from someone whose life has been changed by whatever program I'm visiting. At Premier, I heard one of those stories—not from the member herself but in a private conversation with Val, Premier's director. It was a story about prisoners who are reentering the community.

During the time that Val served as director, there were two such programs in Michigan. Not just anyone who is leaving prison can be accepted, and the state defines limitations regarding what kind of crimes are acceptable—those in which the criminal behavior of the perpetrator does not seem to present a risk factor to the community. One year before my visit to Premier, a prisoner with a long history of legal troubles, Beth, who had grown up in a troubled family and who had spent four years in prison for arson (she had burned down her mother's house), was recommended to Premier by her parole officer, in spite of the fact that the officer doubted she would make it into the program.

Val and Joe picked up Beth at the prison when she was released in July of 2007 and took her straight to the Lodge. Normally, any prospective new Lodge member is interviewed by the residents to determine whether or not that person is a good fit for that Lodge. That step was not possible in this case—a case where it would have seemed to be a necessity. But this was my happy-ending story for this trip. Val reported to me that as of July 2008, Beth had an apartment of her own (well, she shared it with two cats), she was on the board of D&M Consultants, and she had her own cleaning contract with the state to clean a client site on her own.

In Belgium, individuals with mental illness who have been hospitalized or have lived in another community may become boarders in Geel. There are certain criteria for potential boarders, and a history of violent behavior is a vote against such an assignment. However, in some cases, someone who had exhibited violent behavior might be given a chance to live as a boarder, based on a belief that their living conditions or social environment had evoked that behavior and an accompanying belief that the support of a fostering family and community would be a calming factor. When the needs of the boarder and the environment offered by the family have been carefully considered and matched, it has often worked in Geel. It's worked at least once in this country as well—in Southfield, Michigan. Who knows how many other people's sense of community acceptance and their opportunity to live a meaningful life has worked, or could work, for them and the community?

# 9

# Therapeutic Communities

We no longer bear the shame of overcrowded asylums and hospitals. Yet, though an acute mental health crisis can lead to a stay in a psychiatric hospital or ward until the patient is stabilized, there may be no long-term treatment goals. Neither the duration of the stay nor the treatment offered allows time to develop skills and habits necessary for successful transition into a community setting. Outpatient treatment is available, but many fail to use these services, and when they do, the services seldom offer the structure required for adjustment to community life, and the ex-patient is apt to withdraw over time. In most cases, the programs you've read about in previous chapters were founded to provide affordable supportive housing where residents are linked to community treatment programs. Under those circumstances, patient compliance is likely to be better.

Another option, not yet described, provides long-term treatment *within* a residential community. Some of the best of these facilities are members of the American Residential Treatment Association—more than thirty facilities in fifteen states, primarily along the East Coast.[1] Programs included in the ARTA directory are not affordable for most people, certainly not for those in need, and these programs are not covered by Medicare or Medicaid. While some health-insurance policies may cover part of the cost, policy holders will still have to bear a portion of the expense, and that portion may exceed their ability to pay. The programs you'll read about in this chapter may offer financial aid to cover some of the cost, but only for a limited number of patients when need exists. It is true that, with an average stay of six to twelve months, residential treatment programs can create a heavy financial burden for the family. Though it is an "upfront" expense that can be hard to assume, some treatment facilities will assist the family in securing third-party financing. And it is an investment, for a recovered individual able to work and live independently can represent a long-term savings to the family and even to the community in terms of taxpayers' contributions to mental health care.

With only thirty such treatment programs in the United States, and with so few patients having the financial means to avail themselves of such programs, is it even appropriate to include this option in this book? Is a program truly exemplary if there are those who do not have access to it?

I include residential treatment programs for several reasons. Some of them were explicitly or implicitly modeled after Geel, in terms of focus on a family lifestyle *and* the opportunity to find meaning within a working community. That hope isn't necessarily inspired by a single program, for there are diverse programs that all strive to create meaningful lives for those with mental illness. Any one community has its own unique resources. Understanding what succeeds in one setting can motivate potential pioneers to replicate elements using their own available, and unique, resources. For, in spite of the expense of existing residential treatment programs, those programs borrowed elements of success from more affordable programs. Elements of residential treatment programs can be adapted to fit the financial resources of existing small communities. Geel offered, and still offers, a sense of family and the opportunity for meaningful work—both offered in residential treatment programs. In how many other settings might these elements of success be incorporated?

ARTA programs include four main styles: clinical residential, group residential (group homes), farm- and work-based, and apartment-based. Is one "better" than another? Proximity of the program to the family is desirable, for most of these programs include the family in the recovery process. However, the nearest program may not be the best match. There is overlap in features of the four categories, but there are also differences. However, in spite of the diversity, all ARTA facilities seek and promote healing through the use of basic practices and principles that produce improved quality of life through participation in meaningful activities and nurturing relationships. Some principles focus on the *individuals*—their strengths and weaknesses and their ability to form supportive relationships by understanding how their behavior can affect the behavior of others. The client moves to achieve individual goals—taking small steps to establish new habits—in a structured daily life, receiving support from staff and fellow residents, opportunities for community integration, and a sense of *belonging* to a community, all of which increase the individual's sense of self-worth.

In spite of common practices and principles, success is strongly influenced by the clients' sense of "rightness"—a feeling of being "at home" in a program of their choice. The reputation of a facility or a visit to their website can be appealing. Either can be a starting point, but it is critical that the client and family speak with staff members before and/or during a personal visit.[2]

As I began to identify exemplary mental health programs, I learned of two ARTA sites in the Eastern United States—both operating as working farms—whose beginnings predated deinstitutionalization. Given the fact that Geel started as a rural program, these sites were on my "must visit" list. In March 2014, I was able to move them to my "been there—wow!" list. One of those programs was responsible for another ARTA program, and since it was in my home state, I was able to visit during a trip to visit family. I learned of the fourth ARTA site in this chapter from an acquaintance in Atlanta.

I've also included a fifth program with similar social and work environments but serving a different population—those with intellectual disabilities (until September 2013, referred to as *mental retardation*). Parents of children diagnosed with severe mental illness (SMI), such as schizophrenia or bipolar disorder, have concerns for the future of their children. What if they need continued care throughout their lives and they, the parents, are no longer able or available to care for them? Normally the onset of SMI does not occur until the late teens or early twenties, after up to twenty years of parenting and preparing one's child for the future, anticipating the pride and joy of the child's success. When symptoms first appear, in the face of too many unknowns, the future is cloudy. There is hope that this will be an acute episode and all will be well. Yet parents are often in emotional limbo as various medications are tried and a diagnosis is too long in coming. Then, when an effective medication is found, there is hope that it will manage symptoms—in the same way that insulin manages diabetes—allowing a meaningful life for the child and a sense of relief for the parent. But a prescribed medication can lose its effectiveness over time, and the search for management must begin anew. Parents of children with SMI may cycle through hope and despair many times.

Not so for parents of a child with intellectual disabilities. At birth, or early in the child's life, parents know the source and symptoms and even name of a disability that won't go away. This kind of knowing can be easier to deal with, especially at this time in our history when there are more educational and social opportunities for those with intellectual disabilities. In many cases, the child can lead a meaningful life and may even be able to hold a job and take care of their personal needs. But parents also know that, while there might be progress in the course of development, in many cases developmental delays will not completely disappear, and from the beginning of the child's life, parents are apt to wonder, "What will happen to our child when we're gone?" In the 1970s, a group of parents had that concern and founded Innisfree Village, which provides a secure and meaningful life for children and a sense of peace for parents. In this chapter, you'll also read the story of permanent housing for this population as it exists in Crozet, Virginia.

## SPRING LAKE RANCH—CUTTINGSVILLE, VERMONT

On March 23, 2014, I flew into Albany, New York, and drove to Spring Lake Ranch in Cuttingsville, Vermont.[3] Spring Lake Ranch was established in 1932 by Wayne Sarcka, born in Finland in 1890, and his wife, Elizabeth Man, born in Long Island in 1894. Though they were born an ocean apart, their life experiences led to a shared dedication to those in need.

Wayne's family moved to Vermont in 1895, when he was a child. As a young adult, he worked for the YMCA in Vermont and, with the outbreak of World War I, was recruited by his employer to work with shell-shocked British soldiers in youth camps. In those camps, he came to value outdoor group work and play as a way to strengthen those who had lived through troubled childhoods or the trauma of wartime combat.

After the war, he returned to the United States and began a career as a fundraiser in New York City, the home of Elizabeth Man, commissioner for the Girl Scout Council in the borough of Queens. She also served as a social worker in New York City settlement houses, established in poor urban neighborhoods where the rich and poor could live together. Living with middle-class workers helped the poor become more knowledgeable and cultured, hopefully to break the cycle of poverty. While fundraising for the Girl Scouts of America, Wayne asked for a communications officer. In answer to his request, he was introduced to Elizabeth, and the chemistry of a shared value system led to their 1928 marriage.[4]

It was on their honeymoon, while hiking the Appalachian Trail, that they came upon Spring Lake in Cuttingsville, Vermont, and fell in love with the beauty of the surroundings, which surely nurtured their love for one another. One year later, they purchased land that included the lake and a farmhouse, intending to turn the house into a summer home. But the property needed work. The need for renovation offered an opportunity to fulfill a dream of Wayne's, born during his World War I work with troubled boys. Taking in teenage boys from a New York City settlement house and a YMCA, Wayne began an experimental camp offering these young men a balanced schedule of work and play to prepare them for life as mature, responsible adults.

In 1932, three years after the boys were brought to the farm, its success impressed a friend, New York City psychiatrist Bernard Glueck who, in the era of institutionalization, believed there was a need to explore alternative care approaches for those with mental illness. While the young men were not mental health patients, Glueck believed that the camp setting would offer those with mental illness the time and space to come to terms with the fact of their illness and to go beyond that fact to find new strength. When he urged the Sarckas to offer that kind of opportunity on their farm, they accepted his challenge, and, as Glueck and his colleagues referred patients selected for such a setting, the first year-round halfway house in the United States—dedicated to family care of the mentally ill—was established as Spring Lake Ranch (SLR).

The Sarcka family continued to live at Spring Lake Ranch and, even when Wayne entered state politics, Elizabeth and their daughter, Anne, born in 1931, ran the ranch. In 1962, the family moved to Jamaica, where Wayne developed an educational facility. When her husband died in 1969, Elizabeth returned to New York, and was involved in social campaigns until her death in 1992.

Today, residents come to SLR from their homes, hospitals, or schools to a place that does not *feel* like a hospital and that offers structure and nurturing that cannot be provided in a hospital. The typical stay for residents is six to eight months, and when they leave, many enter an aftercare program in the nearby community of Rutland, where they can begin the process of integration into the larger community as well as continue growth and stability by participating in activities and services at the ranch.

Residents have a diagnosis of mental illness or substance abuse, and some have a dual diagnosis of both. They can have no history of aggression, fire starting, or commission of verbal or physical abuse. And, perhaps most importantly, they must show a willingness to enter SLR's program. Both the family and the resident meet with staff prior to admission, and, once a prospective resident is accepted, he or she goes through a twenty-four-hour orientation that includes a psychological assessment. Throughout the resident's stay, the family receives weekly updates.

Residents live in small houses on the campus, with four to eight residents in each house, each having their own room and a shared bath. An advisor, available for after-hours support, also lives in the house, with a private room and bath. Each day, the Ranch comes to life with a seven-thirty breakfast in the dining hall followed by a daily meeting at nine. On the day of my visit, I sat in on the morning meeting. Announcements were casual and diverse, including introduction of me as a visitor. Note was made of a missing sauté pan, and residents were reminded of an upcoming art show. They were advised to check the psychiatrist's weekly visit schedule. Announcements, in the context of a working farm, reminded residents of the birth of a baby lamb and the "lamb watch" as well as the "lettuce" watch for sprouting baby lettuces.

All residential treatment programs seek to foster a sense of community cooperation and the residents' value in the community through working together with fellow residents and staff members. Teams are a critical part of treatment at SLR. During the morning meeting, residents sit with their teams, and, once a week, team members meet to discuss current activities and responsibilities related to the work of their team. For each team, a staff member with a clinical education background (a master's degree and/or licensing in social work) provides oversight. In addition, a resident advocate supervises day-to-day activities and connects residents with various SLR resources.

After the meeting, by nine forty-five, residents begin their daily work schedule and spend the next one to two hours with their work crews. Residents are not assigned to a crew indefinitely and can change crew membership every five to seven days. Though residents pay for their housing and treatment,[5] Spring Lake Ranch is self-sustaining in that residents grow or raise their own food, make their own furniture, chop their own firewood, and have income-producing gardens and animals. Each of those tasks is handled by a work team. That morning, I walked around with a staff member to observe the work environment of several different crews.

With my love for wood, one of my favorite visits was the woodwork shop. (My grandfather was a train conductor, but his avocation was carpentry, and as a child, I was in love with whittling.) Here, with supervision, residents make all of SLR's furniture. In addition, when I visited, they were working on a sheltered gazebo for resident smokers, since smoking is not allowed in any SLR building.

The woodwork shop is a place where residents can "find themselves." I was told of one resident who, on first coming to SLR, was prone to staying in his room, doing nothing. But when he expressed an interest in getting some exercise, the head carpenter helped him make a squat bench. While in the shop, I engaged in conversation with a female who seemed to hold some level of leadership. I soon learned that she was a resident who had discovered her love for carpentry at SLR. She told me that her interest and newly discovered skills were a healthy escape from "mental illness," to the extent that she was independently making furniture for SLR and, when she left the ranch, was prepared to make a living as a certified woodworker. I wasn't off base when I sensed that she was a "leader." She led herself along the path to a meaningful life and a sense of purpose.

Next stop—the sugarhouse, critical to SLR's syrup making. In February, sap for the syrup is collected in buckets that are hung on thousands of sugar-maple trees in the SLR woods, while in the sugarhouse, an evaporator maintains the sugar lines. Later on my campus tour, I spotted two old WW II Navy trucks that, I was told, had been donated to SLR and repaired by residents. Mounted on the back were tanks used to bring sap from the woods to the sugarhouse. SLR syrup is sold at the local farmers' market, sent to family and friends during the holidays, and, of course, tops breakfast pancakes at SLR. Attached to the sugarhouse is a sewing room, and I understood the charm of a working farm when I walked through a room filled with bags of wool sheared two weeks earlier and waiting to be turned into cloth. (Later, during my tour, I saw the shorn sheep and, with my empathetic nature, could imagine how cold the Vermont spring must have felt, having lost the comfort of their warm wool coats.)

My campus tour ended in the people's kitchen, separate from the main kitchen where meals are prepared. Since it was still winter in Vermont, garden-crew members were divided among other crews—doing chores for or with them. That morning, they were helping out in the people's kitchen, finishing up with granola making, while others were either making soup to be served at lunch the next day or making bagels, which was an ongoing need at SLR.

Residential treatment programs commonly use a *continuum of care* model that addresses the individual needs and progress of the program's residents. In the context of that model, Spring Lake Ranch began the Rutland Program for transitional living more than twenty years ago. With a 2010 population of close to seventeen thousand, Rutland is a relatively large city by Vermont standards (the third largest in the state), but it offers a small-city community environment. Theater and the arts, local sports and recreation, a weekly farmers' market, street festivals, restaurants, and shops are all available in a downtown area listed as a historic district by the National Register of Historic Places list. Rutland is a working community where residents can meet new people and develop new interests, often through volunteer work, where they can give back to the community. Rutland might be considered a perfect place for transition to independent living from the structured and sheltered life on a working farm. The city is not so big as to be overwhelming, but it is large enough to offer opportunities for community integration.

Prior to moving from the Ranch to Rutland, residents may have already been involved in the community—through volunteer work, an internship, a sheltered job, or in a class at the local college. Throughout treatment—even from the Ranch to Rutland—individual needs, skills, and level of adjustment are carefully evaluated and considered for each resident. In addition, medication management and addiction issues are considered, and thus, before moving from the Ranch to the Rutland Program, residents establish a relationship with an advisor as well as with a general-practice doctor and a therapist in the city.

The Rutland Program offers four alternatives for living, all providing staff support in varying degrees. Some residents, able to live independently, rent apartments on their own, though they may get help from staff, family members, and peers as they choose their apartments. And though they can manage their own finances, medication, and daily routines, the Ranch provides support service as needed.

In Rutland, Spring Lake Ranch maintains three residential buildings that can house up to twenty-three residents. The Royce Street structure, where residents participate in a full schedule of activities, including therapy and recovery group, has six private bedrooms, a community living room and kitchen, and office space for staff who are available to provide support twenty-four hours a day. Once a week, a resident and a staff member team up to cook dinner for the house, creating a sense of family. Some residents may continue to work on the farm during the day, while others may do volunteer work in the city. Since the house is within walking distance of city sites, some use their free time to engage in recreational activities.

The Townhouse is a 1940s home located in the center of Rutland's historic district. Office space for staff is on the ground floor, and the remainder of the house has been converted to eight apartments. Some are used for short-term stays, while some residents may stay in a Townhouse apartment for years.

The newest addition to SLR's Rutland Program, McGee House Integrated Recovery, opened in February 2014 and focuses on recovery from addiction, a growing problem in recent years. Residents (all male) of the nine-bedroom renovated Victorian mansion are either in recovery from addiction or have a dual diagnosis of addiction and mental illness. Given the nature of recovery from addiction, McGee offers a more supported housing environment. As with other Rutland Program participants, McGee residents come from the Ranch work program and begin a relationship with their Rutland advisor while still at the Ranch.

On my second day with Spring Lake Ranch, I arrived at McGee House in time for the morning meeting and was welcomed by residents and staff, who sat around a large table. The meeting included discussion of resident goals for the day, with residents being encouraged to share the source of any inspiration they experienced. By ten o'clock, the morning meeting became a psychotherapy group meeting. Though residents would be sharing personal information, I was invited to stay. Going around the table, the members introduced themselves; when it was my turn, I told them what brought me to SLR and the topic of my book—stigma. With casual comments, several expressed their personal familiarity and experience with the topic.

After introductions, each of the residents told of triggers to drug use they had faced during the week and shared the coping mechanisms and positive thoughts that had helped them through those difficult times. Triggers included TV commercials that sparked memories associated with their drug use, lack of money (most likely creating anxiety), wondering what they had done "wrong" in the past, and finally (one I could identify with) *dreaming* about using drugs. I was a three-pack-a-day smoker until I quit in 1980, thanks to an eight-week cognitive-behavioral program. After I quit, I taught the class, and several times, as I prepared to teach, I dreamed that I was smoking. The dreams did not evoke a longing but rather a feeling of anxiety—as though I had actually gone "off the wagon," but then I reminded myself that I was still smoke-free.

The resident dreamer also coped by realizing, when he awoke, that the dream was *not* reality, giving him a welcome sense of relief. Several talked of sobriety anniversaries or their progress on the road to recovery. One resident, sober for one year plus one month—his longest period of sobriety ever—talked of his propensity to worry. One coping mechanism he used was to think about the amount of time wasted in worrying. Reinforcing this perspective, the counselor suggested to him and others at the table the concept of "thought training," where they think about possible solutions to what is bothering them, rather than worrying about it.

After a tour of the upper floors of the newly renovated McGee, with sincerity and admiration, I wished them all luck and thanked them for their hospitality.

That afternoon, as usual, McGee residents would have time to participate in activities consistent with their individual goals—vocational rehabilitation, college classes, volunteering, Narcotics or Alcoholics Anonymous, or a Rutland club such as the Sober Social Club.

My afternoon would be spent on the highway, headed south to another residential facility on a working farm and thinking, as I drove, about the people and the place that I had come to know in the previous twenty-four-plus hours. All of the thoughts were good, and I wanted the world to know the value of work and community and a belief in one's self. I knew that I would see more of the same at my next stop—another working farm 110 miles south of Rutland, in Monterey, Massachusetts.

## GOULD FARM—MONTEREY, MASSACHUSETTS

William J. Gould, known as Will or Brother Gould, born in 1868, was known for the sound of his laughter and his propensity for evoking laughter from others. He enjoyed playing the clown and was said to come in from working the fields with a lace cap on his head and lace mitts on his hands. From childhood, he also struggled with depression, which he is said to have valued because when it got the best of him, he sought solitude in nature to contemplate what troubled him, and he often came away with new perspectives and a new glow on his face.

Will liked to talk—about anything, from potato crops to the League of Nations to electric pumps, of the power of prayer and the fading role of the horse on the modern farm. He was dedicated to family life and Christian principles—a dedicated pioneer for social reform. Based on his belief that a society is healthy only to the degree that the most vulnerable can thrive, he envisioned a setting where respectful discipline, wholesome work, and benevolent kindness could lead to emotional rehabilitation.[6]

For over ten years, Gould experimented with social service on various farms. His first serious effort, founded with the assistance of a New York City pastor, was a "fresh-air camp" in Becket, Massachusetts. Gould moved to Becket in 1902, and it was here that he met his soon-to-be wife, Agnes Goodyear. They moved many times over the next ten years until finally, in 1913, they purchased a 650-acre farm in the Berkshire Hills of Massachusetts. Initially named Social

Service Farm, Gould Farm is now considered to be America's oldest therapeutic community for people with mental illness. But it wasn't always about mental illness.

As with Wayne Sarcka, Will was initially motivated to work with boys—molding their character to help change society. Over the years, even before Gould Farm was established, he recognized that others were also serving that population, so even though he continued to open his home to boys, his focus switched to adults. In 1908, for example, he ran a successful camp for the rehabilitation of postsurgical patients.

In 1910, in a small rented house in the New York village of Delanson, he moved in the direction of the kind of social work he had envisioned. His wife called it his "gathering of people in the home" approach. In that small Delanson home, the people he gathered were those with serious emotional problems, the homeless, a few children, and some of his wife's family members.

The Farm had been operating for four years when the cold winter season of 1917–1918 caused Gould to close it to guests, sell the cows, and leave a young man from Monterey in charge of the property and the horse. He and the remaining family members moved to Brooklyn, where Gould and his wife did volunteer work at the Neurological Institute and at Bellevue Hospital, serving as advisors to social workers. Professionals with whom they worked subsequently sent patients to the Farm, where the only criterion set by Gould was that his home would serve a need of the guest. Gould found that often his guests' needs were the consequence of what was then referred to as nervous breakdowns or some physical condition related to their minds. Thus, Gould began to give greater attention to those with needs related to their mental conditions, believing that they may have somehow lost their love of life and/or their will to live. In 1921, he was quoted in the *New York Times* as wanting to bring back the desire of living and working to people who had lost it "through loss of faith in themselves and mankind."[7]

Today, guests (never called *patients,* always *guests*) are recovering from, and adapting to, a diagnosis of mental illness—primarily schizophrenia, schizoaffective disorder, depression, or bipolar disorder. As guests at the Farm, they must show no denial of their mental illness and must show some insight about the reality of their illness, coupled with a desire for success—a belief that Gould Farm will allow them to live meaningful lives in spite of a diagnosis of mental illness. It must also be established that when they are ready to leave the Farm— usually after a nine-to-eleven-month stay, they will not simply be released to their own devices but will have family partnerships waiting for them. Families are also involved with treatment during the course of guests' stays, though the type and frequency of involvement is dependent on where the families live.[8]

The minimum age for admission is eighteen, with most guests in their twenties or thirties and a few older guests. As a service to the community, there are two continuing-care rooms available for guests older than fifty-five. At any one time, the Farm can accommodate forty guests. As guests leave, beds become available, but no matter how many might be available, the Farm will take no more than one new guest in any week.

The beginning of life at Gould is similar to that at most residential treatment programs. The first two weeks for a guest are a period of orientation and adjustment. In the case of Gould Farm, since many guests have no experience with farm, or even rural, life, they get a feel for what it's like to live on a working farm and begin to participate in the work program. As with other programs, they are also assessed by a psychiatrist and engage in one-on-one therapy sessions with a clinician. As they become familiar with farm life and the work program, they get to know other guests along with staff members and their families who all reside on the Farm, all fellow members of a community that will be home to them for almost a year.

Weekdays begin with an eight o'clock morning meeting where upcoming or current activities are announced, newcomers are introduced, a weather report is given, and other casual items are shared. The meeting always ends with a poem, a reading, or a group song, accompanied by any available guitarist—a long-standing tradition established by Will Gould. On Wednesday afternoons, more important or urgent issues can be discussed during the community meeting. Also at this meeting, spontaneous recognition and appreciation is offered to those who have helped guests in their daily lives.

As with Spring Lake Ranch, though Gould Farm guests are charged for treatment services and room and board,[9] it is a self-sustaining working farm where guests participate in the work program on one of seven teams, achieving a sense of accountability, learning about group planning, and developing the art of working cooperatively. New guests generally start as members of the forest-and-ground team, which allows them to become familiar with the layout of the campus. At the same time, they get to know their fellow workers and learn various skills required to maintain and repair forestry equipment.

The farm team meets every morning to set a schedule for their day of taking care of farm animals and discuss any special assignments. Members of the garden team raise vegetables, from seed to harvest, for use on the Farm. The harvest-barn team works in a commercial kitchen in the barn, preparing food products for the Farm. Staff and their family members live on the Farm, and the kitchen team prepares three meals a day for at least seventy-five guests, staff, and family members. Thirty-five buildings on campus necessitate an all-important maintenance team, where working guests learn skills that can prepare them for finding jobs when they become independent.

On a road just off campus, a small, twenty-eight-seat restaurant and café is open to the public for lunch and breakfast Wednesday through Saturday from 7:30 a.m. until 2:30 p.m. The restaurant is run by the Roadside Store and Café team. For guests who are preparing to transition off the Farm, this team offers a chance to experience the faster pace that they're apt to encounter as they gain independence in the larger community.

Though an average stay on the Farm is nine to eleven months, some stay for a shorter period of time, and some stay longer. When appropriate, it is possible for a guest to stay up to three years. However, as with all residential treatment programs, most will transition to a new life of independence, and thus, continuum of care is a critical aspect of recovery. Most Gould Farm guests will leave the structure and warmth and security of family life on the Farm. That life is therapeutic, and for most guests, is an experience never to be forgotten. But it isn't just about making memories. It's about gaining self-respect and learning to cope with symptoms of mental illness as independent members of a larger community where life is different from life on the Farm. It's a transition potentially fraught with the anxiety of adjustment that any of us might feel when we move on to a new life. And so, preparation for the transition of Gould Farm guests occurs at a reasonable pace and includes a variety of activities. A psychiatric-rehabilitation practitioner assesses the guest's work and cognitive skills. Guests participate in exercises to explore options for life beyond the Farm. They attend a series of Transition Group meetings and may take classes to prepare them for a GED or a driver's license. For those who plan to stay in the area once they leave the Farm, they visit Boston to explore available services in that city.

Gould Farm offers two types of nonresidential support. Guests who have developed a level of self-reliance and want to live in the Berkshires or Boston area can continue in the Gould Farm program as nonresident clients. Through thirty hours of structured staff support, they learn transition skills that lead to an increasing ability to manage their lives and their medication. They also continue with individual therapy and prepare for a new independent life-style through volunteer work or goal planning for further schooling and/or employment.

Others who have moved into their own homes near Gould Farm and who have a well-established sense of self-sufficiency may still want to maintain an ongoing relationship with Gould Farm. That can be arranged for a minimal monthly fee through an individualized contract with Gould's Extended Community Services Program. That contract provides for case management, in which the guests meet with staff advisers weekly for an indefinite period of time in order to review their treatment goals. If necessary, a guest may return to the Farm for respite, and all alumni are encouraged to maintain their connections to the Farm for as long as they desire.

As I made plans to visit Gould Farm, I was thrilled to learn that there was a two-bedroom (with living room) lodge house available for guests. For two days and a night, I would be a Gould Farmer! After nearly a three-hour drive from Rutland, I got to the farm in the late afternoon and entered the main building for directions to the lodge. Though no one made a fuss over my arrival, I felt instant warmth emanating from the surroundings and the people who were in the building. Sometimes we simply get what we expect. From what little I knew of Gould Farm, that is probably what I expected. But by the time my visit was over, I found that my expectations were *not* unreasonable. As I write this entry now, eighteen months after my visit, I can still feel the reassuring embrace of the Farm, its guests, the staff and their own family members, including their children---all live-in residents of Gould. I felt that I was visiting the home of a caring and hospitable family.

In arranging my visit, I had communicated with Donna Burkhart and met her soon after my arrival. Throughout my stay, I was drawn to her appealing combination of loving warmth and gentle leadership. As my visit was ending, she took time out to invite me into her office so that I could ask questions and talk with her about what I had experienced as well as what *she* had experienced since she and her husband had arrived at Gould Farm in 1984.

When I asked her about her responsibilities and contributions to the Gould Farm environment as Director of Admissions and Client Service, she described her role as being that of a fulcrum between the outside world and clinical goals for the guests. Through her guidance and/or indirect communication, she helps guests balance their goals by considering three critical questions. The first question is "Who am I?" and not just in a solitary sense but as a member of the community. And to consider that question, the guest must also ask a related question: "Who is the community?"

Secondly, guests are led to think about the clinical consideration of "*How* am I?"—a question that deals with any and all health-related issues, encouraging them to see themselves as whole human beings. As they address those questions, they can more readily and accurately answer the third question, "What do I do?"—which leads them to identify talents, skills, and abilities that will allow them to feel like whole people with a place in the community.

Donna didn't talk much about herself, except in the context of her responsibilities. I only knew that she'd been there since 1984. But later, as I wrote about my experience and pondered the Farm and Donna and the guests, as I'm prone to do, I wanted to know more and needed to do some research. Why had she come to Gould Farm, and why had she stayed there for so long? I learned that Donna had come to Gould Farm in 1984 because her husband, Wayne, took a job as a part of the Farm's work program. They brought with them their two sons—one in third grade at the time and the other in kindergarten. Both Donna and Wayne had grown up in a Mennonite community and, prior to coming to Gould, had spent four years with the Mennonite Central Committee working on agricultural projects in Africa. On returning to the United States, they had both begun work on advanced degrees—Donna in teaching, and Wayne in community development—preparing for further travel. However, while Wayne was writing his dissertation, he visited Gould Farm for research. During that visit, he learned of a job opening for a gardens-and-grounds manager—and the rest, in terms of the Burkharts at Gould Farm, is history. Donna has served as an administrator, and Wayne is the agricultural director.

Beyond the kind of job description that one might find on paper, Donna understands that many guests are seeking to find adult identities that may not have been available to them as they struggled with limited identities—people with mental illness. Many want to return to where they were before mental illness became part of their lives. Their families might have the same goals. It's seldom an obtainable goal, but what they do achieve is a new path and a sense of acceptance—what Robert Frost might call *not against, with.*

Fourteen years after moving to Gould, Wayne and Donna were faced with a family crisis of their own. They wanted to "run away" from the pain but looked at the community that was their family and said, "We can turn our backs, or we can do what we ask every guest to do: embrace what we cannot bear." They encouraged themselves by learning from those whom they had encouraged and have never looked back. They found a life at Gould Farm.[10]

I understand how they could come to consider Gould Farm their home and guests as their family, and I treasure a post visit note from Donna in which she rewarded me with a simple sentence: "You're a Gould Farmer now!" renewing the sense of inclusion that I felt everywhere on the farm and especially in the main building where guests and staff gathered as social equals and, as they played and mingled, children of all ages created a sense of joy and family

## ROSE HILL CENTER—HOLLY, MICHIGAN

In 1987 Dan and Rosemary Kelly—fellow "Michiganders"—also became Gould Farmers. However, what led them to the Farm was quite different from what motivated my visit. In July 2008, I visited the outcome of *their* experience with Gould Farm.

Dan, a senior member of a large accounting firm, and Rosemary, a former teacher, have four children. John, next to youngest, was born in 1961, and when he was two years of age, tests indicated mild retardation (what is now referred to as an intellectual disability). Doctors could only guess at the cause but wondered if a high fever as an infant—most likely due to an infection—was to blame.

In spite of his diagnosis, John was a diligent student at an academically demanding high school and received daily tutoring from his mother. When he graduated in 1981 and went to work for a Detroit marketing firm, his parents surely breathed a sigh of relief that, in spite of any early brain insult, their son was working and living a meaningful life while living with them in their home. However, five years later, John expressed some troubling perspectives and exhibited troubling behaviors, beginning with obvious agitation and escalating to paranoid and delusional thinking—believing that, when he was driving, other drivers were staring at him, and even more troublesome, a belief that painters working in their home were, in fact, spies.

When this kind of symptom begins to emerge, while worrisome, it's difficult for friends and family members to know exactly what is happening—particularly since possible conclusions may be too painful to accept. However, on November 25, 1986—a few weeks after John's agitation began—any doubt or hope that John's parents held vanished. That day, when Dan came home from work, his son pointed to a box with a blinking light. Dan knew it was a burglar alarm. John did not see anything that simple or rational and told his father, "The FBI and CIA are bugging the house!" Dan went into the bedroom to tell Rosemary, who was in bed, still recovering from a serious automobile accident. When he told her what had happened, she expressed her own concern about John's recent behavior.

Dan returned to the living room, perhaps hoping that their fears were exaggerated. Instead, John screamed at him, "You're not my father!" and ran out of the house to the front porch of a neighbor's home, where he huddled in fear. That night, John was admitted to a psychiatric unit in Royal Oak, Michigan.

For weeks, the family rode an emotional rollercoaster of doubt and hope, not knowing what was in store for their son or what they should, or could, do to help him. His mother visited every day for weeks and saw him alternate between silence and incoherence. Though they hoped that physicians could explain their son's condition and rescue him from his emotional pain, there was no relief to be found, not even from available medication. With no improvement, doctors told them that there was little hope for full recovery and suggested that John should be placed in a long-term care facility.

With the desire and the means to provide what was best for their son, in March 1987 Dan and Rosemary took John to the Institute for Living, a long-term private hospital near Hartford, Connecticut. Here he was diagnosed with paranoid schizophrenia, but in spite of the diagnosis, John's parents felt some sense of relief when, with medication, their son showed improvement. Voices that had taunted him went away. He warmed to his parents. However, now over a year had passed since the onset of John's symptoms, and, in the summer of 1988, the family took steps that would allow him to leave the hospital. They had learned of Gould Farm, and with hope in their hearts, they moved John to the Farm.[11]

Given what had transpired since John thought the FBI and CIA were bugging their house, his transformation at Gould Farm must have seemed like a miracle. In the warm and nurturing environment of the Farm, with meaningful work to be done, John improved to the extent that his drug dosage was reduced. He showed new energy, and his cheerful personality was resurrected. However, after eighteen months at Gould, encouraged by his improvement, the Kellys wanted their son to be closer to home.

Rosemary set out to find a place in their home state that would offer John the same kind of physical and social environment he had experienced at Gould Farm. She visited group homes and state mental hospitals in Michigan, but nothing came close to what Gould Farm offered. In one group home, Rosemary was appalled to learn that residents had to leave the building by nine each morning and were not allowed to return until late in the afternoon. A few facilities offered more intensive care but cost as much as two thousand dollars a week.

In light of their positive experience with Gould Farm and given that there didn't appear to be anything like it in Michigan or adjoining states, in December 1988, the Kellys decided to create a Gould Farm type facility in their home state. As a successful businessman, Dan Kelly understood the steps necessary to launch such a venture. Experienced advisers were necessary, and he sought the advice and guidance of Gould Farm's treasurer and development officer. Next, steps were taken to create a private nonprofit corporation to be known as Rose Hill.[12]

While Dan had business knowledge, he humbly admitted to a group of friends and business leaders,

> I don't pretend to be an expert in mental illness. But no one has to be a rocket scientist to understand what we need—a center to help rehabilitate the mentally ill. We want to teach them basic living skills and how to work again. I've seen this succeed—not only with my son but with other mentally ill people as well. They need a chance.[13]

He took that message to the mental health community, to business contacts, and to civic and church groups, and his message was convincing. Support and funding grew. The marketing firm that had employed John to do clerical work prior to the onset of his paranoid symptoms donated two hundred and fifty thousand dollars from a charitable trust. Donations, big and small, came from other companies and citizens, and soon Rose Hill met its funding goal of $5.3 million.

It was time to choose a site for Rose Hill Center, a setting that would allow development of a Gould Farm–like environment. They found that setting in 372 acres located in a rural community sixty miles north of Detroit. Here they would create Rose Hill Center, where people like John could experience the same kind of client/staff interactions that Gould Farm had offered their son.[14]

Building began, and in the spring of 1991, Rose Hill's first resident, John Kelly, moved into a small cottage, where he lived independently and worked as Rose Hill's first staff member. As the property was developed and buildings were erected, John cut down trees, built fences, split wood, and sometimes even recruited his sisters to join in the effort.

A year later, in May 1992, six years after John Kelly had screamed, "You're not my father!" Rose Hill Center opened. As the family stood together for the opening, there were no doubts about family unity and devotion. John was ready to greet Rose Hill's guests in the same way that Gould Farm had welcomed him.

On opening day, Rosemary and John noticed a "haggard and wary" woman emerge hesitantly and fearfully from the back seat of a car. With no hesitation on his part, John walked toward her, held out his hand, and in a gentle voice that echoed the approach of Will and Agnes Gould—a couple he had never met in person but whose legacy had given him new life—John said, "Welcome to my home. Now it's your home too." The woman he was welcoming was Doris, a thirty-four-year-old woman who had been raised in a stable and happy home. As a teenager, she had won a state beauty contest, had designed many of her own clothes, and aspired to a career in television. Then, at the age of eighteen, Doris suddenly became withdrawn and frightened and experienced visual and auditory hallucinations, and, as John Kelly had been at the age of twenty-five, Doris was diagnosed with paranoid schizophrenia.

When John welcomed Doris into "his home," she was still symptomatic. At first she resisted any change, refused to tidy her room or do farm chores—the latter was "man's work," she insisted—and when staff tried to coax her out of her room, she screamed in fear, as John had screamed at his own father, "Get away from me!" Staff did not force themselves on her. They understood her fear, and they didn't give up. Then one morning, John Kelly—now a Rose Hill staff member who knew what Doris was feeling—casually asked, "Want to come see the animals?" She accepted, and together they walked to the barn. They continued to the pasture, where wire fence was being installed. Doris hated farm work, but the setting—perhaps the warm sun and outdoor environment along with the gentle demeanor of John Kelly—evoked something in her, and she began to help.

The door to healing had been opened. Before her illness, she had enjoyed cooking, and one day, she admitted to John that she hadn't cooked for a long time. When John suggested that she cook something at his place, she used apples from the nearby orchard to make applesauce. Using fruits and vegetables from Rose Hill, she continued making food items and, even better, offered them to other residents, to staff, and to her family when they visited.

One year after John Kelly extended the hand of welcome to Doris, she took a job at a local fast-food restaurant, the first job she'd held in fifteen years. From a visit to the barn, to helping with installation of wire fences, to making applesauce, to holding a job, in a snowball effect manner, Doris became more and more self-sufficient and graduated from Rose Hill on July 2, 1993.

Rose Hill continues to offer those with mental illness an opportunity to create a life of meaning and purpose. Gould Farm was the inspiration and model for

Rose Hill, but it wasn't a precise replication. The property that became Rose Hill had been a private working farm, but it is not a self-sustaining farm like Gould Farm and Spring Lake Ranch. However, as with Gould and SLR, Rose Hill's therapeutic program is based on structured work environments where residents serve with staff on one of four teams—housekeeping, kitchen, horticulture, or farm-animal care. Also, as with Gould and SLR, Rose Hill offers opportunities for recreational and academic activities. Skills that guests learn in the classroom or on work teams help prepare them for future employment.

Those who apply to Rose Hill's program must be at least eighteen years old and not currently dangerous to themselves or others. They must be capable of independent personal care, be able to participate in a structured daily program according to their personalized treatment plan, and be willing to collaborate with a psychiatrist in order to find an effective medication regimen. Though Rose Hill now has a program for those with co-occurring mental illness and substance-abuse disorder, when entering Rose Hill, residents may not be abusing drugs or alcohol or be in need of detoxification.

The stay of a Rose Hill resident starts with thirty days of assessment to determine how well they function in various areas of independent living. With that information, a Master Individual Treatment Plan is created for each resident to address specific needs. The Residential Rehabilitation Program can accommodate up to thirty-nine residents, who live in private or semiprivate rooms in one of two buildings, with additional rooms available on the second floor of a community center that also houses the community dining room and administrative offices.

Rose Hill also offers programs for those who have developed a greater degree of independence and who need less support. For those with a dual diagnosis, the Co-occurring Residential Rehabilitation Program opened July 2014 and uses an individualized treatment plan that includes therapy and activities specific to the resident's addiction. Those in the Transitional Living Program live in an on-campus townhouse and engage in a minimum of twenty hours of meaningful daily activity every week. Individuals who have shown improvement but still need some assistance are included in the Extended Residential Program, living in one of two buildings that accommodate a total of seventeen residents. For those who have returned to the community but do not have adequate support, the Community Support Program offers fee-based services appropriate to the client's needs.[15]

When pilgrims filled the homes of Geel citizens, it was natural and practical for them to participate in whatever work needed to be done—most commonly farm work. To this day, work matched to their interests or skills will be found for those Geel boarders who are able to work. When reviewing our own history with treatment approaches to mental illness, you may recall Benjamin Rush observation that "maniacs of the male sex in all hospitals who assist in cutting wood, making fires, and digging in a garden, and the females who are employed in washing, ironing, and scrubbing floors, often recover, while persons whose rank exempts them from performing such services languish away their lives within the walls of the hospital."[16]

We are wise to be cautious about forced labor, particularly from those who are vulnerable to stress or abuse. But must we be "all or none"? It appears that there is therapeutic value in work, and with the proper approach, those who are living with mental illness are entitled to work that will give them meaningful lives—without suffering loss of financial support to provide necessary medical care. Opportunities to live a meaningful life with necessary medical care occur easily and naturally in privately funded residential treatment centers. Given the success and long term cost saving of such an approach, implementation of a similar environment is something to consider when we build and support community mental health programs.

## SKYLAND TRAIL—ATLANTA, GEORGIA

A friend of mine knew of my interest in exemplary mental health programs and the stigma of mental illness. Thus, she suggested that I drive from Birmingham to her Atlanta home, in September 2013, to hear a panel discussion on "Mental Illness in America from Stigma to Strategy." CNN's Dr. Sanjay Gupta would be the moderator, and Skyland Trail would be the site, offering me a chance to tour this nationally recognized nonprofit treatment program.

Skyland Trail has much in common with many of the programs in this book. As with other programs described in this chapter, they hold membership in the

American Residential Treatment Association. Skyland Trail's founder, like others in this book, was motivated by personal knowledge of the problems associated with mental health care. Also, no matter the cost of treatment or services, for the purpose of this book, I've defined exemplary programs as those that, explicitly or implicitly, offer the opportunity for a meaningful life, as does Geel, by addressing the needs of the *whole person.*

In 1951, Atlanta received an All-America City Award due to its rapid growth and high standard of living in the South. By 1980, the population of Atlanta's metropolitan area was close to two million. However, in spite of its size and standard of living, hospitalization was the primary treatment for mental illness, with no available residential treatment facility that could prepare those with mental illness for reentry into their community. Charles B. West (1921–2013), born and raised in Atlanta, was recognized for his contribution to the building and growth of the city. When the daughter of a close friend was diagnosed with a mental disorder, West became keenly aware of the lack of residential treatment in the town that he loved and nurtured. Recognizing a void that needed to be filled and nearing retirement from his family-owned business, he decided to make another contribution to Atlanta—the George West Mental Health Foundation (named for his father). The board of directors was assigned the task of studying programs around the country in order to guide them in the creation and funding of a program to provide long-term recovery, not simply short-term stabilization, as did hospitalization.

In 1989, Skyland Trail opened—without a hospital atmosphere or lockdown—to house a community of voluntary clients. The thirty-thousand-square-foot building housed a gym, dining room, meditation pavilion, vocational services and computer lab, a greenhouse, and—surrounding, the building—gardens and trails. Consistent with the continuum of care[17] approach, treatment begins in a residential or day-treatment program but proceeds with deliberate step-down and reintegration points. Skyland Trail now includes Skyland Trail South, with the most intensive support—where most residential treatment clients begin their stay—and Skyland Trail North, a "step-down" residential facility where clients receive continued support as they develop independent-living skills. Some clients come to Skyland Trail from hospital stays and, on the average, will be ready to live independently in the community in four to six months. The length of the stay allows for gradual progress through levels of care that are consistent with improvement in symptoms and skills.

In 1991, an aftercare program was established as a part of the continuum of care that supports reintegration into the community. In the context of Skyland's whole-person approach, they have one of the few treatment programs in the country to integrate medical and mental health treatment, and they are currently affiliated with Atlanta's Emory University for the provision of clinical services and research. To meet the needs of young clients, in spring 2016, Skyland Trail will open a young adult campus on 3.5 acres adjacent to the main campus. The twenty-four-thousand-square-foot building will include a thirty-two-bed residential wing and community areas for recreation, dining, and treatment.

The criteria for admission to Skyland Trail are similar to other residential treatment communities. Clients must be at least eighteen years of age with a primary psychiatric diagnosis—a mood or thought disorder such as bipolar, major depression, schizophrenia, or anxiety disorder. However, most clients have a co-occurring diagnosis of alcohol or substance abuse, borderline personality disorder, or secondary anxiety disorders.

Thoughts and behaviors associated with mental disorders seldom fit neatly into a single diagnosis. Diagnosis is useful, even important, but at Skyland Trail, as with most other mental health programs, treatment and recovery are based on an awareness of the whole person, not the diagnosis. The holistic-treatment model includes a variety of services and goals: finding an effective medication regimen; gaining new perspectives and insights through psychotherapy; and the use of art, music, horticulture, and recreational therapy to help the client discover new interests and/or skills. In a classroom setting, clients learn about mental illness—not just their diagnoses—and with that knowledge, they learn strategies that will help them cope with their diagnoses, thus preventing relapse.

A personalized recovery plan is created for each client who is then assigned to one of five recovery communities, each made up of ten to fifteen clients, all of whom have similar diagnoses. However, they may transition from one recovery community to another as their goals and clinical needs change. The recovery community, led by a primary counselor and a team of therapists, is the client's primary support system. The recovery group, as an affinity group, offers a learning environment similar to what we called "homeroom" in our school days.

In order to understand the recovery process of family members *and* to support them in their recovery, Skyland Trail offers programs addressed to family recovery and recommends a one-day family-orientation program. This program is offered once a month and familiarizes family members with what the clients will experience and/or be offered during their stays at Skyland. One presentation, presented by a family therapist, specifically addresses the family's role in recovery. In addition to gaining useful information, presentations are made by specialists on each topic, offering family members an introduction to staff members.

The cost of treatment at Skyland is linked to the type of service being offered and the length of time spent in any one treatment level. Adult residential treatment lasts an average of four to six months. Nonresidential treatment is also available, but it is not considered a good starting place for those who are coming out of hospitalization. Clients in this program live in the community and come to campus for treatment and social-integration activities that are available from ten to four, Monday through Friday. Two to six months (with a minimum of eight weeks) are recommended for those in nonresidential treatment.

Stand-alone treatment options for those who are not currently enrolled in one of the programs already described include vocational services. Independent coaching is also available for those in either a transitional-housing program or for recent Skyland Trail grads. Also, with referral from a mental health provider, Independent coaching is available to community members.[18]

Finally, the Life Enrichment Program (LEAP) meets Tuesday and Thursday evenings for structured social interaction, and on weekends for community-based activities. LEAP is included in residential programs or as an add-on to day treatment intensive outpatient programs. And, as with vocational services, it is available to community members with a referral from a mental health provider.

Atlanta businessman Charles B. West was responsible for founding Skyland Trail. Dorothy Chapman Fuqua, wife of businessman and philanthropist John Brooks "JB" Fuqua, who fought a fifty-year battle with depression,[19] also made significant contributions to Skyland Trail, serving as a Skyland Trail board member and then as an emeritus board member. The Dorothy C. Fuqua Conservatory and Orchid House in the Atlanta Botanical Gardens are evidence for her love of gardening, which is also evident at Skyland, where she helped establish their horticultural-therapy program. In 2005, Skyland Trail raised $11.7 million for capital enhancements, making possible the 2010 opening of the Dorothy C. Fuqua Center, which houses the administrative and admissions office, a training and education center, and the Skyland Vocational Services Program with a computer learning center.

In 2011, her son and daughter-in-law honored Mrs. Fuqua's ninetieth birthday by establishing a lecture series to be held annually at Skyland Trail. It was that lecture series that featured Dr. Sanjay Gupta in September 2013 when I visited. The evening started with opening remarks by Mrs. Fuqua's son, Rex, and Tom Johnson, who, like Fuqua's father, J. B. Fuqua, had fought his own battle with depression, even as he served as the third president of CNN. However, understanding the stigma of mental illness, he did not reveal his illness publicly until after his retirement in 2001.

Sanjay Gupta, MD, a familiar name and face to anyone who watches CNN, where he serves as their chief medical correspondent, made brief comments and introduced the panelists. Panelist Ray Kotwicki, MD, MPH, is chief medical officer for Skyland Trail and a faculty member at Emory University. Thus his position at Skyland Trail includes research on integrated treatment of mental and physical health.

In addition to CNN, the Centers for Disease Control (CDC) is also located in Atlanta. As medical epidemiologist in the CDC's Division of Violence Prevention, Alex Crosby, MD, discussed the public-health approach to mental illness, including adolescent suicide clusters and school-associated violence.

The experts provided a useful perspective on "Mental Illness in America: from Stigma to Strategy," but it was probably the last two speakers—mother and daughter, Cinda and Linea Johnson—who captured the hearts of audience members. As individuals and family members, they knew the personal impact of mental illness and stigma. They told their story in the book *Perfect Chaos*,[20] which many in the audience had read, but now, as they spoke of the pain and confusion they encountered on their journey through mental illness, the story came alive. It was real. It was more than words on pages.

As a Seattle University professor and director of its special education graduate program, Cinda Johnson, EdD, was professionally prepared to understand bipolar disorder. But no one in their typically well-adjusted family of four— two parents and two daughters—was adequately prepared for the changes and demands the family would face when suicidal depression escalated and led to a diagnosis of bipolar disorder for Linea, the youngest daughter, who seemed to be lost from the family. As is often the case in terms of diagnosis and appropriate treatment, finding a successful drug was a trial-and-error experience. And in the process, electroconvulsive shock therapy (ECT) was added to the mix that helped Linea escape from the symptoms of her illness. But it wasn't just the treatment approaches that led her along the path to recovery; it was also her family's indefatigable support and faith. It was the resilience of Linea and her family.

Together, in *Perfect Chaos,* Linea and Cinda alternate narratives—from two equally touching perspectives of the family story. The public asks questions about mental illness. So, too, do those who experience the symptoms of mental illness—personally or through a family member.

The book begins with Cinda describing questions that taunted her as she removed the strings from Linea's sweatpants while standing outside the locked entry to a psychiatric unit where her daughter was on suicide watch:

> How did I get here? What signs did I miss over the last few years? Could I have saved my daughter from this pain? Could I have prevented my family this agony?[21]

A few pages later, Linea describes a time, after the agent had sold the book to a publisher, all of the editing was complete and both women were asked to write a preface. While visiting her boyfriend's apartment, she begins to cry and escapes to the bathroom in the hope that she can get her emotions under control and pretend that she only went to the bathroom "to pee." In an effort to stop crying, by identifying the source of her tears, she questions herself.: "What started this? Why am I crying when I am so happy with my current life? When I know that I am not experiencing any form of depressions?" With the book now a reality that would soon be in print for all the world to read, Linea understands the source of her tears: That book.

> Why is divulging my story so hard? Why do I want to expose my deepest insecurities and fears and pain to the public? Why, when I can't even show my boyfriend…would I want to show more people the dirty chaos of mania, the humiliation of a drug test, the blood, pain, and starvation that accompany a suicidal depression?[22]

She continues to explore her sense of self-stigma, asking herself,

> Are you afraid of sharing your story with unknown and known readers? Could this be the fear of perhaps not sharing this story at all? The fear of continuing to hide your true self and feelings from the world? Could these tears mean that perhaps you haven't quite accepted all of your past feelings and memories, all of the hospitalizations and misery and sadness? That you haven't yet processed what it means to have bipolar, how to live with it, how to carry on? Why, then, if sharing all of this creates such an onslaught of pain, are you continuing on?[23]

We can be grateful the Linea and Cinda's agent asked them to consider a preface. That final step in preparing the book for publication caused Linea to ask herself questions that likely reflect questions that the public asks, a public that would like to hide from the "fact" of mental illness. And Linea has the courage to share her humiliation, because it isn't just about her. It's about all the people who have and will experience the same pain that she and her family have experienced. It's about standing emotionally naked before a public that doesn't understand a pain they haven't experienced.

> I want to share my story because I want to help society see that this is a common illness…people don't choose to get sick and

don't wish to live dangerously unstable lives…this can happen to anyone…this is something that is normal…the people we see as having a mental illness, those on the streets or in the hospitals, are those who need the most help…the people who we read about in the headlines…are merely people who didn't get the help they needed and…represent one small sliver of those living with mental illness.[24]

The Johnson family summoned the courage and caring necessary to live with Linea's mental illness. They had no choice. They couldn't hide from it. But they took their courage and caring one step further with the decision to share their story. It is not a unique story but it is a story that the public needs to hear in order to allay fears, born of innocence or ignorance, regarding mental illness, and in order to offer support to those whose experience has, or will, echo the experience of the Johnsons and others like them. Linea and Cinda chose a *not against, with* approach to dealing with their pain, and their own courage can evoke the courage of public citizens as well as evoking resilience in others who face mental illness in their own lives or the lives of family members.

## INNISFREE VILLAGE—CROZET, VIRGINIA

Heinz Kramp—German by birth, American by choice—remembered the serenity and beauty of an early mental institution that was located near his childhood hometown in Germany. He held onto and cherished the image of beautifully designed apartment complexes, lovely gardens, and fruit trees that grew up to the third floor of the buildings. He remembered his early experience when, later in Washington, DC, he worked in a facility for the handicapped, where he often visited with parents of disabled children and young adults. He heard their concerns about what would happen to their children when they were no longer able to provide the kind of care that anyone would want for their children. They were haunted by the possibility that their children might have to live out their later years in an institutional setting,

However, some of these parents became aware of Camphill Village, founded in upstate New York in 1961 as part of a movement to reform treatment of people with special needs. They had friends who had moved their children to Camphill, where concern for them was replaced with hope that they could live meaningful lives, even after their parents were gone. The idea of such a place offered hope for a group of Maryland parents whose children had been born with intellectual disabilities. A place such as Camphill could insure a meaningful and challenging adult life for their children, who would share work and play with caregivers and would be treated as family members. And thus a dream of Camphill on the Potomac was born in the hearts and minds of those parents. They needed a place to plant the seed of that dream, and they found it in the Blue Ridge Mountains of Central Virginia, outside Charlottesville. In 1971, with the purchase of Walnut Level Farm, Camphill of the Potomac became Innisfree, Inc., a registered Commonwealth of Virginia tax-exempt, charitable, and educational foundation corporation whose stated purpose was to create a living and working environment for adults with mental disabilities. Inspired by the beauty of the setting, the first line of a poem by William Butler Yeats provided a fitting name: "I will arise and go now, and go to Innisfree." The second verse reflects what the founding parents must have felt and envisioned for the future of their children: "And I shall have some peace there, for peace comes dropping slow; Dropping from the veils of the morning to where the cricket sings."

Walnut Level Farm came with a three-story estate house, more than two hundred years old, and Joe Coleman, manager of the farm since 1950, stayed on as manager for thirty-six years, taking care of a few hogs and managing a beef herd. And in spite of the addition of many more residential structures, the Walnut Level house is still standing and used today.

Heinz Kramp assumed the position of executive director, and in June of 1971, he, his wife, and their five children moved into Innisfree. Those adults with mental disabilities who would live at Innisfree Village were not referred to as *patients* or *clients* or even *residents,* but, consistent with the parents' desire that their children live as family members of caregivers, they were referred to as *coworkers.* Innisfree's first two coworkers, Kenny and Margie, arrived in December of 1971, and more followed in that first year as construction of a woodshop and a new residence was completed. By 1974, there were four new residential buildings and more than twenty-five coworkers in residence.

The Innisfree experience is described as, and literally *is*, a life-sharing experience in which coworkers and volunteer caregivers learn from each other as they live, work, and play together. Caregivers are referred to as *volunteers,* because that's what they do, committing to at least one year of service at Innisfree, though many stay much longer. In the life of Innisfree, close to three hundred volunteers from all walks of life and from all over the world have lived for a year or more. They range in age from early twenties to midseventies, and many bring with them their own children, who also have the privilege of life sharing. In addition to live-in volunteers, service groups of five to fifteen often visit Innisfree for a few hours or a day of work—painting farm outbuildings, cooking special community dinners, or deep-cleaning the community kitchen. As they experience the joy or work, they learn about Innisfree's mission and become a part of that mission, interacting with volunteers and coworkers. They give their time and gain an understanding of, and appreciation for, people with disabilities, along with an appreciation for the value of community living and life sharing—lessons that will serve them as residents of their own communities.

Today, life sharing takes place among seventy-five village members—thirty-nine coworkers, twenty volunteers, and fifteen long-term staff. Acreage has grown to 550 acres, with 280 acres of open fields. There are thirteen residential homes, including two located in nearby Charlottesville, where coworkers can hold part-time jobs.

Coworkers are all born with some form of intellectual disability, sometimes of unknown cause, but including conditions such as Down syndrome, autism, Fragile X syndrome, and cerebral palsy. When coworkers take up residence at Innisfree, they must be older than eighteen and younger than thirty-five. Many who had been in that age range when they took up residence at Innisfree are now aging, less mobile, and less able to take care of themselves. Consistent with Innisfree's policy of flexibility—evolving to meet the needs of coworkers, volunteers, and long-term staff—in 1996, a house was built to serve the needs of aging Innisfree coworkers.

Coworkers must be capable of making decisions and must have participated in the decision to live at Innisfree, being content with rural living. As life-sharing members of a large family, they cannot have a history of doing physical harm to themselves or others. Because coworkers work and play at Innisfree, they must be able to orientate and walk from place to place. And they must be able to eat and use the toilet independently.

All coworkers live in either a family-style house or a semi-independent apartment building where full-time, live-in volunteers serve as house parents. In either case, they have their own private bedrooms and bathrooms that they share with one or two other coworkers. While their bedrooms are fully furnished, they can personalize them with their own private possessions. Shared living space consists of a kitchen and dining area, a living room with a television, and a laundry room. Coworkers all have assigned chores that allow them to contribute to household management. While a community lunch is served in the Community Center on weekdays, other meals are prepared and eaten either in their own homes or with coworker friends in other Village homes.

I was there for both lunch and dinner during my visit. Lunch was served in the large community dining room, offering me a chance to observe and mingle with the family of Innisfree residents—coworkers and volunteers—in a lively, comfortable family atmosphere. After lunch, Izrael "Iz" Zak, my guide for the day, gave me a tour. As he told me of his background and association with Innisfree, I became aware of the kind of person who is drawn to live there. Iz was born in the USSR and earned a degree in sociology from Rutgers University. He, his wife, and their two children had come to Innisfree in 1996 when Iz accepted a two-part job. He ran a fitness program, coordinating Special Olympics events and working with coworkers in Innisfree's gym, and he also served as a financial assistant.

Coworkers spend four days a week in workstations. What goes on at the workstations isn't "busy work." It is meaningful work that provides food for the village and, in some cases, income. Before and after lunch, Iz took me on a tour of the workstations, describing what each had to offer to coworkers and the Village. In the herb garden when we visited that morning, coworkers harvested herbs for the day's lunch. At the vegetable garden workstation, coworkers harvested and washed fresh vegetables, and in the community kitchen, another team chopped vegetables for lunch.

Some of the items that are grown or made at Innisfree are sold to the public at the Innisfree Community Gardens (CSA), established in 2004—vegetables, culinary and medicinal herbs, flowers, and eggs from Innisfree's farm worksta-tion. In the bakery, coworkers were making bread and granola, an ongoing task. Every week, they make fifty to sixty-five loaves of white and whole-wheat bread to be served in Innisfree houses or sold at special events or to churches. Also, they make more than forty pounds of granola, which is sold to local natural food or gourmet stores such as the local Whole Foods Market.

The farm workstation began in 2008 when Peter and Debra Traverse, both raised on family farms, were hired by Innisfree to establish the station with a fo-cus on animal husbandry. Coworkers now participate in caring for a small herd of cows and more than three hundred chickens. The Traverses also conceived, and now oversee, the Innisfree Village Farm Environmental Services Project, with a critical purpose of regenerating land that has lost its fertility after decades of continuous grazing, a purpose that is of value beyond Innisfree for any farm with grazing animals.

For some coworkers, a full day at workstations can be too challenging or stressful. But one does not find meaning in the context of idle hours, and so the free school workstation gives these people opportunities to explore their cre-ativity through music therapy, art, pottery, and papermaking. Another activity at the free school workstation is observing nature and, for example, understanding the changing seasons—from falling leaves to snow to flowers. They also make a weekly trip to the local library, where they can look for books on any topic of personal interest. For some, this encourages them to improve their reading skills.

The weavery workstation, now home to twenty looms, is one of the original workstations, established shortly after Innisfree coworkers started moving to the site. Open four days a week, it is a favorite station, not just for coworkers but for volunteers and long-term staff as well. All the woven items are made from natu-ral fibers, which are dyed at Innisfree, and every item has a label personalized with the name of the weaver. Items are sold in local stores and craft fairs where weavers commonly work, offering them the opportunity to meet buyers of their items and to feel like members of the community. The woodshop is another one of the original workstations, and some wood products are also sold at local craft fairs. Open three days a week, it serves as a workstation for coworkers *and* a workshop for small construction and repair projects to serve the Village.

When coworkers are not at workstations, they can participate in fitness sessions and weekly expressive therapy classes in music, art, or pottery. In addition, there are regular evening activities—parties or dances. Often coworkers are taken into Charlottesville, home of University of Virginia. We all find meaning not just in our being, but through participating in life—in relationships with others, through learning about our world, and in community activities. Coworkers are given opportunities for that kind of participation.

Later in the afternoon, after we had visited all the workstations, Iz and I went back to the community dining room to chat about Innisfree. As soon as I met Iz when I arrived at Innisfree, and then during my "grand tour," I was taken with his friendliness—to me, to coworkers, and to volunteers—and his easygoing, good nature. As we sat in the dining room, I saw this nature at work when an agitated coworker approached him and expressed a concern that was not particularly well articulated. But Iz responded to what was obviously needed in that moment and calmly suggested that the coworker take a walk on the path that ran past the community-center dining room and around the buildings. The man readily followed Iz's suggestions, and as he began his walk, though he was still mumbling, his agitation began to abate.

In the evening, I was an invited guest for a dinner prepared by coworkers who lived together in a semi-independent apartment building. Before dinner, as some coworkers were busy in the kitchen, I entered into friendly conversation with others in the combination living room/dining room. Soon dinner was on the table, and we all enjoyed a delicious meal that included more friendly conversation in a manner reminiscent of a time before busy family schedules interfered with that part of the day, when the gathering of family members around the dinner table was the norm. It was a warm and friendly social environment that carried me back to memories of my childhood. I felt as though I was having dinner in a neighbor's house back home. In fact, all of Innisfree, with the homes grouped around barns and outbuildings and the large community center, feels like a neighborhood, both physically and socially—the kind one would want to live in "back home."

Residential treatment centers provide months of long-term treatment in an atmosphere of community work and play. They are costly but worth the investment for those who can afford it. But they are not a "forever home" for those with mental illness, and the cost cannot be borne forever. They offer preparation for the client (guest, resident) to live a meaningful and independent life in his or her own community.

Innisfree is not a treatment center. It is a community in which resident coworkers can live out their lives and "have some peace." Thus, costs must be considered somewhat differently.[25] Volunteers receive a small monthly stipend along with medical coverage for nonpreexisting conditions, but their volunteerism is a "financial resource." Innisfree also benefits from private funding and family support, covering room and board, participation in workstations, expressive therapies, and evening recreation. But coworkers and their parents have been guaranteed a lifestyle and peace of mind that is priceless.

# 10

# Using Resources, Filling Needs—Not Against, With

A thousand years ago, those in need made their ways to a village in Belgium, seeking the intercession of a martyred princess. The legend of St. Dymphna was a magnet attracting those with mental disorders. Then, and through the ages, the city of Geel has found the resources to accommodate those who seek healing and solace in its community.

Today, a county in need exists in the state of Alabama, and a city within that county has served as a magnet, motivating those with a need to *serve* community members in need—an attitude similar to what existed in colonial America. Eighteen Alabama counties are included in Alabama's Black Belt. Cities located in those counties include Montgomery, the state capital, and Selma, a focal point for the Civil Rights movement that resulted in the Voting Rights Act of 1965. Hale County, one of the Black Belt counties, is home to Greensboro, the catfish capital of Alabama, population 2,435, 100 percent of whom are rural dwellers, about two-thirds African American. The city has a 2012 median household income almost sixteen thousand dollars less than Alabama's median household income and over twenty-five thousand dollars less than that of the United States.[1]

Geel had a history that beckoned those in need of a particular kind of healing. The history of Greensboro and Hale County didn't beckon to those in need, but the history does account for many of the citizens who are currently in need. Though that history led the *Birmingham News* to refer to the area as "Alabama's Third World"[2] in a 2002 investigative report, the region is cherished by those who have spent their lives linked to the community. In his 1989 book *Historic Hale County*, Randall Curb, the city's unofficial historian,[3] describes the progression of events that created the Greensboro of today:

> The story of early Greensboro is one of the most interesting to be found anywhere in the South...one door invariably opens upon another and then another and there is never any real end—only resting places.[4]

Curb, though legally blind at the age of sixty, still holds a vivid memory of the people and places that tell the story of Hale County. In addition to what Curb and today's residents have experienced and remembered, its history goes back to a time long before current structures existed—back at least twenty-two hundred years, when an ancient Native American tribe established what was, at the time, the largest city in North America. Twenty-six earthen mounds in nearby Moundville are visible reminders of the sophisticated society that used to be.

The Black Belt[5] acquired its name not, as some think, because of the skin color of most of today's residents, but due to its rich black soil and the economic opportunities that soil offered. Though catfish ponds now occupy the fields in which cotton once grew, the area is still referred to as the Black Belt, and evidence of the economic influence of the fertile soil remains. This soil lured those who became plantation owners. Antebellum homes still stand, bearing witness to a time when fertile fields fed the financial success of many.

Since 1966, I have lived in Alabama's largest city, Birmingham—only ninety miles northeast of Greensboro. In their elementary-school days, my now-adult children visited Moundville on field trips. I knew something of the Black Belt and its modern-day association with poverty, but I knew next to no details—of either the past history or current status.

My introduction to Greensboro was too long in coming, and there is a certain irony that I should have been so interested in, and motivated by, a unique community on another continent when a community worthy of attention was right down the road from my own home. But the road to discovery is often an uncharted path along which we encounter unexpected and pleasant surprises, and if it hadn't been for Geel, it's possible I might never have learned as much as I now know about Greensboro.

Without a plan, the citizens of Geel used their resources to address the problems associated with an overwhelming influx of pilgrims in need of a cure for their mental illness. Now that I know Greensboro, it occurs to me that it too has—step by step, without an outlined plan—used its unique resources in a *not against, with* approach to address the many sources of poverty, because, as in colonial times, this population is not in need for one single reason. When my journey to discover mental health programs worthy of recognition began—even after I had started writing this book of hope—I never dreamed that so much of what I learned in my journey would be encapsulated in a single small town in the "third world of Alabama," my home state for two-thirds of my life.

As I visited diverse and exemplary mental health programs around the country, I knew that I hadn't even skimmed the surface of sites worthy of inclusion. And until one of my community funders made me aware of the fact, I didn't know that one of those sites, Project Horseshoe Farm,[6] was only a two-hour drive from my hometown. One visit to the website for Project Horseshoe—a relatively new addition to Greensboro that serves the needs of those with mental health problems—and I was making arrangements to visit the city, with no idea of the many reasons to hope, due to the city's amazing use of resources, that I would encounter just down the road from Birmingham.

Greensboro's median income is a clue to its current economic status. To be more precise, in 2012, 30 percent of community residents lived in poverty, and one in four adults in Hale County were unable to work due to disability.[7] Some assume there are those who could work, but don't. Whether that's an accurate assessment or not depends on your opinion of what it means to be disabled. It shouldn't be a matter of opinion, but disability, in and of itself, is not a diagnosis. And so, to qualify as being disabled, other factors have to be considered. Does the condition prohibit a person's ability to function—especially in a workplace? The answer is not a ready yes or no. The accurate answer is *maybe,* because it depends on the kind of job the person is qualified to hold. For example, does chronic pain, a common ailment in Hale County, prohibit someone's ability to function on the job? Yes, this is highly likely if the job demands constant standing.

You might respond that the solution is easy: let the person find a job that doesn't demand a lot of standing. That is a viable solution only if the job seeker is aware of jobs that would allow him or her to sit down and his or her level of education opens the doors to those kinds of jobs. Seems simple enough, doesn't it? Perhaps, but only for those with knowledge and skills born of experience and/ or education.

A good number of Greensboro citizens have neither the knowledge of available sit-down jobs nor the education to hold such jobs. Why? Across the country, major employers in small towns are shutting down, thus closing the doors to the presence and availability of jobs for those with no more than a high school education (only 11 percent of Greensboro's population over the age of twenty-five are educated beyond high school).

Greensboro's economic status is not a secret, and the documented needs of its citizens have served as a magnet for many with a need to serve. A forty-nine-year-old architect and professor from the state's Auburn University School of Architecture believed that "as an architect, I have the opportunity to address wrongs and try to correct them."[8] A young woman from California's Bay Area left behind eighteen years of product development and management for companies such as Victoria's Secret and BabyGap for product development in Hale County using the county's resources. A dedicated young psychiatrist, co-medical director of an Assertive Community Treatment (ACT) team at Loma Linda University Medical Center, where he provided supportive services to one hundred patients with severe mental illness, sought a smaller community with a true sense of community.

## RURAL STUDIOS—NEWBERN, ALABAMA

Architect Samuel Mockbee migrated from Auburn University, 145 miles east of Hale County, in 1993. From a socioeconomic perspective, Hale County perhaps reminded Mockbee—fondly known as Sambo to his friends—of his personal experience growing up in the state of Mississippi during the Civil Rights movement, where his concern regarding treatment of African Americans was exacerbated by the murder of three civil rights workers from his hometown of Meridian. It's possible that this memory and concern motivated him to establish

Rural Studio in the Hale County community of Newbern (population 183 as of 2013).

After high school, Mockbee served in the army for two years before enrolling in Auburn University where, in 1974, he earned a degree in architecture. He returned to Mississippi and helped establish an architectural firm that explored new approaches to design and construction, approaches inspired by Mockbee's awareness of the need for affordable housing. During its thirteen-year existence, the firm's unique constructions and use of recycled materials to create modern themes earned praise and, at the same time, exposed the tension that existed between social and economic conditions.

When Mockbee joined Auburn's faculty in 1992, he saw an opportunity to motivate future architects. A year later, he established an off-campus program as an option of study for Auburn University architectural students—a hands-on opportunity to design and build affordable housing and, at the same time, because of the studio's location, to better understand the needs of those who would occupy those homes.

A hallmark of Rural Studio's approach is its use of Hale County resources. By now, Mockbee was convinced that recycling, reusing, and remaking was the most practical approach to using available resources. Mockbee's Rural Studio was motivated by his desire to enhance the learning and lives of students by encouraging a broader understanding of the potential of their chosen art form, while at the same time serving the people of Hale County. Mockbee summed up the totality of his motivation:

> Architecture is a social art. And as a social art, it is our social responsibility to make sure that we are delivering architecture that meets not only functional and creature comforts, but also spiritual comfort. All architects expect and hope that their work will act as a servant in some sense for humanity—to make a better world.[9]

One year after the birth of Rural Studio, Alabama Power Foundation grant money allowed students to build their first house in the small Hale County settlement of Mason's Bend, on the banks of the Black Warrior River, where most community residents lived in trailers or shacks. Masons Bend residents Mr. and Mrs. B., along with their three grandchildren, had lived in an unheated shack with no plumbing until Rural Studio designed and built a house that specifically fit their needs. True to Mockbee's approach, the walls of the house were made of donated hay bales. As each house has its own name, this one came to be called the Hay Bale house. Over the next ten years, Rural Studio built five more houses in Mason's Bend and has been responsible for the design and building of Hale County parks and civic structures: a town hall, baseball field, and fire station in Newbern and the Lion's Club Park, County Animal Shelter, and County Hospital Courtyard in Greensboro.

Too often, those with good intentions for improving a community in need are guided by their own "book learning" education to formulate a template, rather than seeking to understand and respond to the unique nature of a community's needs and resources. Not Rural Studio. They are concerned with the specific resources and needs of people in their specific community. To date, more than 150 structures in Hale County owe their existence—their unique design and affordable construction—to more than six hundred students of Rural Studio who have been educated as "Citizen Architects."[10]

# HERO HOUSING RESOURCE CENTER– GREENSBORO, ALABAMA

Rural Studio's unique approach, coupled with motivation and success, became known to those who lived far beyond Hale County limits. The life of one such person was turned around when she read a book about Rural Studio. Pam Dorr, for eighteen years a successful California Bay Area clothing designer, had, in her teens, many years before her success in product development, come to own a house of her own. Though the house needed work, she personally did the work, turning a house into a home—*her* home—using free and found items, similar to what she would learn was Rural Studio's approach. Having lost her mother as a child, she needed to create a sense of home for herself, and once she completed that goal, she looked beyond her home and into her community—talking to community members and learning of their needs. Could she do for anyone else what she had done for herself? She could, and she did. She helped to establish community gardens and, in one of those, heard a homeless man express the need for a "cold-food" garden—a place to grow foods that did not need kitchen cooking. Pam listened, understood, and responded. She met Eddie, a community member diagnosed with schizophrenia, who no doubt felt the "alonenesss"—the social and self-stigma—that often goes with that diagnosis. Pam and Eddie began to walk the beach together as friends, and during their walks, they identified art hidden in pieces of "this and that." Together, they gave life to that art, and to this day, Pam credits Eddie with helping her find herself in the same way they found beauty in discarded items.

Given Pam's early personal experience, it is not surprising that when she read of Rural Studio, she identified with its purpose and approach. Though she had served her community during the time she was climbing the corporate ladder, something within her wanted to do more. Pam applied for and was awarded a one-year fellowship with Rural Studio's Outreach Program. She arrived in Greensboro in 2003 and, twelve years later, is still there, living a life that satisfies her dream of "making a difference" while fulfilling what had once been the impossible dreams of Hale County residents—over and over and over again.

Hale County inspired Pam to use her creativity and the county's resources to serve the community in the same manner that she had served the community around her California beach house. Without a real "plan," her avocation naturally began to evolve into a vocation. At the end of her one-year architectural fellowship, she took a paid position with Rural Studio and, at the same time, did volunteer work for Hale Empowerment and Revitalization Organization (with an apt acronym of HERO). Founded in 1994 by five hundred Greensboro community members, HERO is a nonprofit organization with the goal of ending rural poverty and encouraging a strong community sense of family.[11] Initially, HERO Family Resource Center provided classes, counseling, and services for the families of Hale County. As a volunteer, Pam used her knowledge of how to use "free and found items" and her open-hearted energy to assist those with little in the way of financial resources to make much-needed repairs to their homes. In 2004, those services led to Pam's creation of the HERO Housing Resource Center and HERO's focus on affordable housing. For those who dream of a home of their own, simply providing one is not a practical starting place. Ellen Baxter knew it to be true in New York City. Pam Dorr knew it to be true in Hale County, Alabama. HERO counseling for first-time homeowners includes free monthly workshops as well as scheduled appointments with a HERO housing counselor. Those who are not ready, or even eager, to own homes can receive counseling on how to obtain rental assistance.

Pam's experience with using free and found items to create or repair homes was a valuable resource. What of her eighteen years of experience in product development? The citizens of Hale County needed paying jobs. Pam set out to identify product-development resources available in the area, resources that might lead to job creation. But this type of initiative was a project, a goal that needed input and involvement from community members. People who collaborate and plan need a place to communicate, a place that encourages community dialogue. Thus Pam sought out the experience and expertise of Project M[12] (*m* for mentor), a nonprofit born in Maine in 2003 whose purpose was to encourage and train young designers to address community social problems.

In 2009, on a street corner in Belfast, Maine, Project M began work on a concept meant to encourage conversation among community members. Volunteers handed out free slices of pecan, pumpkin, or good old American apple pie, believing that community consumption of pie—offered in a pop-up, temporary café format—could encourage community conversation. In 2007, prior to Project M's 2009 PieLab idea, they had established a relationship with Greensboro through a "Buy-a-Meter" project in which they helped raise money to hook up community residents to running water. Project M's understanding of the need for community dialogue in Greensboro led them to take Free-Pie Day south using the pop-up concept.

In three weeks' time, with a six-hundred-dollar budget, Project M volunteers created PieLab and managed it through the spring and summer.[13] Success. It was clear that, for Greensboro's purposes, this concept was worthy of more than a temporary pop-up format. And so HERO, with Pam Dorr using her free-and-found approach, created a space in an old home behind HERO's offices.[14] As so often happens, "free and found" was also "clever and charming." The back of cards in an old library card catalog—with book titles and check-out histories on the front—found new life as sketch pads and order pads.

As Dorr had hoped and anticipated, PieLab became a community clubhouse where community members could talk and develop new ideas, listen to a band, or access the Internet in a warm and homey environment while eating a piece of homemade pie. And PieLab was so charming that it began to attract customers from beyond Alabama's "third-world" counties.

PieLab soon moved into a roomier, refurbished Main Street Greensboro brick-fronted building, with large windows, exposed brick walls, counters from old Greensboro shops, and a chalkboard menu that, along with pie choices, now included luncheon items—all prepared right in the building.[15] PieLab is a comfortable site where community members and visitors can feel at home—where no one is an outsider. It has been an inspiration for other communities, in terms of the concept and the physical space, earning recognition and accolades from respected culinary judges. *Southern Living* magazine named PieLab's apple pie as one of the South's best. In 2010, recognizing the inviting environment, the James Beard Foundation named Greensboro's PieLab as one of three finalists for its restaurant-design award.

When PieLab moved from the old house to its new Main Street home, that old house was not retired but became the headquarters for HERO's AmeriCorps Vista volunteers who run BikeLab. Pam is also a master at finding new uses for existing resources, such as bamboo.[16] Bamboo grows well in the rich Black Belt topsoil and requires neither irrigation nor pesticide. It grows *so* well, in fact, that it can take over. Plants that take over are seen as a nuisance for some, but not Pam Dorr. Pam viewed bamboo from a *not against, with* perspective. Anyone who has been to Asia, where bamboo is used for building scaffolding, has seen evidence of its strength. That strength makes it an excellent candidate for the building of bikes. And that's what they're doing with it in Greensboro. Workers harvest the naturally growing bamboo from the fields, cure and dry it in their studio, and in about thirty more hours can produce a ready-to-ride bike. They sell the bikes. They conduct workshops teaching people how to build their own bikes. They ship bamboo to eleven different countries and are the sole suppliers for bamboo to North American cities from Camden, Maine, to Toronto to

San Francisco. They provide job training for at-risk youth through HEROyouth, preparing them to work in green manufacturing companies.

Pam does not bemoan what is lacking in Greensboro and Hale County. With her *not against, with* mind-set, she celebrates the usefulness of what *is* available: materials and talents. In addition to bamboo, there are pecans aplenty in Hale County, which led to a pecan business run by a young woman, a graduate of HERO's youth program who has completed her GED and is now attending college while building a small business (with twenty-seven wholesale accounts) whose profits provide scholarships for local young people who would not ordinarily have a chance to attend college. Greensboro also provides jobs for locals—in the construction business, in a thrift shop, and in a state-licensed day care.

Sambo Mockbee and Rural Studios and affordable housing; Pam Dorr and HERO and pies and bamboo bikes and pecans; identifying available resources; filling the needs of both those *in need* and those with a *need to serve*—all success stories that emerged from a *not against, with* mentality. *With* what is available and works, rather than struggling *against* deficits born of impoverishment.

## PROJECT HORSESHOE FARMS— GREENSBORO, ALABAMA

But as I tell stories that I didn't expect to find when I traveled to Greensboro, I digress from the original purpose of my visit. I traveled to Greensboro to find out what was happening in terms of Project Horseshoe and mental health care. Before my visit, I used the Internet to learn more about Project Horseshoe Farm, and it was on the Internet that I first met John Dorsey, a successful young psychiatrist who came to Hale County from a psychiatric residency in Loma Linda, California, about 450 miles south of San Francisco.

John is dedicated to the needs of those with mental illness and was serving that population in Loma Linda. But for him, something was missing. He wanted more: to live and practice within a small-town community with a more "human feel." When he shared that need for more, a colleague suggested that he might find what he was looking for in Alabama, where he would find communities with a *very* different feel than what he was experiencing in Loma Linda, California.

That suggestion led him to seek and secure a position at Bryce Hospital, Alabama's oldest and largest inpatient psychiatric facility, first opened in 1861 and once considered to be an architectural model for such facilities. In the twentieth century, Bryce had become a model of a different sort when it became known for its overcrowded conditions and poor care, resulting in the Wyatt v. Stickney class-action law suit,[17] begun in 1970 and reaching its final conclusion in 2003—thirty-three years of litigation that cost the state of Alabama fifteen million dollars but also produced a final agreement that established a nationally recognized model for care. The Wyatt Standards were defined by four criteria for institutional care: (1) a humane psychological and physical environment, (2) presence of qualified and sufficient staff for administration of treatment, (3) treatment plans individualized to specific patient needs, and (4) minimum restriction of patient freedom.

Though Bryce continues to provide services for the mentally ill, the original building is now owned by another Alabama institution, nationally known by college-football fans, particularly those who know the legend of Coach Bear Bryant. Both Bryce and the University of Alabama are located in Tuscaloosa, the fifth largest city in Alabama and the county seat of Tuscaloosa County, north of and adjacent to Hale County, thirty-eight miles from Greensboro, and a long way from the experiences and environment that had been a part of the first thirty-two years of John Dorsey's life.

The quality and diversity of Dorsey's educational background and experience are impressive. His academic journey began with a bachelor of arts degree in Neuroscience from Pomona College, a highly rated California liberal-arts college. From California, he moved east to Philadelphia to earn his MD from Jefferson Medical College, at the same time earning a master's of business administration with a focus on health and medical services administration from Chester, Pennsylvania's, Widener University. For his residency in psychiatry, it was back to California and the University of California, Davis, Medical Center, where faculty presented him with their Outstanding Resident Award and medical students selected him to receive the Resident Medical Staff Outstanding Teaching Award. He had an alphabet soup of academic credentials and awards that evidenced approval from mentors and peers. But he had become more self-aware of something that can't be defined by the number of degrees or awards one holds—the need for a sense of community.

Based on his colleague's suggestion, at the end of his psychiatric residency, he sought employment at Bryce Hospital. He got the job, but as he made his way east to Bryce, he learned that the psychiatric post he had accepted was no more. Still, Dorsey kept driving to a place where he knew no one but where he began to meet new people, creating a sequence of events that led him to Greensboro and life in a trailer. He didn't know exactly what he would do in Hale County, but as he settled into a small-town sense of community, he became aware of a general aura—people simply and naturally wanted to help one another. In their own way, they were kindred spirits with this highly educated psychiatrist from California.

John Dorsey is as humble as he is enthusiastic and energetic. He is not the kind of person who would want to be the star of the show, and as you've seen, he's not the only person responsible for what has happened in Greensboro. When he arrived in the area in 2005, Rural Studio had been making its contribution to the county for twelve years. Though Pam Dorr had arrived on the scene only two years prior, she had already begun to change things through her work with HERO. But John's arrival was clearly an important and valuable addition—one more person with a need for community. Greensboro met his criteria and he, in turn, had something to offer to this small Black Belt community.

John Dorsey brought with him valuable credentials in terms of his ability to serve those with mental health problems. But those credentials might not have had the same impact if not for the personal need for community that led him to this area and has informed his work in the region. It was, in fact, his compassion that led him to a career of caring for those with severe mental illness. But in Greensboro, he found "a chance to put together good psychiatric care with good support for people to help them have a good quality of life and live successfully in their community."[18] As he made contacts in the area, opportunities to serve in the Black Belt emerged. He was recruited by Bryan Whitfield Memorial Hospital in nearby Demopolis (thirty miles northeast of Greensboro) to establish an Adult and Geriatric Behavioral Health Program, where he now serves as co-medical director. In addition, he has assumed the duties of staff psychiatrist at the Hale County Jail and the Perry County Correctional Facility in Marion, Alabama (thirty miles east of Greensboro).

Reminiscent of colonial motivation, it wasn't long before Dorsey recognized a host of community needs that justified a new program, an umbrella program meant to address any community need. In 2007, on a former sixty-acre dairy farm, Project Horseshoe Farms was established. The project began to serve the community with an after school program for at-risk students in Greensboro elementary school. By 2014, close to one hundred young people were served by this program.

Dorsey was professionally aware of the needs of those hospitalized with mental health disorders who eventually faced the difficult transition from hospital life to home life. He knew that those in transition were at risk for returning to the hospital or some institutional setting. Thus, in 2009, Dorsey began to address this particular problem when he bought and restored a Victorian house, giving the structure new life as a residency program for women fifty and older who had been diagnosed with a mental disorder. Here, the residents live in a supportive family-type environment, experiencing companionship from their housemates as well as other community members, including those who work within the Project Horseshoe structure. The house opened to its first six residents (all female, primarily geriatric) in 2009. Many of those women have since graduated back to their families or even to independent living, fulfilling Dorsey's goal of helping former patients live the most independent lives possible. And as residents leave for new lives, there is a waiting list of women waiting to move in.

PieLab is a place for community members to meet and plan. Project Horseshoe's Community Clubhouse, located on Main Street directly across the street from PieLab, provides a place for Project Horseshoe residents and other elderly or mentally disabled community members to escape a sense of isolation when they gather to enjoy a host of activities. During my August 2014 visit to Greensboro, my first stop was the clubhouse, where I was greeted by one of the Project Horseshoe Fellows who showed me around and gave me an overview of what happened in that building in the course of a day. The Horseshoe Farm Fellowship program offers a gap-year opportunity for those who have completed their undergraduate studies and plan to attend a graduate program, usually medical school. Most of the Fellows are from the Southeast, but other states are represented as well. During their year at Horseshoe, Fellows live together in a building located on Horseshoe property, offering them opportunities for peer interaction and support. And, most important, they experience a brand of community life that may be new to them. In addition to their interactive work with Horseshoe Farm and community members, they also participate in weekly discussions, following a syllabus that focuses on citizenship, community, and the start-up and operation of nonprofit organizations. Because of their firsthand experience and onsite education, many Fellows who have gone on to medical school have chosen to follow a "rural track," preparing them to serve populations that are far removed from large-city medical centers and services.

One of the first things I noticed when I entered the clubhouse, even before my orientation began, was the effect of storefront-type windows at the front of the building, letting in the sunshine and all that sunshine brings with it. At the front of the clubhouse, sofas and chairs created a sense of being in a friend's home. The charming environment was representative of what I later learned was the free-and-found approach of HERO and Rural Studio. The clubhouse—the original site of the youth program that now meets at the local school—is located in an old Western Auto Building, and there has been little effort to hide that former identity. Western Auto store images that once identified the entry door are now displayed as works of art and hang on the wall bordered by window frames. There is a small kitchen area open to the large room that, in its reincarnation, is filled with tables and chairs rather than automotive supplies.

When I arrived, I soon joined a group of clubhouse participants, community volunteers, and Horseshoe Fellows, who sat around a large table chopping vegetables for lunch. We engaged in friendly chatter, with some interested in the chatter and some more intensely, and seriously, interested in the chopping task. Later, while the meal cooked, klutz though I am, I felt no sense of self-consciousness as I participated in movement activities with recorded background music, beginning, in a fitting manner, with Pharrell Williams's "Happy." We danced, we stretched, we learned something about the nutritional value of the lunch we would eat, and we played some board games.

This was not the first time I'd observed or participated in body-movement exercises in a mental health clubhouse environment. I was familiar with the fact that if some participants didn't seem to be as actively involved as one would hope, it wasn't necessarily their lack of enthusiasm but rather the dulling side effects of medication. And so, the joy evoked by "Happy" was amplified when I saw that with casual and friendly encouragement from the Fellows, *all* of the participants were active. I felt like I was in the midst of a group of friends simply gathering together for the fun of it.

Later that day, I paid a visit to the women's independent-housing facility, where some of my fellow vegetable choppers made their home. Once again, I felt the warmth that makes a house a home: an inviting front porch, a spacious green lawn, and the fact that residents had their own rooms. It is hard to know which of those factors is most important. It's likely that it was a mix in which "the whole was greater than the sum of the parts" (my favorite cliché because I so often see evidence of its truth).

For one with a need for community, John Dorsey found a close-to-perfect setting in Greensboro. He also found an enthusiastic collaborator in Michael Lynch, who, as managing director and manager of external relations until 2015, held the only paid position in Project Horseshoe and helped to initiate and activate programs that addressed the needs of Greensboro. Compassion is, and was, the motivating factor for both Michael and John. Though they do not have identical-twin personalities—far from it—the common thread of compassion evoked energy and dedication from both men.

Though Michael is no longer a member of the Project Horseshoe staff, he played a significant role in acquiring an old downtown hotel that had been empty and unused for many years but where restoration is now underway in order to create a space that will serve the needs of Greensboro residents. It may house programs for people with dementia. It may house medical students on rural rotations. It may serve as a medical-education hub for rural West Alabama. Whatever its future function, one thing is for sure: it will be used in a *not against, with* fashion—as a resource for a community in need, populated by citizens in need.

Project Horseshoe Farms, along with Rural Studio and HERO, are parts that create a whole far greater than their sum—services to meet the needs of at-risk children, senior citizens, and adults with mental illness…those who are unemployed but are eager to work and be self-sufficient. In Greensboro, everything and everyone is a potential resource for community well-being and even growth. The common denominator, the secret to success, is always community support and integration. Greensboro is a community that is creating a legacy, a new history, using its resources to serve those in need for a variety of reasons, as surely as Geel has always used its resources to service those in need of healing. In each case, as with other programs described here, the community identified the needs of its citizens and used available resources to fill those needs.

# 11

# Silencing the Voice of Stigma

Stigma is insidious. It seldom, if ever, develops overnight. The stigma of mental illness can grow from diagnostic words uttered by amateurs without full knowledge of what the words mean. It can be the product of media or literary images, likely to present extreme cases for the sake of news or drama. Stigma evolves as damning evidence, feeding on itself. It gains in strength as the evolution proceeds. It is tenacious and does not easily yield to reason.

Patrick Corrigan, in one of his many professional responsibilities as Director of the National Consortium on Stigma and Empowerment (NCSE), has been a leader in research that seeks successful ways to break through that tenacity, to attenuate stigma. Corrigan has investigated the effectiveness of three common approaches traditionally used to reduce stigma: protest, education, and contact. Across the ages, protest—letters to the editor, demonstrations, etc.—has played a role by making known the need for social change in a variety of situations. In modern times, it is often used in response to unfair representations of those with a mental disorder. That kind of pressure has been successful, for example, in motivating a change in images that are presented to the public by the entertainment industry, resulting in SAMSHA's Voice Awards. But protest normally originates from individuals or special-interest groups. The question remains as to whether or not that protest, and any accompanying change, actually edifies the larger community. And, unfortunately, publicized protest can even have the opposite effect of what is intended—a rebound effect such that the stigmatized group may "pay the price" of protest.

If replacing a myth-based stigma or perception of mental illness with a more accurate understanding is the goal, it would seem that, of the three techniques, education would be the most obvious road to success. The meaning of the word *variable* in scientific language is the same as it is in casual conversation: anything that can be measured and can change or be changed. When scientists measure two or more variables, they can look for a statistically significant relationship between those two variables—either a positive or negative *correlation*. If measurements of both variables go up or down at the same time, a *positive* correlation exists; for example, increased TV viewing by children may be correlated with an increase in aggressive social behavior, decreased TV viewing with a decrease in aggression. A significant *negative* correlation exists if one variable increases while the other decreases (a seesaw effect). For example, increased TV viewing by children may be correlated with decreased academic performance. It can be useful to understand these relationships, but when all we do is measure variables, we cannot assume that movement of one *causes* the movement of another. We can't assume cause and effect. In fact, when variables have only been measured, a positive or negative correlation may *suggest* a possible cause-and-effect relationship, but if such a relationship does exist, it's impossible to know which variable is the cause and which is the effect. And there may in fact be *no* cause-and-effect relationship between the measured variables at all. In the example given above, there *could* be an unmeasured variable (a third variable) that causes changes in both increased TV viewing and decreased academic performance. Or, in the other example, a third variable could be driving both increased TV viewing *and* aggressive behavior. Though it doesn't take a social scientist to identify possible third variables, the public too often ignores their presence. It's easier to think in terms of cause and effect.

When all researchers do is measure variables, they can only hope to find correlations. But in the social-science laboratory, it is possible to exert systematic control over certain variables (that is, hold them constant across multiple groups), and then present other variables of interest at specified levels or in diverse form, thus isolating the effect of that variable. In addition, the social science researcher can create a *control* group for comparison. Using these forms of systematic control, it *is* possible to make objective cause-and-effect statements about the relationship between variables of interest. Corrigan and his colleagues have done that with interesting results, providing insight into ways to decrease stigma.

They took the three approaches to stigma reduction—protest, education, and contact—plus a control group and randomly assigned subjects to one of the four groups. Three groups were presented with information regarding mental illness in one of three contexts (protest, education, or contact), and a fourth group, the control group, simply received information on a benign topic unrelated to mental illness.[1] The attitude of all subjects regarding mental illness was measured *before* they experienced one of these four types of presentation and again *after* the presentation. Would the three presentation styles produce a change in attitude? And even more important, would one presentation style work better than another?

One of the approaches had no effect on attitude. Those who were exposed to statements meant to induce a sense of moral outrage about the treatment of the mentally ill (protest group) showed no reduction in stigma after the presentation compared to prepresentation. But compared to the control group (benign presentation) and the protest group, subjects presented with facts that challenged myths about mental illness (education group) showed a statistically significant change in attitude regarding both depression and psychosis from pre- to postpresentation. Their postpresentation attitude reflected less blame toward persons with mental illness along with greater confidence in their chances of recovery. And subjects who heard a presentation made by a stranger presenting his own personal history of dealing with mental illness (contact group) also showed a similar attitude change. In an immediate sense, education and contact were equally effective.

What is more interesting, and important, was demonstrated in the second phase of this experiment, when all subjects were shown the same videotape of an actor playing the role of someone with mental illness. Subjects were unaware of his status as an actor and were led to believe that he was actually mentally ill. In the video, he told his "life story," and in the course of telling his story—in the context of the story—they heard him make two types of statements about his life: (1) delusional statements such as "Sometimes I believe I'm George Washington," and (2) an equal number of believable fact statements, such as "I work as an engineer." Ten minutes after seeing the video, subjects were asked to write down as many statements as they could recall from the video.

Researchers were interested in knowing what subjects had paid attention to and remembered from the story of someone who they believed was mentally ill. They were even more interested in knowing whether previous experience in the first stage of the experiment would affect what they paid attention to during the viewing. It did.

When "meeting" someone with mental illness in the video, subjects who earlier had contact with a mentally ill presenter recalled more of the believable statements and fewer of the delusional statements than did the education group. These second-stage results suggest two very important things about how to defuse the stigma of mental illness. First, civil interaction (contact) with a person who has been labeled as mentally ill can have a positive impact on future encounters with someone who is known to be mentally ill, even when the person in the subsequent encounter fits a negative stereotype, such as making delusional statements. It appears that positive experiences beget positive perceptions in future encounters. Secondly, in terms of improving one's future appraisal of someone with mental illness, previous contact (experience) seems to be more important than previous education. Whereas certain kinds of experience can feed the stigma of mental illness, the voice of other experiences has the power to reduce the stigma of mental illness. There is reason to hope that those who have been dealt a diagnosis of mental illness can be accepted in their communities *if* they are lucky enough to live in communities that have not avoided contact with mental illness and do not rely on the distant contact of discouraging news stories. It appears that community contact with stigmatized individuals might create willingness for more contact. It's been happening in Geel for centuries, and it can happen in other settings when community members have opportunities for casual contact with those who have been diagnosed with a mental disorder and/or show symptoms associated with a mental disorder.

Recently, Dr. Corrigan encouraged those who have lived with the challenges of a mental disorder to consider sharing their story by "coming out proud" and offering their friends and coworkers the opportunity to have contact with mental illness. He himself courageously led the way by publically sharing his own experience with mental illness as the opening story in his 2015 book *Coming Out Proud to Erase the Stigma of Mental Illness: Stories and Essays of Solidarity.*[2]

# COMPEER, INC.—ROCHESTER, NEW YORK

You've read of programs that offer services to those with a diagnosis of mental illness, particularly programs that offer those services in the context of community integration. In the 1980s, during a Local NAMI meeting, I heard noted psychiatrist E. Fuller Torrey speak and first learned of Compeer, whose purpose was to coordinate friendship matches between community members and those with a diagnosis of any type of mental disorder. Compeer doesn't simply provide a service to those with a diagnosis of mental illness. Its primary function is to bring together consumers and community members purposely in one-on-one friendship matches. Compeer's story is another example of how needs are recognized and available resources are used to address those needs.

In 1973, Bernice Skirboll of Rochester, New York, was severely injured in an automobile accident. She promised herself that if she recovered, she would do something to make a difference in her community. As she rejoiced in a successful recovery, she did not forget her promise. Between 1970 and 1986, in the era of deinstitutionalization, Rochester's Mental Health Association established an Adopt-a-Patient program, which allowed formerly institutionalized patients to live in the community.[3] In that first year, twelve community volunteers were matched with twelve community members who had been institutionalized due to a mental disorder. In 1977, Adopt-a-Patient adopted a new name, Compeer, a word that perfectly fit the purpose of Adopt-a-Patient. Consistent with the spirit of the organization, a *compeer,* by definition, is a person of equal rank, status, or ability—a companion or comrade. In 1983, after affirmation from the state of New York and the National Institute of Mental Health Services as a model program and a Presidential Recognition Award from the United States Department of Health and Human Services, Compeer became Compeer, Inc., and held the first national conference attended by eighteen Compeer programs from fifteen states. In that same year, the value of Compeer was recognized by the American Psychiatric Association with its Certification of Significant Achievement Award. Compeer continued to collect awards and recognition, and in 1996, the organization became international with the addition of a Compeer program in Australia.

By 2011, close to four thousand volunteers from more than fifty affiliates in the United States, Canada, and Australia were serving as Compeers. Volunteers associated with the original Rochester, New York, agency served more than seven hundred children and adults with mental illness. Today there are sixty Compeer affiliates worldwide. Compeer programs serve adults, the elderly, veterans and their families, and youth, including children of prisoners. The model is simple. The most common type of match is a one-to-one friendship match in which community volunteers make a commitment of at least one-year to meet with their friends for one hour a week. The match is a cooperative effort between Compeer, the volunteer, the therapist, and the client. For example, before being matched with friends, volunteers participate in a three-hour training session to learn more about practical issues related to mental illness, relationship building, and the Compeer process. An example of a practical issue could be related to side effects of certain medications that can cause photosensitivity, which would mean that a Compeer friend should avoid social activities that involve being in the sun for too long, such as a daytime baseball game. Before the match is finalized, there is a three-way meeting between the volunteer, the client, and the therapist. After the match is made, volunteers receive a second training, and every month, the client and volunteer complete a progress report together that is submitted to the therapist, who uses the report as a guide in ongoing therapy. Furthermore, throughout the life of the friendship, Compeer staff offer continued support to all participants in the match.

Compeer provides contact with a stigmatized group, one of two critical variables identified in Patrick Corrigan's research. In addition, Compeer offers access to the other important variable: education. During volunteer recruitment programs, staff members talk to schools, corporations, churches, and civic organizations, constantly educating the public and increasing awareness and understanding of mental illness.

After learning of Compeer in 1993, I was privileged to be involved in the development of a Compeer affiliate in Birmingham, Alabama. My interest and motivation were keen as I set out to identify community members who shared my eagerness to establish an organization that would provide a valuable service to our community. Little did I realize the effort and frustration associated with establishing this kind of resource in a community.

In June of 1993, I invited a small group of interested individuals to meet in my home—to learn about Compeer and to evaluate community need for such a program. Enthusiasm was high, and this group became a task force to identify resources and recruit other interested individuals. This was not my first experience with a nonprofit agency, but it was my first experience in founding such an agency. We soon learned that the composition of a nonprofit board is critical. Members must include not only those interested in mental illness (in our case) but also experienced fundraisers and community leaders who can get the attention of influential allies. Almost one year later, we had at last put together an advisory board that included such individuals. In the coming years, this advisory board would become the governing board of directors.

There was much to do, however, before advisors could become directors, and at times it seemed that everything had to be accomplished all at once. A proposal had to be submitted to the International Affiliation of Compeer Programs (IACP). We quickly enlisted the *pro bono* services of an attorney, who would help us to establish status as a nonprofit corporation so that donations would be tax deductible. Even in those early days, it was important to have an operating budget to pay startup fees and annual membership fees to IACP, giving our agency the right to use the Compeer logo and materials, and even more importantly, to receive IACP direction and support throughout the development stage and beyond.

So even as we prepared and filed for nonprofit status, we were soliciting donations from individuals and corporations. Once our nonprofit status was established, we could submit grant requests to local and national institutions. However, while organizational donors will give limited funds for development, they prefer to give their money to functioning agencies. And so, as we addressed and completed the startup process, we also began to recruit volunteers and contact therapists for future client referrals.

After establishing our agency and making matches, we encountered both success and frustration, with each new frustration a learning experience that led us to a new and higher plateau of growth and development. For example, when we lost donated office space, we were quickly able to find space in a newer building at a better location because of our established community presence. All nonprofit volunteer agencies deal with similar struggles. But the stigma of mental illness presents Compeer with an additional hurdle to overcome.

For example, a lack of understanding regarding mental illness can hamper volunteer recruitment. During a volunteer training session, one of the potential volunteers asked me what to do if their Compeer friend called too often or talked too much. I asked her if she had any existing friends who might do that. As I expected, she did. I asked what she did under those circumstances. Her response laid the foundation for my response to her original question. Compeer volunteers are not therapists; they are simply friends sharing whatever is of mutual interest with their Compeer friends. And when matches are made, the need for some kind of mutual interest is considered. They can go to a movie, share a cup of coffee, shop, play cards or games, go for a walk, or just talk—about their children or grandchildren or a book they've both read. What they do isn't important. Being together is what counts. And if there are "rules" or guidelines for a satisfying friendship, a Compeer friendship operates according to the same guidelines.

Funding, staffing, and recruitment challenges led to the end of Birmingham's Compeer agency in 2002. We were disappointed, but after close to ten years of operation, we felt we'd made a contribution to the community. We knew of successful friendship matches that had changed lives. We had educated community members as we spoke to civic and church groups. And perhaps our proudest, surely grandest, moment came in 2001 when we partnered with our local Habitat for Humanity agency to build a house that we chose to name Hope House. It represented what Compeer is about: uniting therapist, consumer, and volunteer in an effort to help the community understand and cope with mental illness. It was the product of labor by individuals whose lives had been touched by mental health issues in some manner and who, at the building site, worked together to literally and metaphorically build the foundation, erect the walls, and install the windows and doors of Hope House. Whereas those with a diagnosis of mental illness are often isolated from the rest of the community, at the building site, they were able to break free of their isolation. And when I visited the site and saw all the workers together—dressed in work clothes, swinging hammers, rolling paint—it was impossible to know which workers were consumers or therapists or family members or pharmaceutical reps[4] or psychology or sociology college students. Their differences were invisible and unimportant.

It was their similarities and mutual caring that was most obvious. As Greater Birmingham Habitat for Humanity (GBHFH) and Compeer collaborated to build the walls of a home, they tore down walls created by attitudes, fears, and misunderstandings. They removed barriers to acceptance and offered social support and meaning to those dealing with mental illness.

The groundbreaking for Habitat Hope House—the first Habitat for Humanity home in the nation to be built exclusively by volunteers with mental health challenges, their families, and mental health caregivers—occurred on April 12, 2001. Compeer of Birmingham originated the idea, which was fully supported by GBHFH, as evidenced by the organization's board chair at that time, Jan Bell, who stated at the groundbreaking, "As the Hope House walls are raised, myths and stereotypes about persons with mental illness will be torn down." In order to sponsor the building of a Habitat House, the sponsor must provide workers and funding. Forest Laboratories, an American pharmaceutical company, provided full funding in the amount of forty-five thousand dollars. Ken Goodman, president and chief operating officer for Forest Laboratories at the time, also offered verbal support of the project, stating, "We believe this project sets an example of people from various walks of life joining together to overcome misperceptions."

Those who are chosen to occupy and own a Habitat home must fulfill certain obligations, including the contribution of three hundred hours of "sweat equity" toward a down payment. There is always a waiting list of potential Habitat homeowners. Those on the list must have completed their sweat-equity payments, and since they may be first-time homeowners in their family, they must have completed classes that will help them understand how to assume this privilege and responsibility.

When Jan Bell considered an appropriate family for this project, she recommended one in which the head of the household had cerebral palsy, a physical disability. There seemed to be a lovely symmetry that those with one category of disability should be working on behalf of a family with another type of disability. And it made the experience all the more meaningful to those workers who were accustomed to being referred to as *consumers*. The term, adopted by NAMI, makes sense in some ways, but workers liked the idea of being *producers*, lending something to the community, rather than consumers, dependent on community services.

The new residents of Habitat Hope House, in fact, represented members of two different families, bound by a common loss. The father of a three-year-old daughter had cerebral palsy. He was also a recent widower, and when his wife passed away, leaving him alone to care for his daughter, his mother-in-law, the child's grandmother, became a part of the family unit. Prior to moving into their new home, the family had lived in substandard conditions, but now the "woman of the house" experienced the joy of selecting carpet and vinyl colors and expressed gratitude for the blessing of "a wonderful partnership of people helping people."

In April, the mere seed of an idea was planted. Nine months later, Habitat Hope House was a home, because from the moment the seed was planted, every individual and organization that became involved was almost instantly enthusiastic about the project. I like to believe that the enthusiasm was so spontaneous because this idea made sense; it felt right. It makes sense that people with mental illness should be given the opportunity to do productive work. It makes sense that they can work alongside members of the community. It makes sense because they *are* members of the community.

Over a period of nine months, more than fifty psychology and sociology students hammered and hauled and painted. More than fifty mental health professionals and pharmaceutical company employees worked at the site. And most importantly, there were at least thirty-two builders who had a diagnosis of mental illness, along with twenty who had a family member with some form of mental illness. I say "at least" thirty-two with a diagnosis of mental illness, because some of the workers from other volunteer categories quietly made me aware of their own personal struggles with mental illness.

In spite of the number of people who will experience some form of acute or chronic mental disorder at some time in their lives, fear and stigma still persist. And as long as they persist, too many will avoid seeking help even in the face of troubling symptoms, while others who *have* sought help will, because of the social and self-stigma associated with their diagnosis, suffer social isolation. At the Hope House site, there was no sense of fear or stigma or isolation. There was only laughter and good clean sweat and a loving community effort. We were all the same. Side by side we all laughed, and we all sweated. Habitat Hope House was about friendship and a community working together. As with all the sites you've read about—including Geel and Compeer—our voice of hope is clearest, most harmonious and melodious, when we work together to tear down walls of fear and build foundations of hope—*not against, with.*

# Epilogue

## The American Dream

In 1992, the Office of Consumer Relations in the Alabama Department of Mental Health and Mental Retardation first sponsored what has become the nation's largest statewide mental health conference organized for and by consumers—founded as the Alabama Consumer Recovery Conference, now known as the Alabama Institute for Recovery. Since 1997, the conference has been held in a large rural conference center near Talladega, Alabama. In May 2006, I attended the three-day conference—along with seven hundred consumers and two hundred staff members who were all there to hear speakers, participate in workshops, put on a talent show, and enjoy the pastoral setting.

On Tuesday morning, May 2, the day that I drove to Shocco Springs Conference Center, fifty miles west of my home, I woke up, as usual, to the morning news coming from my clock radio. There were no major catastrophic events reported that morning, but the news did present a story, including aspects of the American Dream, that evoked some serious pondering on my part. (I "ponder" a lot. For most of my life, I've been told that I think too much, but as a researcher and college professor, I've been lucky enough to earn my keep by thinking—and by encouraging others to do the same.)

So what was the news on May 2 that troubled me? Well, it wasn't a single news item, but rather the coming together of seemingly unrelated comments and events that caught my attention. That morning I heard that Enron CEO Ken Lay, in court, had defended a more than two-hundred-thousand-dollar birthday celebration for his wife—coming much too close to the demise of Enron. How could he defend such an expenditure at that time? He explained that it's hard to "give up on the American Dream." That statement started my day with a jolt and some serious thinking about what it means to be an American and to pursue the American Dream.

Even as I tried to digest Lay's justification for what can, in my view, only be described as overspending, I recalled a news story from the previous evening, when a Columbia University economist had talked about issues related to legal and illegal immigration. He made one point that, like Lay's comment, lodged in my mind, when he described how the immigrant's battle to become an American is viewed differently by those trying to cross the border and those who were born on the "right side" of the border. In 2015, undocumented immigrants are still in the news, but that's a separate issue, not truly relevant to my story, except to gain insight into what America means to those who seek what I take for granted. I do know and cherish the story of my own grandparents and their immigration from Denmark to the United States at the beginning of the twentieth century.

For my grandfather's family, it began in Sweden in the late 1800s when they moved to Denmark due to poor economic conditions in Sweden. My grandfather had many siblings—some perhaps born in Sweden, some in Denmark (my grandfather was in the latter group). They were a large family, and my great-grandmother was the head janitor of a building on a street in Copenhagen that is now lined with posh shops. On a visit to Copenhagen in 2000, I stood in front of that building and imagined my grandfather, as a child, playing on the narrow street or perhaps helping his mother as she toiled inside the building. I knew that their dream of living a better life did not end in Denmark. One by one, the adult children came to the United States to earn money and send it back home—to help with living expenses in Denmark and to, in time, allow for the next family member, or two, to make the trip until the whole family was together in America, ready to live the American Dream.

Motivation is similar today for all immigrants, documented or undocumented, and in many cases, families faced hardships to get here and often experienced rejection due to their immigrant status once they arrived. But still they came, and they continue to come—seeking a better life for themselves and their families. In many cases, they mustered up some kind of courage and made some kind of sacrifice in order to become Americans and pursue the American Dream. But, my guess is that *their* American dream isn't defined by anything akin to a two-hundred-thousand-dollar birthday celebration. But enough of the digression regarding immigrants. What does it have to do with "hope" for those with mental illness?

On that Tuesday morning, with an undercurrent of thoughts on Ken Lay and immigrants and the American Dream and a one-hour drive to attend a statewide mental health conference organized for and by consumers, the various thoughts overlapped so that I couldn't completely push aside current news events. But mostly I was thinking about the stigma of mental illness—in anticipation of this conference. I read and write about stigma, but this conference was an opportunity to mingle and learn in the midst of seven hundred of those whom I champion, an opportunity to be reminded of *why* I have chosen to advocate for those who live with a diagnosis of mental illness---in my role as an academic, but mostly as a plain and simple person.

On Tuesday evening, during a consumer talent show, the American Dream once again came to mind. Sitting in the audience, I looked at my watch with trepidation when the director of Alabama's Consumer Relations began the evening program by announcing that ninety-six people had signed up to present their talents. Somewhat tired after a long day, I assured myself that I didn't have to stay for the whole show and settled in to see what was in store. In the first half hour, I was amazed at the quality of some of the talent, amazed at the courage of some presenters in the face of limited talent, and touched by the support and adulation of an audience of consumers. I looked at those on stage, and I looked at the faces of those in the audience; I listened to comments, among themselves, of audience members, and heard their sincere applause (sometimes a standing ovation). I thought about the fear and avoidance that some people feel regarding those with mental illness. And I wondered, "How can anyone possibly be *afraid* of these people?" Though most of those in the audience and all of those who took the stage were living with a diagnosis of some form of mental illness, there was great diversity in the presence and degree of symptoms and in their very demeanors (just as there is great diversity among any group of people). But what they all, collectively, as a group—even in their diversity—represented to me was a powerful sense of unadulterated love. Those who face intolerance and rejection from the rest of the world have somehow learned the beautiful art of tolerance and acceptance for one another. Oh that all of us could show that same degree of tolerance and acceptance, not only for consumers but for one another.

A young woman made her way up the steps to the stage with an older woman whom she introduced as her grandmother, her moral support. When she got to the mic, she explained that this was her third time attending this conference but her first time without a wheelchair, her first time to walk up those steps unaided. (What many don't know is that side effects of mental illness and/or necessary medications can also cause physical symptoms.) A small tear of awe leaked from my eye, and the phrase *American Dream* came to mind.

The next day, at lunch, I sat across from a mental health professional who just happened, unprompted by me, to tell me about the work that she does with consumers in which she asks them to talk about their dreams. She shared with me some of those dreams: a job, a home, independence—pretty ordinary stuff, the things that many of us take for granted. Many of their dreams are the same as those that have motivated immigrants to take bold journeys to a new home.

My whole life, I've heard of the American Dream. I'm sure my immigrant grandparents were pursuing that very thing when they came here, one or two family members at a time. But from what I know about my family history and legacy, that dream was more closely linked to a dream of living in a country where "all men [and women] are created equal in that they are entitled to life, liberty, and the pursuit of happiness." That pursuit translated as the *opportunity* to live (life) independently (liberty) in order to pursue their own individual dreams. They worked hard to make the most of that opportunity. And because of their labors, I am a second-generation American who enjoys relatively good mental and physical health. I take for granted the privilege of living where I want to live, pursuing a profession that fits my interests and abilities, and being able to speak out in support of people and issues that I find worthy. I have chosen to work on breaking down the stigma of mental illness and in support of those with mental illness. I don't fully understand my passion on behalf of this particular cause, but I do know that when I am in the midst of those who fight the battle of mental illness, I am invigorated by the courage that they show in *their* pursuit of happiness.

We all find happiness in different ways and in different forms, and indeed we all have the right to pursue our own form of happiness if our pursuit does no harm or impede others. If being rich and throwing quarter-of-a-million-dollar birthday parties for one's spouse is a happiness worthy of pursuit by some, so be it. *But*…that is a personal choice; it is *not*, in and of itself, *the* American Dream, at least not in my book.

Call me a dreamer, an idealist, but if you are a believer in the American Dream, may I recommend two things? First of all, do everything in your power to treat these people—any group of people who must struggle with what you take for granted—with respect and support for their courage. And perhaps you might reconsider your own version of the American Dream based on their motivation, rather than that of the likes of Ken Lay. Try it. You may find for yourself and provide for others, including those with a diagnosis of mental illness, the *real* meaning of "happiness" ---*not against* anyone's *dis*abilities including our own, but *with* our unique abilities and the contribution that each of us can offer.

# End Notes

## Introduction

1. "The Fearless Wisdom of Robert Frost," *Vogue*, 141, no.6 (March 15, 1963): 118–9.

2. The actual spelling is *Geel*, even though in English publications, the city is often spelled *Gheel*, with the *Gh* meant to emphasize the Flemish guttural pronunciation of *G*.

3. James C. Coleman, James N. Butcher, and Robert C. Carson, *Abnormal Psychology*, 6th ed. (Glenville, IL: Scott Foresman, 1980), 11.

4. A variety of terms related to abnormal behavior, thinking, or mood are currently used. *Mental illness* or *mentally ill* are now seen as stigmatizing terms, evoking a negative stereotype. *Disorder*, with a descriptive adjective, is used in the *Diagnostic and Statistical Manual of Mental Disorders (DSM-5)*, published by the American Psychiatric Association. Clinicians often use a term identifying a professional relationship (e.g., *client* or *patient*). The National Alliance for the Mentally Ill (NAMI) uses consumer, short for *consumers of mental health services*, acknowledging that those with a diagnosis of mental illness using the service of providers, have the kind of consumer rights as do those who use *any* kind of service. A preferred designation is *person(s) with* but this can become wordy. The power of language to support or reject a given image cannot be ignored. However, the purpose of this book is not to label or diagnose. Thus, acknowledging variability in preferred terms, the author will alternate various terms with an effort to match the context in which the term is used.

5. Coleman et al., *Abnormal Psychology*, 41.

6. Aring, Charles D., "The Geel Experience: Eternal Spirit of the Chainless Mind," *Journal of the American Medical Association* 230, no. 7 (1974): 998–1001.

7. P.C. Sham, C. J. McLean, and K. S. Kendler, "A Typological Model of Schizophrenia Based on Age at Onset, Sex and Familial Morbidity," *Acta Psychiatrica Scandinavica* 89, no. 2 (1994): 135–41.

8.  Goldstein, Jackie. "The 'Geel Project': Historical Perspectives on Community Mental Health Care" (Presentation at the 106th American Psychological Association Annual Convention, San Francisco, CA, August 16, 1998). http://faculty.samford. edu/`jlgoldst/apa98talk.pdf.

9.  Goldstein, Jackie. "A Community Mental Health Care Legend? Whatever Happened to Geel?" (Roundtable discussion at the 129th Annual Public Health Association, Atlanta, Georgia, October 22, 2001).

## Chapter One: The Voice of Stigma

1.  US Department of Health and Human Services, *Mental Health: A Report of the Surgeon General* (Rockville, MD: 1999).

2.  For example, see *New York Times* 2002 series: Levy, Clifford J. "For Mentally Ill, Death and Misery," April 28, Section 1, 32, 35, 36; "Here Life Is Squalor and Chaos," April 29, A1, A26–27; "Voiceless, Defenseless and a Source of Cash," April 20, A1.

3.  Elias, Marilyn. "Mentally Ill Die 25 Years Earlier on Average," *USA Today,* May 3, 2007.

4.  Early, Pete, *Crazy: A Father's Search Through America's Mental Health Madness* (New York: Berkley Books, 2006).

5.  Johnson, Linea and Cinda Johnson, *Perfect Chaos: A Daughter's Journey to Survive Bipolar, A Mother's Journey to Save Her* (New York: St. Martin's Press, 2012).

6.  Kissinger, Meg. "Chronic Crisis: A Quest for Care (four-part series)," *Milwaukee Journal Sentinel,* July 20, 2013.

7.  Smedes, Lewis, *Keeping Hope Alive* (Nashville, TN: Thomas Nelson, 2000).

8.  Bandura, Albert, *Self-Efficacy: The Exercise of Control* (New York: W. H. Freeman, 1977).

9.  Bandura, *Self-Efficacy*, 477.

## Chapter Two: The Voice of Legend

1. Aring, Charles D. "Gheel Revisited," *Journal of the American Medical Association* 230, no. 6 (1974a): 849.

2. Aring, Charles D "The Gheel Experience: Eternal Spirit of the Chainless Mind," *Journal of the American Medical Association* 230, no. 7 (1974b): 998–1001.

3. Godemont, Marc. "600 Years of Family Care in Geel, Belgium: 600 Years of Familiarity with Madness in Town Life," *Community Alternatives: International Journal of Family Care* 4 (1992): 155–68.

4. Parry-Jones, William. "The Model of the Geel Lunatic Colony and Its Influence on the Nineteenth-Century Asylum System in Britain," in *Madhouses, Mad-Doctors and Madmen: The Social History of Psychiatry in the Victorian Era,* ed. Andrew Scull (Philadelphia, PA: University of Pennsylvania Press, 1981), 201–17.

5. Literature and legend use diverse spellings of the young princess's name. These include Dymphna, Dimphna, and Dimpna.

6. Belgium, as it is today, did not exist as an independent state until 1831 when The Netherlands, France, and Germany each "contributed" a part of their own territory to make a new ("artificial") country, with a mixture of different religions, languages and traditions.

7. Deutsch, Alfred. *The Mentally Ill in America* (New York: Columbia University, 1949), 14.

8. Officers of the New York State Lunatic Asylum, Utica (ed.), "Article III: A Village of Lunatic," *The American Journal of Inanity* 4 (1847–81): 217–22.

9. Kernodle, R. Wayne. "Three Family Placement Programs in Belgium and the Netherlands," *Hospital and Community Psychiatry* 23, no. 11 (1972): 329–45.

10. Parry-Jones, *Model of the Geel Lunatic Colony,* 201.

11. M. Koyen, *History of Geel and Family Care: 1250–1790.* Unpublished manuscript translated by Ellen Baxter (n.d.).

12. Daly, B. O. "St. Damhnat," *Journal of the County Louth Archaeological Society* 11, no. 4, 19 (1949): 243–51.

13. Robert C. Carson, James N. Butcher, and Susan Mineka, *Abnormal Psychology and Modern Life, 10th ed.* (New York: HarperCollins, 1996).

14. Maher, Winifred B. and Brendan A. Maher, "Psychopathology: I. From Ancient Times to the Eighteenth Century," in *Topics in the History of Psychology*, Vol. 3, ed. Gregory A. Kimble and Kurt Schlesinger (Hillsdale, NJ: Erbaum, 1985).

15. M. Koyen, *History of Geel and Family Care,* "The Ritual," 3.

16. M. Koyen, *History of Geel and Family Care,* "The Sick Room," 2.

17. Roosens, Eugeen. *Mental Patients in Town Life: Geel—Europe's First Therapeutic Community* (Beverly Hills/London: Sage Publications, 1979).

18. Roosens, *Mental Patients in Town Life.*

19. "Autonomous Statute for Age-Old Foster Family Care in Geel," *Flanders* 2 (1991): 15–17.

## Chapter Three: A Dying Voice

1. Dumont, Matthew P. and C. Knight Aldrich, "Family Care After a Thousand Years: A Crisis in the Tradition of St. Dymphna," *American Journal of Psychiatry* 199 (1962): 110–21.

2. Phillipe Pinel (1745–1862) was a French physician best known for advocating humane treatment for those with mental disorders.

3. From 1815 to 1830, Belgium was under Dutch administration.

4.  Tuke, D. H. "On a Recent Visit to Gheel," *Journal of Mental Science* 31 (1886): 481–97.

5.  Aring, Charles D. "Gheel Revisited. Commentary," *Journal of the American Medical Association* 230, no. 6 (1974a): 849.

6.  Aring, Charles D. "The Gheel Experience: Eternal Spirit of the Chainless Mind," *Journal of the American Medical Association* 230, no. 7 (1974b): 998–1001.

7.  J. Y. Choe, L. A. Teplin, and K. M Abrams, "Perpetration of Violence, Violent Victimization, and Severe Mental Illness: Balancing Public Health Concerns," *Psychiatric Services* 59, no. 2 (2008): 153–64.

8.  In 2007, 50 percent of boarders were between ages of thirty-five and fifty-four, 25 percent were older than fifty, and 20 percent were older than sixty. In that same year, 72 of 122 boarders were living with their first foster family.

9.  Most foster families are couples (63.5 percent in 2007), and most have only one boarder (in 2007, there were 138 families with one boarder, 48 with two boarders, and 7 with three boarders).

10. Depending on age of boarder and where they live, there are several transportation options. OPZ provides van service, the city has a public transportation system using buses, and many community members and boarders gladly ride their bikes.

11. Leo Srole, Thomas. S. Langner, Stanley T. Michael, Marvin K. Opler, and Thomas A.C. Rennie. *Mental Health in the Metropolis: The Midtown Manhattan Study* (New York: McGraw Hill, 1962).

12. Fowler, Glenn, "John D. J. Moore, an Executive and a Former Envoy, Dies at 77." *New York Times,* (September 13, 1988) http://www.nytimes.com/1988/09/13/obituaries/john-d-j-moore-an-executive-and-a-former-envoy-dies-at-77.html.

13. The United States of America and Northern Ireland (2012), website by the John Moore Newman Fellowship. *John Moore*, 3-5, accessed January 17, 2015, http://usaandni.com/about.

14. Moore, John D. J. "What Gheel Means to Me," *Look*, May 23, 1961, 35–9.

15. Srole, Leo. "Geel, Belgium: The Natural Therapeutic Community—1475–1975," in *New Trends of Psychiatry in the Community*, ed. G. Serban (Cambridge, Mass: Ballinger, 1977), 111–29.

16. Leo Srole, personal communication, August 19, 1974. Archived at Hobart/William Smith Colleges Library, Geneva, NY.

17. Gasthuismuseum Geel, *History of the Museum*, http://en.gasthuismuseumgeel.be/History/default.aspx?id=2721.

18. Aring, "The Gheel Experience," 998–1001.

## Chapter Four: The Voice of History

1. Geel's experience with mental illness began when pilgrims taken into homes of community members were logically referred to as *boarders*. While the number of boarders has decreased, other mental health services are available for citizens of Geel and surrounding communities. These citizens, though not referred to as boarders, also benefit from the community's tradition of acceptance.

2. Eldridge, Larry D. "'Crazy Brained': Mental Illness in Colonial America," *Bulletin of the History of Medicine* 70 (1996): 361–86. With no diagnostic criteria in colonial days, community members referred to those who exhibited erratic or socially unacceptable behavior with labels describing the behavior. Citizens could apparently distinguish between erratic behavior and intellectual disabilities, for the latter were commonly referred to as *simple* or *dumb*. In the seventeenth century, those who displayed more troublesome behavior were identified by a number of terms. Based on ancient

belief in the moon's effect on behavior, some were identified as *lunatics,* a label that lingers today, though *not* in a clinical context. Other terms from the seventeenth century include *out of their wits, deluded, mad, distempered, distracted,* and simply *crazy* (362–364).

3.  Rothman, David J. *The Discovery of the Asylum: Social Order and Disorder in the New Republic,* rev. ed. (Piscataway, NJ: AldineTransactions, 2005).

4.  Jimenez, Mary Ann. "Madness in American History: Insanity in Massachusetts from 1700 to 1830," *Journal of Social History,* 10, 1 (1986), 25–44.

5.  John Langdon Sibley, (Vol. X, 1933, 281–288) as cited in Jimenez, "Madness in American History."

6.  Shipton, Clifford J., *New England Life in the Eighteenth Century* (Cambridge, MA: The Belknap Press of Harvard University Press, 1963), 221.

7.  Shipton, *New England Life,* 217.

8.  Jimenez, Mary Ann. *Changing Faces of Madness: Early American Attitudes and Treatment of the Insane* (Hanover, NH: University Press of New England, 1987).

9.  Jimenez, *Madness in American History*, 218.

10. Eldridge, *Crazy Brained*, 386.

11. Grob, Gerald N. *Mental Institutions in America: Social Policy to 1875* (New York: Free Press, 1973), 12, fn 9.

12. Eldridge, *Crazy Brained*, 7.

13. Grob, *Mental Institutions in America,* 7.

14. David S. Roby, "Pioneer of Moral Treatment: Isaac Bonsall and the Early Years of Friends Asylum," as recorded in Bonsall's diaries 1817-1823, Friends Hospital, accessed March 6, 2006, http://friendshospitalonline.org/isaacbonsall.htm.

15. In annual Asylum reports, the Bonsells were always identified as co-superintendents, consistent with the progressive attitude of Quakers who accorded women respect equal to men.

16. Rush, Benjamin. *Medical and Observations Upon the Disease of the Mind* (1812), Kindle edition, 224.

17. Grob, *Mental Institutions in America,* 103.

18. Grob, Gerald N. *The Mad Among Us: A History of the Care of America's Mentally Ill* (New York: The Free Press: 1994), 48.

19. Clark, Tom Foran. *The Significance of Being Frank: The Life and Times of Franklin Benjamin Sanborn* (2005), eBook.

20. State Correction and Poverty Reports, Massachusetts, State Board of Charities, Annual Report 1-15, 1863/64-1877/78 (as cited in Baxter, 1978, 3).

21. Beers, Clifford Wittingham. *A Mind That Found Itself: An Autobiography*, Kindle edition.

22. From time to time, *A Mind That Found Itself* is republished, most recently by Doubleday in 2013.

23. Grob, *The Mad Among Us,* 155.

24. *Mental Health America*, accessed November 15, 2015, http://www.mentalhealthamerica.net/who-we-are.

25. Nominees must (1) be, or have been, consumers of mental health services; (2) have made, or be working to make, major contributions to improve lives of people with

mental health conditions, substance use, or co-occurring disorders; (3) demonstrate a strong ability to effectively educate the public about mental health, mental illnesses, substance use, or co-occurring disorders; (4) effectively promote the concept of recovery to local, statewide, and/or national audiences; and (5) illustrate commitment to consumer advocacy despite risks to career, finances, and public acceptance.

26. Norman Endler, "The Origins of Electroconvulsive Therapy (ECT)," *Convulsive Therapy,* 4 (1) (1988): 12-16.

27. *Metrazol Therapy*, accessed September 27, 2014, http://fairfieldstatehospital.com/metrazol.html.

28. Kotowicz, Zibigniew. "Gottlieb Burckhardt and Egas Moniz: Two Beginnings of Psychosurgery," *Gesnerus* 62 (2005): 84, fn14.

29. Pressman, Jack D. *Last Resort: Psychosurgery and the Limits of Medicine* (Cambridge, UK: Cambridge University Press, 1998).

## Part Two Introduction: Community Recovery in the United States

1. Goldstein, Jackie. "Geel, Belgium: A Model of 'Community Recovery,'" http://faculty.samford.edu/~jlgoldst, last updated July 23, 2009.

2. Office of Civil Rights, "Sharing Health Information with Family Members and Friends," accessed August 11, 2015, http://www.hhs.gov/ocr/privacy/hipaa/understanding/consumers/sharing-family-friends.pdf.

## Chapter Five: The Twentieth Century: A New Voice of Hope

1. Bryan L. Roth, Douglas J. Sheffler, and Wesley K. Kroeze, "Magic shotguns Versus Magic Bullets: Selectively Non-Selective Drugs for Mood Disorders and Schizophrenia," *Nature Review* 3 (2004): 383–9.

2. Avid *Seinfeld* fans, of which I am one, will recognize the inspirational role that Loewi's experience played in one of the show's episodes. Another episode

demonstrated the script-writers' knowledge of the phenomenon of left-side neglect following injury to the brain's right hemisphere.

3.  Torrey, E. Fuller, as cited in Ronald J. Comer, *Abnormal Psychology, 5th ed.* (New York: Worth Publishers, 2001), 19.

4.  Ewalt, Jack R. "Goals of the Joint Commission on Mental Illness and Health," *American Journal of Public Health Nations Health* 47 (1) (1957): 20.

5.  Aviram, Uri. "Community Care of the Seriously Mentally Ill: Continuing Problems and Current Issues, *Community Mental Health Journal* 26, no. 1 (1990): 69–87.

6.  Gillon, Steven M. *That's Not What We Meant to Do* (New York: W.W. Norton and Co., 2000).

7.  Kenneth. Heller, Richard A. Jenkins, Ann M. Steffen, and Ralph W. Swindle, Jr., "Prospects for a Viable Community Mental Health System," in *Handbook of Community Psychology,* ed. Julian Rappaport and Edward Seldman (New York: Kluwer Academic/Plenum Publishers, (2000), 445–70.

8.  Jimenez, *Madness in American History*, 9–10.

9.  Grob, *Mental Institutions in America*, 12.

10. Javier Arnedo et al., "Uncovering the Hidden Risk Architecture of the Schizophrenias: Confirmation in Three Independent Genome-Wide Association Studies," *American Journal of Psychiatry* 172 (2) (2015), 139-153.

11. Blog post by CNN reporter Anderson Cooper, http://ac360.blogs.cnn.com/2014/06/09/anderson-takes-part-in-an-experiment-to-help-understand-how-people-live-with-mental-illness/, accessed October 13, 2014.

12. It is difficult to gather census-style data on those who are homeless and living on the streets. Thus it is difficult to assess how many homeless individuals living on the streets suffer from some type of mental disorder.

13. Gillon, *That's Not What We Meant to Do,* 111.

14. Wahl, Otto F. *Media Madness: Public Images of Mental Illness* (New Brunswick, NJ: Rutgers University Press, (1994).

## Chapter Six: Pioneers and Innovations

1. Pan, Deanna. "Timeline: Deinstitutionalization and Its Consequences," *Mother Jones,* http://www.motherjones.com/politics/2013/04/timeline-mental-health-america.

2. "Our History: Thresholds Is Born," Thresholds (n.d.), 1, accessed January 23, 2003, http://www.thresholds.org/history_pl.htm.

3. "2014 Thresholds Annual Report," Thresholds, October 20, 2014, accessed August 15, 2015, http://thresholds.org/wp-content/uploads/2013/04/2014AnnujalRe port_FINAL_reducedfor web.pdf.

4. "Become a Certified Peer Specialist Today," NY Peer Specialists, 2015, accessed August 15, 2015, http://nypeerspecialist.org/.

5. Community Access, "Howie the Harp Advocacy Center," accessed August 15, 2015, http://www.communityaccess.org/what-we-do-/hth-peer-advocacy-ctr.

6. "Frequently Asked Questions," The Supportive Housing Network of New York, 2015, accessed August 15, 2015, http://shnny.org/learn-more/faq/.

7. "Welcome to Geel Community Services," Geel Community Services, 2011, accessed August 15, 2015, http://geelcs.org/about.

8. "About Way Station" (n.d.) accessed November 15, 2015, www.waystationinc. org/aboutwaystation.htm.

9. "Way Station Community Employment Program," Way Station (n.d.) accessed August 16, 2015, http://www.waystationinc.org/CEP.htm.

10. "Press Release: Way Station Model for Treating Mental Illness Expands Statewide," Way Station (n.d.), accessed August 16, 2015, http://www.waystationinc.org/index.htm.

11. MHA Village, "History," The Village Integrated Service Agency, Mental Health America of Los Angeles (copyright 2012), accessed November 25, 2015, http://mhavillage.squarespace.com/history/.

12. Anthony, William B. "Recovery from Mental Illness: The Guiding Vision of the Mental Health Service System in the 1990s," *Psychosocial Rehabilitation Journal* 16, no. 4 (1993): 11.

13. Ragins, Mark. "A Road to Recovery," *Mental Health Association in Los Angeles County,* accessed September 10, 2015, http://cpr.bu.edu/wp-content/uploads/2013/05/Road-to-Recovery.pdf.

14. For eat-in or catering menu see http://mhavillage.squarespace.com/our-businesses/.

15. For offerings and ordering on-line (and an opportunity to "meet" Village members who run the shop), see http://www.villagecookieshoppe.com/.

16. "Immersion Training," Mental Health America of Los Angeles, 2003–2008, accessed August 18, 2015, www.mhala.org/immersion-training.htm.

## Chapter Seven: Spirit of Dymphna in New York City

1. Anderson, David C. "Ellen Baxter," *New York Times*, December 19, 1993. http://www.nytimes.co/1993/12/19/magazine/ellen-baxter.html.

2. Thomas J. Watson Fellowship Overview, Watson Foundation, 2015, accessed April 12, 2015, http://watson.foundation/fellowships/tj.

3. Broadway Housing Communities, 2015, accessed April 18, 2015, http://www.broadwayhousing.org/about/.

4.  Baxter. Ellen. "Geel and New York City: Housing People Living with Mental Illness,"Paper presented at *Symposium OPZ Geel—Community Care: Foster Family Care as an Inspiring Model*, Geel, Belgium, May 16, 2014.

5.  Baxter. Ellen and Kim Hopper, *Interim Report: Quality of Life of Mentally Disabled Adults in Community Settings* (New York: Community Service Society, September 1979).

6.  Baxter, Ellen and Kim Hopper, *Private Lives/Public Spaces: Homeless Adults on the Streets of New York City* (New York: Community Service Society, February 1981).

7.  *"Why Are So Many People Homeless?"* Coalition for the Homeless (n.d.), http:// www.coalitionforthehomeless.org/the-catastrophe-of-homelessness/ why-are-so-many-people-homeless/.

8.  "The Callahan Legacy: Callahan v. Carey and the Legal Right to Shelter," Coalition for the Homeless (n.d.),

9.  "History of SROs and Homelessness in New York,"The Network of NY, History of Supportive Housing, 2015, accessed July 11, 2015, http://shnny.org/learn-more/ history-of-supportive-housing.

10. "The Heights," Broadway Housing Community, 2015, accessed July 8, 2015, http://broadwayhousing.org/housing/heights/.

11. Anderson, *Ellen Baxter*, 7.

12. The Petra Foundation, "Petra Foundation Fellow: Ellen Baxter" *Broadway Housing Communities*, 1–4, accessed March 21, 2015, http://www.broadwayhousing. org/1993/01/150/.

13. Burke, Daniel Burke. "Diaries Shed Light on Unlikely Would-Be US Saint," *National Catholic Reporter*, May 29, 2008, accessed March 21, 2015, http://www.broadway-housing.org/1993/01/150/.

14. "Dorothy Day Apartments," Broadway Housing Community (2015), accessed July 8, 2015, http://www.broadwayhousing.org/housing/dorothy-day.

15. Sugar Hill Children's Museum of Art & Storytelling (2015), accessed July 12, 2015, http://www.sugarhillmuseum.org.

16. Common Ground (2011–2014), accessed July 12, 2015, http://www.sugarhill-museum.org.

17. "The State of Homelessness in America 2014," National Alliance to End Homelessness, May 27, 2014, http://www.endhomelessness.org/library/entry/the-state-of-homelessness-2014.

## Chapter Eight: A Meaningful Life

1. The history and status of Rockland is fascinating; online pictorial tours are worth a visit. For example, see: Jinwoo Chong, June 25, 2015, "The Abandoned Rockland Psychiatric Center in Orangeburg, NY Is Now the Stuff of Nightmares," Untapped Cities, 1–10, accessed August 25, 2015, http://untappedcities.com/2015/06/25/once-a-bustling-state-hospital-the-abaneon3e-rockland-psychiatric-center-is-now-the-stuff-of-nightmares/.

2. "About Us: History," International Center for Clubhouse Development, dba Clubhouse International, 2015, accessed August 24, 2015, http://www.iccd.org/history.html.

3. Interview with Dr. Fairweather: "Starting the First Lodge Society," accessed September 22, 2015, https://www.youtube.com/watch?v=kEg4zlWJ-bc. In this interview, Fairweather describes motivation for this research and initial complications when groups were first moved from the hospital into the community.

4. Kelly, James G. "The 1985 Division 27 Award for Distinguished Contributions to Community Psychology and Community Mental Health: George W. Fairweather," *American Journal of Community Psychology* 14 (1986): 126–8.

5.  The Coalition for Community Living, accessed August 31, 2015, http://www.theccl.org.

6.  Tasks Unlimited: "About Tasks Unlimited," 2015, accessed September 2, 2015, http://www.tasksunlimited.org/.

## Chapter Nine: Therapeutic Communities

1.  "Mental health Communities of Hope and Healing," American Residential Treatment Association, accessed September 17, 2015, www. Artausa.org/.

2.  "How to make the best match," American Residential Treatment Association, accessed September 14, 2014, http://www.artausa.org/best_match.pdf.

3.  "Spring Lake Ranch: Therapeutic Community Working Toward Wellness," Spring Lake Ranch, 2015, accessed September 20, 2015, www.springlakeranch.org.

4.  Davidson, Helen K., review of *Giving a Lift in Time: A Finnish Immigrant's Story*, by Wayne A. Sarcka with Elizabeth Man Sarcka, *Vermont History* 76, no. 1 (Winter/Spring 2008): 76–77, http://vermonthistory.org/journal/76/VHS760106_67-84.pdf.

5.  "Billing and Insurance," Spring Lake Ranch, 2015, accessed October 1, 2015, http://www.springlakeranch.org/admissions/billing-insurance.

6.  McKee William J. *Gould Farm: A Life of Sharing* (Monterey, MA: Wm. J. Gould Associates, 1994).

7.  McKee, *Gould Farm*, 38.

8.  "Gould Farm: Since 1913 We Harvest Hope," Gould Farm, 2009, accessed September 22, 2015, http://www.gouldfarm.org/home.

9.  "Admissions Overview," Gould Farm, 2014, accessed October 1, 2015, http://www.gouldfarm.org/home.

10. Abbott, Kate, "Community Finds Sustenance on Gould Farm in Monterey," *Berkshire Eagle,* August 28, 2013, http://www.berkshireeagle.com/berkshiresweek/ci_23964197/community-finds-sustenance-gould-farm-monterey.

11. Pekkanen, John. "Journey Out of Darkness," *Reader's Digest,* Issue 858 (August 1994): 115–20.

12. Miller, Krystal. "At Rose Hill, the Mentally Ill Blossom," *Wall Street Journal*, December 22, 1992, A10.

13. Pekkanen, *Journey Out of Darkness*, 117.

14. "The History of Rose Hill Center," Rose Hill Center, 2015, accessed September 22, 2015, https://rosehillcenter.org/about/rose-hill-center-history/.

15. "Financial Considerations," Rose Hill (n.d.) accessed October 1, 2015, https://rosehillcenter.org/financial/financial-considerations/.

16. Rush, Benjamin. *Medical Inquiries and Observations Upon the Disease of the Mind* (1812), Kindle edition.

17. "About Us," Skyland Trail, 2015, accessed September 26, 2015, www.skylandtrail.org/About/HistoryMission.aspsx.

18. "Estimated Program Costs," Skyland Trail, 2015, accessed October 1, 2015, Https://www.skylandtrail.org/AdmissionsReferrals/Programcosts.aspx.

19. McKenzie, Martha Nolan. "Executive Life: Overcoming His Torment from Within," *New York Times,* March 31, 2002.

20. Johnson, Linea and Cinda Johnson, *Perfect Chaos: A Daughter's Journey to Survive Bipolar, A Mother's Struggle to Save Her* (New York: St. Martin's Press, 2012).

21. Ibid., 1.

22. Ibid., 5.

23. Ibid., 7–8.

24. Ibid., 8–9.

25. "Residents," Innisfree Village (n.d.) accessed October 1, 2015, http://www.innisfreevillage.org/resident/.

## Chapter Ten: Using Resources, Filling Needs: Not Against, With

1. Greensboro, Alabama, http://www.city-data.com/city/Greensboro-Alabama.html.

2. Archibald, John and Jeff Hansen, "Life Is Short, Prosperity Is Long Gone" *Birmingham News*, May 12, 2002. http://www.al.com/specialreport/birminghamnews/index.ssf?blackbelt/blackbelt1.html.

3. Theroux, Paul. "The Soul of the South," *Smithsonian Magazine*, July 2014. http://www.smithsonianmag.com/travel/soul-south-180951861/

4. "Hunting History in Hale County," *Cherokee County Herald,* July 25, 1990.

5. Tullos, Allen. "The Black Belt," *Southern Spaces*, April 19, 2004, http://southernspaces.org/2004/black-belt.

6. "Welcome to Horseshoe Farm," accessed January 21, 2015, http://projecthsf.org.

7. Toff-Walt, Chana "In One Alabama County, Nearly 1 in 4 Working-Age Adults Is on Disability" NPR Radio, *All Things Considered,* March 25, 2013.

8. "About Samuel 'Sambo' Mockbee," accessed February 4, 2015, http://samuel-mockbee.net/quotes/.

9. Ibid.

10. "Rural Studio Projects by Year," accessed March 15, 2015, http://www.ruralstudio.org/projects.html.

11. HERO Housing, accessed November 15, 2014, www.herohousing.org/.

12. Edge, John T. "Pie + Design = Change," *New York Times,* October 8, 2010, http://www.nytimes.com/2010/10/10/magazine/10pielab-t.html?pagewanted=all&_r=0.

13. Ibid.

14. Ibid.

15. Bleiberg, Larry. "The Sweet Spot," *AAA Alabama Journey,* May/June 2003, 19–20.

16. Strassmann, Mark. "An Entrepreneur Who Turned a Town Around," *CBS News,* September 8, 2013. http://www.cbsnews.com/news/an=entrepreneur-who-turned-a-town-around/

17. Carr, Lauren Wilson, "Wyatt v. Stickney: A Landmark Decision" Reprint from *Alabama Disabilities,* July 2004. http://www.adap.net/Wyatt/landmark.pdf

18. McDonald, Jan. "Dorsey Named Pillar of West Alabama," *West Alabama Watchman,* May 23, 2014 http://www.westalabamawatchman.com/dorsey-named-pillar-of-west-alabama/.

## Chapter Eleven: Silencing the Voice of Stigma

1. Patrick W. Corrigan, et al., "Three Strategies for Changing Attributions About Severe Mental Illness," *Schizophrenia Bulletin* 27, no. 20 (2001): 187–95.

2.  Patrick W. Corrigan, Jon E. Laron, and Patrick J. Michaels. *Coming Out Proud to Erase the Stigma of Mental Illness: Stories and Essays of Solidarity* (Collierville, TN: Instant Publisher, 2015).

3.  Compeer, Making Friends, Changing Lives, Compeer, Inc., 2011, accessed May 3, 2015, http://www.compeer.org.

4.  In order to sponsor a Habitat for Humanity house, the sponsoring organization must provide financial support and a work force. When Compeer of Birmingham offices were housed in a building of doctors' offices, the Forest Pharmaceutical representative became familiar with Compeer and wanted to do something to help and support the work of the agency. That opportunity came when Compeer knew they had to raise money to fund the construction of the house. It was the agency's intention to recruit funding from a number of sources; however, Forest offered to provide financial support for the entire project. In addition, the project cost increased when Compeer decided to build a barrier-free home for a family that included a man with a physical disability. Without hesitation, Forest Pharmaceuticals provided the additional financial support.

34562537R00146

Made in the USA
Middletown, DE
26 August 2016